THE PRINCETON REVIEW

Cracking the GMAT®

with Sample Tests on CD-ROM

Cracking the ACT
Cracking the ACT with Sample Tests on CD-ROM
Cracking the GED
Cracking the GMAT
Cracking the GMAT with Sample Tests
  on Computer Disk
Cracking the GMAT with Sample Tests
  on CD-ROM
Cracking the GRE
Cracking the GRE with Sample Tests on Computer Disk
Cracking the GRE Psychology Subject Test
Cracking the LSAT
Cracking the LSAT with Sample Tests
  on Computer Disk
Cracking the LSAT with Sample Tests on CD-ROM
Cracking the SAT and PSAT
Cracking the SAT and PSAT with Sample Tests
  on Computer Disk
Cracking the SAT and PSAT with Sample Tests
  on CD-ROM
Cracking the SAT II: Biology Subject Test
Cracking the SAT II: Chemistry Subject Test
Cracking the SAT II: English Subject Tests
Cracking the SAT II: French Subject Test
Cracking the SAT II: History Subject Tests
Cracking the SAT II: Math Subject Tests
Cracking the SAT II: Physics Subject Test
Cracking the SAT II: Spanish Subject Test
Cracking the TOEFL with Audiocassette
Flowers & Silver MCAT
Flowers Annotated MCAT
Flowers Annotated MCATs with Sample Tests
  on Computer Disk
Flowers Annotated MCATs with Sample Tests
  on CD-ROM

Culturescope Grade School Edition
Culturescope High School Edition
Culturescope College Edition

SAT Math Workout
SAT Verbal Workout

Don't Be a Chump!
How to Survive Without Your Parents' Money
Speak Now!
Trashproof Resumes

Grammar Smart
Math Smart
Reading Smart
Study Smart
Word Smart: Building an Educated Vocabulary
Word Smart II: How to Build a More Educated
  Vocabulary
Word Smart Executive
Word Smart Genius
Writing Smart

Grammar Smart Junior
Math Smart Junior
Word Smart Junior
Writing Smart Junior

Business School Companion
College Companion
Law School Companion
Medical School Companion

Student Access Guide to America's
  Top Internships
Student Access Guide to College
  Admissions
Student Access Guide to the Best
  Business Schools
Student Access Guide to the Best
  Law Schools
Student Access Guide to the Best
  Medical Schools
Student Access Guide to the Best
  309 Colleges
Student Access Guide to Paying for College
Student Access Guide to Visiting College Campuses
Student Access Guide: The Big Book
  of Colleges
Student Access Guide: The Internship Bible
Student Advantage Guide to Summer
Hillel Guide to Jewish Life on Campus
The Princeton Review Guide to Your Career

Also available on cassette from Living Language
Grammar Smart
Word Smart
Word Smart II

THE PRINCETON REVIEW

Cracking the GMAT®

with Sample Tests on CD-ROM

BY GEOFF MARTZ, JOHN KATZMAN, AND ADAM ROBINSON

1997 EDITION

RANDOM HOUSE, INC.
NEW YORK 1996
http://www.randomhouse.com

Princeton Review Publishing, L.L.C.
2315 Broadway, 3rd Floor
New York, NY   10024
E-mail: info@review.com

ISSN: 1062-5550
ISBN: 0-679-77113-1

GMAT is a registered trademark of the Graduate Management Admission Council, which does not endorse this book.

Macintosh is a registered trademark of Apple Computer, Inc.
System 7 is a registered trademark of Apple Computer, Inc.
Windows™ is a registered trademark of Microsoft® Corporation

Edited by: Bruno Blumenfeld
Designed by: Illeny Maaza
Illustrations by: The Production Department of The Princeton Review

Manufactured in the United States of America on partially recycled paper.

9 8 7 6 5 4 3 2 1

1997 Edition

ACKNOWLEDGMENTS

Our GMAT course is much more than clever techniques and powerful computer score reports; the reason our results are great is that our teachers care so much about their students. We would like to thank all the teachers who have made the GMAT course so successful, but in particular the core group of teachers and development people who helped get it off the ground: Alicia Ernst, Tom Meltzer, Paul Foglino, John Sheehan, Mark Sawula, Nell Goddin, Teresa Connelly, and Phillip Yee. We would also like to thank Diane Reverand and our agent, Julia Coopersmith.

Finally, we would like to thank the people who truly have taught us everything we know about the GMAT: our students.

ACKNOWLEDGMENTS

CONTENTS

Foreword

In 1981, I founded The Princeton Review in order to help prepare high-school students for the SAT (Scholastic Aptitude Test). My first course had nineteen students, and it was held in my parents' apartment. A year later, I began working with Adam Robinson, a highly regarded tutor. Within five years we had become the largest SAT course in the country.

Our SAT techniques are based in part on what we feel to be essential flaws in the design of the test—flaws that could cause students to score well below their true potential. When we looked at the GMAT (Graduate Management Admission Test), we realized that it contains many of the same flaws as the SAT (both tests are written by the Educational Testing Service). We felt that our techniques for tackling the SAT could be equally useful in tackling the GMAT. So, along with Geoff Martz, one of our veteran teachers and development experts, we designed a course specifically geared for the GMAT. For the past nine years, this course has been taught across the country. It has helped GMAT students attain the same phenomenal score improvements as our SAT students.

How do we do it?

First, unlike many coaches, we do not insist that the student learn dozens of math theorems or memorize all rules of written grammar. Our extensive examination of the GMAT has shown that the information needed to do well on this test is surprisingly limited. Thus, we concentrate on a small number of crucial concepts.

Those who have sweated through the GMAT and who have felt that the scores did not reflect their college grades or their business acumen probably suspect that there is more to mastering a standardized test than just reviewing rusty math and verbal skills. So we take our preparation a step further and teach techniques specifically designed to master multiple-choice standardized tests.

Finally, The Princeton Review offers even more than a thorough review and great techniques. Our classes are small (eight to fifteen students) and are grouped according to ability. For students who require extra help, we provide smaller group work sessions and even one-on-one tutoring. In addition, we administer several diagnostic GMATs under actual exam conditions.

Unfortunately, many students can't get to our courses. So for you we have written this book. Although the book explains our strongest techniques, it cannot substitute for small classes and great teaching. Still, careful study and practice of the techniques will provide you with the means to boost your score significantly.

To get the maximum effect of our approach, you must practice on actual GMATs. The only source of real GMAT questions is a book published by the Educational Testing Service called *The Official Guide for GMAT Review*. Available in bookstores, it contains three complete GMATs plus sample sections of each question type. Applying our techniques to the questions in *The Official Guide for GMAT Review* will prove to you that they work. Make the techniques an integral part of the way you think about tests and you will be comfortable and confident using them when it counts—on the day of your actual GMAT.

When our first book, *Cracking the System: The SAT*, was published in 1986, many people asked us when we'd be coming out with books on other tests and other subjects. Since then we've published not only the book you are reading but also *College Admissions: Cracking the System*, *Word Smart*, and guides to the GRE, LSAT, and MCAT.

If you have any questions about our course, or about academic matters in general, give us a call at 1-800-REVIEW 6.

Good luck on your GMAT!

John Katzman
President and Co-founder

PART I

Orientation

1

Orientation

WHAT IS THE GRADUATE MANAGEMENT ADMISSION TEST?

The Graduate Management Admission Test (GMAT) is a four-hour standardized test used by business schools as one tool to decide who they are going to let into their M.B.A. programs.

How Has the Test Changed?

Until recently, the GMAT was a three-and-a-half-hour multiple-choice test. However, on the October 1994 exam, the GMAT was changed to include an essay-writing section known as the Writing Assessment. The seven multiple-choice portions of the test remain—but to accommodate the Writing Assessment, these sections have been shortened from 30 minutes to 25 minutes and contain slightly fewer questions. The total testing time has been lengthened to four hours.

Here's what you will find on the GMAT:

1. a one-hour writing assessment during which you will be asked to write two essays

The rest of the test will consist of 25-minute sections of multiple-choice problems:

2. a 16-question, problem-solving math section

3. a second 16-question, problem-solving math section

4. a 20-question math section called Data Sufficiency

5. an 18-question Reading Comprehension section

6. a 22-question grammar section called Sentence Correction

7. a 16-question Critical Reasoning section

8. an Experimental section

Each administration of the GMAT will begin with the writing assessment, but after that the other seven sections can appear in any order. The Experimental section will look just like a regular section and can be from any of the section types. For example, on the test you take you might find that there are two Sentence Correction sections (one real, one Experimental). The Experimental section is never included in the scoring process. The test publisher uses it to try out new questions for future tests and to gauge the relative difficulty of your GMAT. We'll have more to say about the Experimental section later.

We're Different

Although its guiding philosophy is that people's positions in society should be determined by their scores on a series of multiple-choice tests, ETS does not hire its own executives on the basis of their test scores.

WHERE DOES THE GMAT COME FROM?

The GMAT is published by the Educational Testing Service (ETS) under the sponsorship of the Graduate Management Admission Council (GMAC). The council is supposed to oversee ETS. Both ETS and GMAC are private companies. We'll tell you more about them in this chapter.

HOW IS THE GMAT SCORED?

Four or five weeks after you've taken the GMAT, you will receive a report from ETS containing four scores:

1. your total score
   (This is reported on a scale that runs from 200 to 800.)

2. your verbal score
   (This is reported on a scale that runs from 0 to 60.)

3. your math score
   (This is also reported on a scale that runs from 0 to 60.)

4. your Writing Assessment score
   (This is reported on a scale of 1-6, in half-point increments, with 6 being the highest score.)

Business schools tend to focus on the total score, which means that you can make up for your weakness in one area by being strong in another. For example, if your quantitative skills are better than your verbal skills, they will help pull up your total score. Total scores go up or down in ten-point increments. In other words, you might receive 490 or 500 on the GMAT, never 494 or 495.

You will also see a percentile ranking next to each score. For example, if you saw a percentile of 72 next to your verbal score, it would mean that 72 percent of the people who took this test scored lower than you did on the verbal section.

ARE GMAT SCORES EQUIVALENT TO SAT SCORES?

No. Even though they both use the same 200–800 scale, GMAT scores are not the same as SAT scores. For one thing, the pool of applicants to business schools is much more select than the pool of applicants to colleges. People who take the GMAT have already graduated from college. In addition, most have several years of business experience.

The GMAT itself is more complex than the SAT. GMAT questions cover a broader range of topics and have a greater degree of difficulty.

Most people find that their GMAT score is somewhat lower than the score they received on the verbal or math SAT. According to ETS, two-thirds of the people who take the GMAT score between 380 and 590.

GMAT Scores by Phone

If you think you might want to take the GMAT again, and you want to know your scores quickly, a new ETS feature may be useful to you. By calling 1-800-463-GMAT nineteen days after your test day, you can get your scores in just a few minutes. The service costs $10.00 and is roughly twice as fast as waiting for your scores to arrive by mail. ETS accepts all major credit cards. If you decide to call, make sure you have your admission ticket with your registration number on it. This allows you to go the fully automated route, instead of waiting for a human representative to come on the line.

WHAT IS THE PRINCETON REVIEW?

The Princeton Review is a coaching school based in New York City. It has branches in over fifty cities across the country and several branches abroad. The Princeton Review's techniques are unique and powerful. We developed them after studying dozens of real ETS exams, analyzing them with computers, and proving our theories with our students. They work because they are based on the same principles that ETS uses in writing the test.

The Princeton Review's techniques for beating the GMAT will help you improve your scores by teaching you to:

1. think like the test writers at ETS

2. take full advantage of the limited time allowed

3. find the answers to questions you don't understand by using our unique process-of-elimination techniques

4. avoid the traps that ETS has set for you (and use those traps to your advantage)

A WARNING

Many of our techniques for beating the GMAT are counterintuitive. Some of them seem to violate "common sense." To get the full benefit of our techniques, you must trust them. The only way to develop this trust is to practice the techniques and convince yourself that they work.

But you have to practice them *properly*. If you try our techniques on the practice problems in most popular GMAT coaching books, you will probably decide that they don't work.

Why?

Because the practice questions in those books are very different from the questions on real GMATs. These books may have Data Sufficiency questions and Sentence Correction questions and Reading Comprehension questions, but if you compare them with the questions on real GMATs you'll find that the resemblance is only superficial. In fact, studying the practice questions and techniques in some of the other books could actually hurt your GMAT score.

One reason these coaching books do not use real GMAT questions is that the Graduate Management Admission Council won't let them. So far, the council has refused to let anyone (including us) license actual questions from old tests. The council says it is in the process of figuring out an equitable licensing system, but we aren't holding our breath. For one thing, the council has its *own* review book (published jointly with ETS) called *The Official Guide for GMAT Review*. The cover of the book boasts that it has 900 *actual* GMAT test questions. ETS is apparently not in any hurry to let anyone else have access to real questions.

For this reason, we strongly recommend that you purchase the current edition of *The Official Guide for GMAT Review*. Ignore the suggested methods for answering the questions—they are too time-consuming to be of any use during a real test—and concentrate on the real GMAT sections.

The book can be found in many bookstores, or you can order it by sending a check for $13.95 (within the United States) to:

> Graduate Management Admission Test
> Educational Testing Service
> P.O. Box 6108
> Princeton, NJ 08541-6108

By practicing our techniques on real GMATs, you will be able to prove to yourself that the techniques work and increase your confidence when you actually take the test.

A BIG CHANGE IN THE OFFING

ETS has announced that as of October 1997, the GMAT will be administered in a new format. Students will no longer be able to take the test in a paper booklet; instead, they'll have to take the test on computer.

All the question types will stay the same, but clearly this is a radical change. The "computer adaptive" GMAT will contain approximately 60 to 70 questions divided between one math section and one verbal section. Test takers will choose an answer by clicking on it with a mouse.

ETS has been offering a computer adaptive version of another of its tests, the GRE, for the past year—with mixed reviews. Some test takers feel that the computer adaptive tests are more difficult. If the new GMAT resembles the computer adaptive GRE, you will not be able to skip a question or go back to a question, you will have to use a scroll bar to see reading comprehension passages, and you will pay approximately twice as much for the privilege.

If you can take the GMAT before October 1997, we recommend that you do.

Here to Serve, Forcibly

Contrary to popular belief, ETS is not a government agency. It's a monopoly. There is almost no way around taking one of their tests and paying them for the privilege.

How to Think About the GMAT

ARE YOU A GENIUS OR AN IDIOT?

If you're like most people, you think standardized tests measure how smart you are. If you score 800 on the GMAT, you may think of yourself as a genius (and the future manager of a corporate empire). If you score 200, you may think of yourself as an idiot (and the future manager of a convenience store). You may think that the GMAT measures your math and verbal abilities. At the very least, you probably believe that the GMAT is an accurate predictor of how you'll do in business school.

One reason you might believe this is because ETS encourages you to think that it's so.

WHAT IS ETS?

If you went to ETS to interview for a job, you would be impressed with the working conditions: a beautiful 400-acre estate just outside Princeton, New Jersey. The estate used to be a hunting club, and it boasts a swimming pool, a goose pond, a baseball diamond, lighted tennis courts, jogging trails, an expensive house for the company president, and a chauffeured motor pool.

You would also be impressed with the company's financial structure. ETS is a large private company, and it makes a lot of money. (It's also tax exempt.) It sells the GMAT and the SAT of course, but it also sells about 500 other tests—including those for CIA agents, golf pros, travel agents, firemen, and barbers.

However, what would probably impress you the most, businesswise, is the fact that ETS has pulled off a deal that would in any other field have rendered it liable to antitrust action: ETS has a monopoly.

TO GET INTO BUSINESS SCHOOL YOU CAN

A) take the GMAT

B) take the GMAT

If you don't like *Time*, you can read *Newsweek*. If you don't like AT&T, there are a host of competitors to choose from. But if you don't like the GMAT . . . well, you might as well consider going into social work.

ETS won't mind. They write that test, too.

It might strike you that a company could get fat and lazy without any competition to keep it honest, but you can't really blame ETS for trying to hold on to a deal that's as sweet as this one. And in order to do that, ETS must convince both you and the business schools to whom you are applying that the GMAT actually measures something.

There's just one hitch. It doesn't.

WHAT DOES THE GMAT MEASURE?

The GMAT is not a test of how smart you are. Nor is it a test of your business acumen. **It's simply a test of how good you are at taking ETS tests.** ETS says that "the GMAT is not a test of knowledge in specific subjects." This is also untrue. In fact, you will learn that by studying the very specific knowledge outlined in this book, you can substantially improve your score.

Not Just the College Board

Here is a partial list of organizations that buy tests from ETS:

The CIA
The Defense Department
The National Security Council
The government of Trinidad and Tobago
National Contact Lens Examiners
The American Society of Heating, Refrigerating, and Air-conditioning Engineers

The GMAT as Job Interview

The first axiom of any how-to book on job interviewing is that you must always tell your interviewer what he or she wants to hear. Whether or not this is good job-hunting advice, it happens to be a very useful strategy on the GMAT. The test writers at ETS think in very predictable ways. You can improve your score by learning to think the way they do and by learning to anticipate the kinds of answers they think are correct.

Who Writes the GMAT?

Many people believe that GMAT questions are written by university professors or successful executives. This is not true. Virtually all questions are written by ordinary company employees or by college students and other people who are hired part time from outside ETS. Sometimes the questions are even written by teenagers. The daughter of one ETS vice-president spent the summer after she graduated from high school writing questions for ETS tests.

ETS "examiners" try to write each question so that it can be used in as many as four different tests. Some of the questions from the GMAT have turned up on the SAT. As you struggle with a difficult question on the GMAT, it may console you to know that somewhere in America a hapless barber is having even more trouble with it than you are.

How Much Does the GMAT Change from Test to Test?

Not very much. Imagine that you're one of ETS's test writers struggling to produce tests that will be taken by over 7 million students each year. Not only must your test question be suitable for the test you are now writing, but it must also be good enough to be included in a file from which future test questions for other tests may be chosen. Under these circumstances, what is needed is a kind of generic question written according to established formulas. While ETS has tried several different question types over the years, the essential philosophy of the GMAT hasn't changed much since the test was first administered in 1954.

Will ETS Change the Test in Response to The Princeton Review?

To make a significant change in the GMAT, ETS would have to alter its most fundamental notions of standardized testing. Until ETS is willing to give up its essential philosophy, the GMAT will remain a flawed test, and our techniques (which are based on those flaws) will continue to work just fine.

However, we are not asleep. We monitor each new GMAT very closely. Each year, we will publish a new edition of this book to reflect the subtle shifts that happen over time, as well as any changes in question type.

Forget About the "Best" Answer

The instructions for the GMAT tell you to select the "best" answer to every question. What does "best" answer mean? **It means the answer ETS believes to be correct.**

Is the GMAT Just Like the SAT?

The GMAT and the SAT are both prepared by the same organization, so they share the same philosophy. But there are substantial differences between the two tests. The GMAT is a much tougher test, and it contains question types not found on the SAT. Many of the techniques developed by The Princeton Review for the SAT are useful on some sections of the GMAT, but we have also developed new techniques and expanded on some of the old ones.

Scapegoats

According to David Owen, in his book *None of the Above*, declining test scores have been blamed on many things in the last thirty years: the assassination of President Kennedy, the increased incidence of marriage among female teachers, communism, the American Civil Liberties Union, fluoridated water, feminism, witches, the Vietnam War, the civil rights movement, and the use of anesthesia in childbirth.

Is This Book Just Like the Princeton Review Course?

No. You won't have the benefit of taking four proctored GMATs that are analyzed and scored by our computers. You won't get to sit in small classes with ten other highly motivated students who will spur you on. You won't get to work with two expert instructors who can assess your strengths and pinpoint your weaknesses. There is no way to put these things in a book.

What you *will* find in this book are some of the techniques and methods that have enabled our students to crack the system—plus a review of the essentials you cannot afford not to know.

If at all possible, you should take our course. If that is impossible, then there is this book.

How to Crack the System

In the following chapters we're going to teach you our method for cracking the GMAT. Read each chapter carefully. Some of our ideas may seem strange at first. For example, when we tell you that it is sometimes easier to answer hard GMAT questions without actually working out the entire problem, you may think, "This isn't the way I conduct business."

The GMAT Isn't About Business

We're not going to teach you business skills. We're not going to teach you math and English. We're going to teach you the GMAT.

3

Cracking the System:
Basic Principles

HOW TO SCORE HIGHER (INSTANTLY) ON THE GMAT

Nothing else we're going to suggest in this book will be as easy to accomplish as what we're about to tell you. In the following pages we will show you many powerful techniques to raise your score, and give you many insights into the way this test is designed, but none will be as simple to make use of as this first basic concept:

DON'T ANSWER ALL THE QUESTIONS!

Most people take the GMAT as if it were a race with points awarded for completing the course. Answering every single question hastily somehow seems preferable to answering most of the questions carefully. Nothing could be further from the truth.

It turns out that you can score extremely well on the GMAT by completely skipping some of the questions. While the scoring formula varies slightly from test to test, here are some general guidelines, taking into account the new, slightly shorter format.

> You can score above 550 (which is itself well above the national average) by getting 20 questions wrong and completely ignoring 20 questions.

That works out to skipping an average of 3 questions on *every* section.

Don't believe us? On the GMAT administered in October 1995, someone who got 20 questions wrong and skipped an additional 20 questions scored a 560.

> You can score above 500 on the GMAT by getting 25 questions wrong and completely ignoring 25 questions.

That works out to skipping an average of 4 questions on *every* section.

On the October 1995 GMAT, someone who got 25 questions wrong and skipped 25 questions scored 510.

YOU MAY THINK YOU ALREADY SKIP QUESTIONS

Most students end up skipping a few questions. Of course, they're not really "skipping" these questions. They look at a question, spend three minutes trying to figure it out and then end up leaving it blank. In other words, they "skip" problems because they don't know the answer.

DON'T YOU DARE SKIP A QUESTION JUST BECAUSE YOU DON'T KNOW THE CORRECT ANSWER

This may sound a little loony, but it turns out that you don't always have to know the correct answer to get a question right.

Try answering the following question:

What is the unit of currency in Yugoslavia?

What? You don't know? You'd better skip it then.

Unless you work for an international bank or have traveled in Eastern Europe, there is no reason why you should know the unit of currency in Yugoslavia. (By the way, the GMAT doesn't ask such factual questions. We're using this one to make a point.) As it stands now, since you don't know the answer you would have to skip this question, right?

Not necessarily. GMAT questions are written in multiple-choice format. One of the five choices has to be the answer. How do you find it?

LOOK FOR WRONG ANSWERS INSTEAD OF RIGHT ONES

Let's put this question into a multiple-choice format—the only format you'll ever find on the GMAT—and see if you still want to skip it.

What is the unit of currency in Yugoslavia?

(A) the dollar
(B) the franc
(C) the pound sterling
(D) the yen
(E) the dinar

HOW TO SCORE HIGHER (ALMOST INSTANTLY) ON THE GMAT

Suddenly this question isn't difficult anymore. You may not have known the right answer, but you certainly knew enough to eliminate the wrong answers. Wrong answers are often easier to spot than right answers. Sometimes they just sound weird. At other times they're logically impossible. While it is rare to be able to eliminate all four of the incorrect answer choices on the GMAT, you will almost always be able to eliminate at least one of them—and frequently two or more—by using Process of Elimination. Process of Elimination (POE for short) will enable you to answer questions that you don't have the time or the inclination to figure out exactly. We will refer to POE in every single chapter of this book. It is one of the most fundamental tools you will use to increase your score.

Try another example:

> Which of the following countries uses the peso as its unit of currency?
>
> (A) Russia
> (B) Canada
> (C) Venezuela
> (D) England
> (E) Chile

This time you can probably only get rid of three of the five answer choices using POE. The answer is clearly *not* Russia, Canada or England, but most people probably don't know for sure whether the answer is Venezuela or Chile.

You've got the question down to two possibilities. Should you guess, or just leave the question blank?

HEADS OR TAILS

A Chilean might flip a peso. You have a fifty-fifty chance of getting this question right—heads you win, tails you lose.

But how much do you stand to win or lose?

ETS figures out your score by adding up all the questions you get right and then subtracting a quarter of all the questions you get wrong. (Blank answers are completely ignored—they don't cost you any points and they don't add any points.) The sum of correct answers minus a quarter of incorrect answers is your raw score. Using a "scoring formula," this is then converted into the number somewhere between 200 and 800 that will be sent to the business schools you're applying to.

> For every correct answer, you get one raw point.
>
> For every blank answer, you get nothing.
>
> For every wrong answer, ETS subtracts one-fourth of a raw point.

In other words, four mistakes will erase one correct answer. ETS does this to prevent you from guessing randomly, but let's see how this really works.

GUESSING IS GOOD

Raw points and scaled scores are confusing. Let's put this in terms of something we deal with every day: money.

For every answer you get right, ETS will give you a dollar. For every question you leave blank, ETS will give you nothing. For every answer you get wrong, ETS will take away twenty-five cents.

If you guessed completely at random on five questions, what would happen? There are five answer choices for each question, so you would have a one-in-five chance of getting the right answer on each of the questions. According to the laws of probability, you should get one out of the five questions correct.

So ETS gives you a dollar.

In the meantime, you got four questions wrong. So ETS takes away a quarter for each of the four questions.

What just happened? By guessing completely at random, you ended up with exactly the same score as if you had left all five questions blank. In other words, guessing didn't hurt you. Guessing *never* hurts you.

HEADS YOU WIN A DOLLAR, TAILS YOU LOSE A QUARTER

Let's go back to the peso problem. We were down to a fifty-fifty guess. The answer was Chile or Venezuela. In this case we're no longer guessing at random. We've eliminated three of the answer choices—the odds are much better now. Heads you win a dollar, tails you lose a quarter.

Suppose there were two problems you didn't know how to solve on the GMAT but POE allowed you to eliminate three answer choices on each of them. This leaves you with two fifty-fifty guesses. The odds say you'll get one of these two questions correct. So ETS gives you a dollar. The odds say you'll get the other one wrong. So ETS takes away twenty-five cents.

You're seventy-five cents ahead.

YOU CAN INCREASE YOUR SCORE BY GUESSING

In the chapters that follow, we'll show you specific ways to make use of POE to increase your score. You may feel uncomfortable about using these techniques at first, but the sooner you make them your own, the sooner you'll start to improve your score.

IS THIS FAIR?

If you took any math courses in college you probably remember that the correct answer to a problem, while important, wasn't the only thing you were graded on. Your professor was surely more interested in *how* you got the answer, whether you wrote an elegant equation or used the right formula.

If your equation was correct but you messed up your addition at the end, did you get the entire question wrong? Most college professors give partial credit for an answer like that. After all, what's most important is the mental process that goes into getting the answer, not the answer alone.

On the GMAT, if you don't pencil in the right oval on your answer sheet, you're wrong. It doesn't matter that you knew *how* to do the problem, or that you marked the wrong answer on your answer sheet *by mistake*. You're just wrong.

This really isn't fair. It seems only fitting that you should be able to benefit from the flip side of this situation. If you fill in the correct oval, ETS doesn't care how you got that answer either.

When you leave a question blank on the GMAT, the impression you give is that you knew nothing about the question. But consider the peso question. While it's true that you probably weren't sure of the exact answer, you did know several things about that problem: You knew three answers that were definitely wrong. Didn't you deserve partial credit for knowing that?

You won't get it unless you guess.

So, What Are the *Appropriate* Uses?

The following is a list of what ETS considers "inappropriate uses" of GMAT scores:

1. as a requisite for awarding a degree

2. as a requirement for employment, for licensing or certification to perform a job, or for job-related rewards (raises, promotions, etc.)

3. as an achievement test

If Guessing Is So Great, Why Leave ANY Questions Blank?

First of all, on some questions you really may not know anything. If there are no answer choices you can eliminate, there is no sense in guessing. Second, POE takes time. Spending time with all the questions in a section will cause you to rush and make careless mistakes, and may cause you to fall into the traps ETS has set for you. On problems where you have to guess, take the time to make sure you guess well.

So Which Questions Should You Skip?

There are two types of questions you should skip.

The ones you don't like. Let's imagine that you're in the middle of a 16-question problem-solving section. If you're shooting for a score of 550, you know that you can safely skip three problems and still have room to make a few mistakes.

This means that all you have to do on this section is find roughly thirteen problems that you like.

If you take one look at problem number 8 and develop an instant, unreasoning hatred for it, skip it and never give it a second thought.

The ones you know absolutely nothing about. If there is absolutely nothing you can think of to do on a problem, then it makes no sense to spend any time on it. Skip it and move on.

SUMMARY

1. You don't need to answer every question on the GMAT in order to get an extremely good score. By skipping some questions, you save time and improve your accuracy on the ones you choose to do.

2. Not knowing the exact answer to a question, however, is not a good reason to leave it blank.

3. When you don't know the right answer to a question, look for wrong answers instead. This is called POE.

4. Guessing blindly will not hurt your score. Guessing well will *raise* your score.

4

Cracking the System:
Advanced Principles

PUTTING THE BASIC PRINCIPLES TO WORK

In the last chapter we reviewed some basic principles about cracking the GMAT. We showed you that it is possible to:

1. find correct answers by using POE, the Process of Elimination, to get rid of incorrect answer choices

2. earn partial credit for partial information

In this chapter we'll show you which choices to eliminate, when you should guess and when it makes sense to skip a question entirely.

You'll also learn how to:

1. take advantage of question order, particularly on the math sections

2. make better use of your time by scoring the easy points first

3. use the Joe Bloggs principle to eliminate obviously incorrect choices

4. find the traps ETS has set for you

5. turn these traps into points

ORDER OF DIFFICULTY

If you've seen an actual GMAT, you probably noticed that the questions in the math sections got harder as you went along. You probably didn't think much of it at the time, but this is always true on the GMAT. Every math section starts out easy and gets progressively harder. In the verbal sections the same principles apply, although you'll see as you get to the chapters that cover these sections that the verbal strategies we will be showing you will make the order of difficulty irrelevant.

Easy, Medium, Hard

In general it's a good idea to think of each math section of the GMAT as having three parts:

1. The easy third: Questions in the first third of a section are easy.

2. The medium third: Questions in the middle third are medium.

3. The difficult third: Questions in the last third are difficult.

If you keep this in mind, you'll have a big advantage on the GMAT. You'll know that it's silly to spend a lot of time trying to answer the last (and therefore hardest) question of a math section before you've answered all the easy questions.

All questions on the GMAT are worth the same number of points. Why not do the easy ones first? Smart test takers save the hard questions for last, after they've racked up all the easy points.

A Little History

In the 1950s, ETS shipped its 368 different tests with what it called "special electrographic pencils" (mechanical pencils with #2 lead). The pencils made marks that could be read by the company's automatic scoring machines, which contained hundreds of electrified metal prongs, one for each square on the answer sheet. The young women on the staff graded test papers by feeding them into these machines one at a time and lowering the prongs to the surface of the paper. Every time one of the prongs touched a blackened square corresponding to a correct answer, the graphite on the paper completed an electrical circuit. Then the women read the number of correct answers from a dial on the front of the machine and wrote it down.

LIES, DAMNED LIES, AND STATISTICS

Why does ETS construct the GMAT this way? ETS is obsessed with statistics. One statistic ETS thinks is important is the accuracy of its tests in measuring low-scoring as well as high-scoring students. The GMAT is supposed to measure "general developed abilities" over a wide spectrum. In other words, it is supposed to be just as fair in assessing the ability of someone who scores 200 as it is in assessing the abilities of someone who scores 800.

If ETS put the difficult questions first, many people would never get to the easier questions that they could answer correctly. So ETS puts the easiest questions first and gradually increases the level of difficulty. It is not much different from a high jump contest in which the bar is raised a notch on each round. The theory is that a student will answer questions correctly until he or she reaches his or her level of ability, and then will get everything else wrong. This is supposed to ensure that each student receives every point he or she "deserves."

The people at ETS are very pleased with the GMAT. After all, they write it, and it makes a lot of money for them every year. In fact, they think this test is so good it can make a meaningful distinction between someone who scores 420 and someone who scores 450. They're especially proud of their statistics. Just about every article we've ever seen about education in America uses statistics compiled by ETS. But ETS has this little problem.

ETS's PROBLEM

The GMAT is a multiple-choice test.

That may not seem like a problem to you, but consider the following situation. Suppose an average student takes the GMAT and answers all the questions he understands. The student is all set to put down his pencil when one last difficult question catches his eye. One of the answer choices just "seems" right. So he picks it.

And gets it right.

ETS gets nightmares just thinking about this situation. That average student was supposed to get 500. He "deserved" 500. But by guessing the correct answer to one extra problem, he may have gotten 510.

Ten points more than he "deserved."

ETS's SOLUTION

ETS's statistics wouldn't be worth much if students could routinely guess the correct answer to difficult questions by picking answers that *seemed* right.

So ETS came up with a wonderful solution:

On difficult questions, answer choices that *seem* right to the average student are always wrong.

CHOOSING ANSWERS THAT *SEEM* RIGHT

When we take the GMAT, most of us don't have time to work out every problem completely, or to check and double-check our answers. We just go as far as we can on each problem and then choose the answer that seems correct based on what we've been able to figure out. Sometimes we're completely sure of our answer. At other times we simply do what we can and then follow our hunch. We may pick an answer because it "just looks right," or because something about it seems to go naturally with the question.

Whether you're a high scorer or a low scorer, this is almost certainly the way you approach the GMAT. You figure out as much of each problem as you can and then choose the answer that seems right, all things considered. Sometimes you're fairly positive that your answer is correct. But at other times—on hard problems—all you can do is follow your hunch and hope you're right.

WHICH ANSWERS SEEM RIGHT?

That all depends on how high your score is.

Suppose you took the GMAT and scored 800. That means every answer that *seemed* right to you actually *was* right. You picked the answer that seemed right on every question, and every one of those answers was correct.

Now suppose your friend took the GMAT and scored 200. That means every answer that *seemed* right to your friend actually was *wrong*.

Of course, most people who take the GMAT don't score 800 or 200. The average person scores somewhere in between.

WHAT HAPPENS WHEN THE AVERAGE PERSON TAKES THE GMAT?

The average person isn't right all the time. But the average person isn't wrong all the time, either. Like everybody else, the average person picks the answer that *seems* right on every problem. Sometimes these hunches are correct; sometimes they are not.

To be specific:

◆ On the easy questions in each section, the average person tends to pick the correct answer. The answers that seem right to the average person actually are right on these questions.

◆ On the medium questions in each section, the average person's hunches are right only some of the time. Sometimes the answers that seem right to the average person really are right; sometimes they are wrong.

◆ Finally, on the difficult third, the average person's hunches are always wrong. The answers that seem right to the average person on these questions invariably turn out to be wrong.

MEET JOE BLOGGS

We're going to talk a lot about "the average person" from now on. For the sake of convenience, let's give him a name: Joe Bloggs. Joe Bloggs is just the average American prospective business-school student. He has average grades from college, and will get an average grade on the GMAT. There's a little bit of him in everyone, and there's a little bit of everyone in him. He isn't brilliant. He isn't dumb. He's exactly average.

HOW DOES JOE BLOGGS APPROACH THE GMAT?

Joe Bloggs, the average person, approaches the GMAT just as everybody else does. Whether the question is hard or easy, he always chooses the answer that *seems* to be correct.

Here's an example of what a difficult problem might look like on a GMAT problem-solving section:

14. The output of a factory was increased by 10% to keep up with rising demand. To handle the holiday rush, this new output was increased by 20%. By approximately what percent would the output now have to be decreased in order to restore the original output?
    - (A) 20%
    - (B) 24%
    - (C) 30%
    - (D) 32%
    - (E) 79%

This question is from the last third of a math problem-solving section. Therefore, according to the order of difficulty, it is one of the hardest problems in that section. Don't bother trying to work the problem out now. You will learn how to do this type of problem (percentage decrease) in the first math chapter.

HOW DID JOE BLOGGS DO ON THIS QUESTION?

He got it wrong.
Why?
Because ETS set a trap for him.

WHICH ANSWER DID JOE BLOGGS PICK ON THIS QUESTION?

Joe didn't think this was a hard problem. The answer *seemed* perfectly obvious. Joe Bloggs picked choice (C). Joe assumed that if you increase production first by 10% and then by 20%, you have to take away 30% to get back to where you started. Joe chose choice (C) as his answer.

Tennis Anyone?

The ETS "campus," in Princeton (actually, Lawrence Township), New Jersey, features lighted tennis courts, a baseball diamond, a swimming pool, a croquet lawn, a private hotel, a sauna, nature paths, and cavorting deer.

ETS led Joe away from the correct answer, and actually may have encouraged him to guess, by giving him an answer that *seemed* right. In fact, the correct answer is choice (B). Here's the same problem with slightly different answer choices. We've changed the choices to make a point:

What's in a Name?

In 1976, *Forbes* Magazine called ETS "one of the hottest little growth companies in US business."

14. The output of a factory was increased by 10% to keep up with rising demand. To handle the holiday rush, this new output was raised by 20%. By approximately what percent would the output now have to be decreased in order to restore the original output?

   (A) 21%
   (B) 24%
   (C) 34.2%
   (D) 37%
   (E) 71.5%

If Joe had seen this version, he wouldn't have thought it was an easy question anymore. Now none of the answers would *seem* right to Joe. He might have left it blank, or he might have guessed. This would have made the question fairer, but ETS didn't want to take the chance that an *average* person might get this question right by mistake.

COULD ETS HAVE MADE THIS AN EASY QUESTION INSTEAD?

Sure, by writing different answer choices.

Here's the same question with choices we've substituted to make the correct answer choice obvious:

14. The output of a factory was increased by 10% to keep up with rising demand. To handle the holiday rush, this new output was raised by 20%. By approximately what percent would the output now have to be decreased in order to restore the original output?

   (A) a million %
   (B) 24 %
   (C) a billion %
   (D) a trillion %
   (E) a zillion %

When the problem is written this way, Joe Bloggs can see that the answer has to be choice (B). It seems right to Joe because all the other answers seem obviously wrong.

PROFITING FROM OTHER PEOPLE'S BANKRUPTCY

Everyone knows about a company that is a textbook example of how *not* to run a company.

Suppose you started your own company, with three partners: Freddie Laker, John DeLorean, and Ivan Boesky. You have an important business decision to make, and each of your partners gives you his advice. Laker says, "Sell your product for less than it cost you to make it. It always worked for me." DeLorean says, "I have a great investment opportunity for you. Get together $200,000 in cash and call this number in Bolivia." Boesky says, "Listen, what you need is good inside information."

Are you going to make use of the advice of these losers? Sure, you now know three things you're not going to do.

Joe Bloggs is a textbook example of how *not* to take a test.

YOUR PARTNER ON THE TEST: JOE BLOGGS

When you take the GMAT a few weeks or months from now, you'll have to take it on your own, of course. But suppose for a moment that ETS allowed you to take it with Joe Bloggs as your partner. Would Joe be any help to you on the GMAT?

YOU PROBABLY DON'T THINK SO

After all, Joe is wrong as often as he's right. He knows the answers to the easy questions, but so do you. You'd like to do better than average on the GMAT, and Joe earns only an average score (he's the average person, remember). All things considered, you'd probably prefer to have someone else for your partner.

But Joe might turn out to be a pretty helpful partner, after all. Since his hunches on difficult questions are *always* wrong, couldn't you improve your chances on those questions simply by finding out what Joe wanted to pick, and then picking something else?

If you could use what you know about Joe Bloggs to eliminate one, two, or even three obviously incorrect choices on a hard problem, wouldn't you improve your score by guessing among the remaining choices?

THE JOE BLOGGS PRINCIPLE

We're going to teach you how to use Joe Bloggs on the GMAT. When you come to difficult questions on the test, you're going to stop and ask yourself, "How would Joe Bloggs answer this question?" And when you see what he would do, you're going to do something else. Why? Because you know that on hard questions, Joe Bloggs is *always* wrong.

Highest Salaries Paid to Dead People

Elvis Presley	$15.0 million
Ian Fleming	$7.5 million
John Lennon	$5.0 million
Jimi Hendrix	$4.0 million
T.S. Eliot	$2.5 million
James Dean	$1.2 million
Jim Morrison	$1.0 million
Marilyn Monroe	$1.0 million
John Wayne	$ .7 million
Abbott and Costello	$ .4 million

Source: *Forbes*, 1990

What If Joe Bloggs Is Right?

Remember what we said about Joe Bloggs at the beginning. He's the average person. He thinks the way most people do. If the right answer to a hard question seemed right to most people, the question wouldn't be hard, would it?

Joe Bloggs is right on some questions: the easy ones. But he's always wrong on the hard questions.

Should You Always Just Eliminate Any Answer That Seems to Be Correct?

No!

Remember what we said about Joe Bloggs:

1. His hunches are often correct on easy questions.

2. His hunches are sometimes correct and sometimes incorrect on medium questions.

3. His hunches are always wrong on difficult questions.

Putting Joe Bloggs to Work for You

In the following chapters, we'll be teaching you many specific problem-solving techniques based on the Joe Bloggs principle. The Joe Bloggs principle will help you:

1. use POE to eliminate incorrect answer choices

2. make up your mind when you have to guess

3. avoid careless mistakes

SUMMARY

1. The questions in each of the three math sections start out easy and gradually get harder. Most people are supposed to get the first question correct. Almost no one is expected to get the last one correct.

2. The questions in the verbal sections generally follow the same pattern, but you will find that our techniques will make ETS's order of difficulty irrelevant.

3. Since you know where the easy questions are located, you should never waste time trying to figure out the answer to a hard question if there are still easy questions you haven't tried. All questions are worth the same number of points. Why not do the easy ones first?

4. Except for Sentence Correction questions, every section of the GMAT can be divided into thirds by degree of difficulty as follows:

   ◆ On the easy third of each section, the average person gets most of the answers right. The answers that *seem* right to the average person actually *are* right on these questions.

   ◆ On the medium third of each section, though, the average person's hunches are right only some of the time. Sometimes the answers that *seem* right to the average person really *are* right; sometimes they are wrong.

   ◆ Finally, on the difficult third, the average person's hunches are *always* wrong. The average person picks the correct answer on the hardest questions only by accident. The answers that *seem* right to the average person on these questions invariably turn out to be wrong.

5. Almost everyone approaches the GMAT by choosing the answer that *seems* correct, all things considered.

6. Joe Bloggs is the average person. He earns an average score on the GMAT. On easy GMAT questions, the answers that *seem* correct to him are usually correct. On medium questions, they're sometimes correct and sometimes not. On hard questions, they're *always* wrong.

7. The correct answer on a hard question could never seem right to most people. If it did, the question would be easy, not hard.

Taking the GMAT

TICK, TICK, TICK . . .

If you've read the first four chapters of this book, you've already begun to see that while doing well on this test involves proper utilization of time, the GMAT isn't quite the race against time you may have thought it to be.

Using the pacing guidelines on page 14, you can begin to map out a strategy of how many questions you actually need to answer in order to get the score you're looking for. There will be many problems you can afford to skip completely.

We're going to show you some powerful techniques in the chapters ahead. To take full advantage of these techniques, it's important that you practice on real GMATs. The practice tests in most other GMAT preparation books won't help you; they aren't sufficiently like real GMATs. The only available source of real GMAT questions is a book we've already mentioned in the first chapter: *The Official Guide for GMAT Review*, which is published by ETS.

Periodically, as you work through this book, you should time yourself while taking real GMAT sections. This will give you practice in using our techniques, and get you used to taking the test under timed conditions.

THE PRINCETON REVIEW DIAGNOSTIC TEST

At the back of this book you will find a complete GMAT diagnostic test designed by The Princeton Review. While not a real ETS exam, our diagnostic offers one important advantage the real ones do not: our answer key (found at the end of the test) not only provides you with the correct answers and a scoring chart but also explains each question in detail, and gives you hints as to which Princeton Review techniques can help to answer each question. We recommend that you take this exam about halfway through your preparation.

ON THE DAY OF THE REAL TEST

Get up early, have breakfast, and do a couple of GMAT questions you've already seen in order to get your mind working. You don't want to have to warm up on the test itself. Bring a snack to the test center. You'll probably get two breaks during the test. Some people spend the breaks comparing answers in the hallway and getting upset because their answers don't match. Ignore the people around you. Why assume that they know any more than you do? Use the break to eat the food you've brought.

At the test site you'll be asked for some form of picture ID. Your driver's license, passport, or employee ID will do. Bring four sharpened No. 2 pencils, a ballpoint pen for the Writing Assessment, and a reliable watch, preferably digital. No calculators are permitted.

Before the test starts, make sure you're comfortable. Is there enough light? Is your desk sturdy? Don't be afraid to speak up; you're going to be spending four hours at that desk.

As you begin each new section, put the last one behind you. Don't get rattled if you think you've done poorly on a particular section. Most people find that their impression of how they did on a section is often worse than the reality. More important, you should remember that one of the seven sections you'll be taking doesn't count. The Experimental section is often harder and weirder than

What to Bring to the Test Center

(1) your registration ticket
(2) a photo ID
(3) a reliable watch
(4) several #2 pencils
(5) a snack

the rest of the test. If you feel you've blown a particular section, there's a good chance it was Experimental.

However, even if you're sure you've spotted the Experimental section, never just blow it off. Take each section as if it counts. You don't want to be wrong about something so important.

At the End of the Test

When you finish the test, there will be some time while the proctor reads you the final thank-you-for-flying-ETS instructions and collects test booklets. Do not use this time to darken the little oval that allows you to cancel your scores then and there. If you choose to cancel at the test site, you will not be able to change your mind later. Even if you're unhappy with the way the test went, you should certainly go home and sleep on it before making a decision. If you still want to cancel, you can do so later by mail. ETS must receive your written request to cancel within seven days of the test.

Do *not* assume that your test has been scored correctly. Send away for ETS's Test Disclosure Service. For $10, ETS will send you a copy of the test you took (minus the Experimental section) and a photocopy of your answer sheet. It is possible that one or more of your responses was too faint to be picked up by the scanning machine but is perfectly visible to the eye. By the same token, an erased answer may have been scored as an incorrect response. Check your answers against the key and complain if you think you've been misscored.

One Final Thought Before You Begin

No matter how high or low you score on this test, and no matter how much you improve your performance with this book, you should *never* accept the score ETS sends you as an accurate assessment of your abilities. The temptation to see a high score as evidence that you're a genius, or a low score as evidence that you're an idiot, can be very powerful.

When you've read this book and practiced our techniques on real GMAT questions, you'll be able to judge for yourself whether the GMAT actually measures much besides how well you do on the GMAT.

Think of this as a kind of game—a game you can get good at.

PART ◆ II

How to Crack the Verbal GMAT

Sentence Correction

6

The Sentence Correction section of the GMAT is composed of 22 sentences, each of which is partly underlined. You have to decide whether a sentence is grammatically correct the way it is written or, if it needs a correction, which of the answer choices best replaces the underlined portion.

Before we begin, take a moment to read the following instructions. They are a close approximation of instructions you will see on the real GMAT. Be sure you know and understand these instructions before you take the GMAT. If you learn them ahead of time, you won't have to waste valuable seconds reading them on the day you take the test.

> <u>Directions</u>: Part or all of each sentence that follows has been underlined. If you think the sentence is correct as written, pick answer choice A, which simply repeats the underlined portion exactly. If you think there is something wrong with the sentence as written, choose the answer choice that best <u>replaces</u> the underlined portion of the sentence.

> This section is designed to measure your correct use of grammar, your ability to form clear and effective sentences and your capacity to choose the most appropriate words. Pick the answer that best states what was meant in the original sentence, avoiding constructions which are awkward, unclear, or which unnecessarily repeat themselves.

THE BAD NEWS

It is important to understand the fine print of the instructions you have just read. The test writers at ETS ask you to choose the "best" answer, by which they mean the answer they think is right. The bad news is that some of the "correct" answer choices in this section will probably not sound correct to you. The rules of English as interpreted by ETS are very different from the rules of English that govern what we read in newspapers or hear on television or speak in our everyday lives.

How many times have you heard your boss, or a television anchorperson, or a president of the United States, make the following statement?

> "Hopefully, we will know the answer to that question tomorrow."

While you probably don't want to make a habit of correcting people's grammar, you should know that this sentence is not technically correct. According to ETS, the president was supposed to say, "It is hoped that we will know the answer to that question tomorrow." It may be of some comfort to you that your boss, the television anchorperson, and the president of the United States would all get a question like this wrong if they took the GMAT.

GMAT ENGLISH

GMAT English should be studied the same way you would approach any other foreign language. It has its own rules and its own internal logic. GMAT English has much in common with American English, but if you rely solely on your ear, you may get into trouble.

Confronted with a badly constructed sentence, most of us could find *a* way to fix that sentence. Most of the time we would probably break the sentence into two separate sentences (GMAT sentences are often too long and unwieldy). Unfortunately, on this test we are forced to find *the* way to fix the sentence; that is to say, ETS's way to fix it.

To do well on this section of the test, you will have to learn GMAT English.

B-School Lingo

Hard Courses: anything with numbers

HP12-C: the calculator of choice for numbers crunching

THE GOOD NEWS

ETS test writers try to stick to the basics. If they tested a controversial point of grammar, they might be proven wrong. They don't want to have to change their minds after a test is given and mail 20,000 letters explaining why they're changing the answer key (something that has happened from time to time in the past). The easiest way to avoid trouble is to test a handful of the rules of standard written English that are commonly agreed upon.

There are huge books devoted exclusively to the correct use of English. You could spend the next six weeks just studying grammar and never even scratch the surface. The good news is that this won't be necessary. Although there are hundreds of rules of standard written English that could be tested, the GMAT concentrates on only a few.

In other words, GMAT English is fairly easy to learn.

SENTENCE CORRECTION: CRACKING THE SYSTEM

In this chapter we'll show you the most common types of errors tested in GMAT sentences, and how to spot them. We'll show you how ETS chooses the four incorrect choices for each question, and we'll show you how to use Process of Elimination to make your life a lot easier.

To forestall the objections of the expert grammarians out there, let us say at the outset that this discussion is not designed to be an all-inclusive discussion of English grammar. You are reading this chapter to do well on sentence correction *as it appears on the GMAT*. Thus, if we seem to oversimplify a point, or ignore an arcane exception to a rule, it is because we do not feel that any more detail is warranted. Remember, this isn't English; it's GMAT English.

ORDER OF DIFFICULTY

According to ETS, the Sentence Correction section usually starts with easy sentences, gets progressively more difficult, and then finishes with a couple of easy sentences. Most of our students find that they can't tell the difference; the first question often seems as poorly worded as the last. You will find that our Sentence Correction techniques make the order of difficulty in this section irrelevant.

PROCESS OF ELIMINATION

Nice Work, If You Can Get It

In 1980, ETS started publishing their books of tests and selling them in bookstores. They took tests developed with money they got from you, the test taker, bound them, and sold them back to you again.

Most people approach Sentence Correction questions the same way. They read the original sentence and then read the entire sentence again, substituting answer choice (B) for the underlined part. Then they go back and do the same thing for answer choices (C), (D), and (E). This approach is both laborious and confusing. It's hard to keep five different versions of the same sentence straight, especially when all five of them are awkward.

The Princeton Review approach will utilize Process of Elimination to narrow down your choices before you have to start reading the answer choices carefully.

Since there are relatively few types of errors that appear on the Sentence Correction section, we will focus on teaching you how to spot these errors. Once you've spotted the error in a sentence you'll be able to go through the answer choices and eliminate any that also contain that error. Then you can decide among the remaining choices.

BASIC PRINCIPLES

Let's look at a Sentence Correction question written in a way that you will unfortunately never see on the real GMAT—with only the correct answer listed:

> Registered brokerage firms have been required to
> record details of all computerized program trades
> made in the past year so that government agencies
> <u>will be able to decide if they should be banned</u>.
>
> (A)
> (B)
> (C)
> (D)
> (E)   will be able to decide if program trades should
> be banned

Piece of cake, right? It gets a little harder when they throw in the other four answer choices. Don't worry if you aren't sure why answer choice (E) is better than the original sentence. We will cover how to spot this type of error (pronoun reference) a little later in the chapter. For now, it's enough to know that the "they" in the underlined portion of the sentence was ambiguous. It wasn't clear whether "they" referred to "registered brokerage firms," "details," or the "computerized program trades."

Don't bother saying it was perfectly obvious that "they" referred to the program trades. This is GMAT English, remember? It doesn't matter if *you* knew what the sentence meant. The sentence had to be clear to the ETS test writer who wrote it.

ZEN AND THE ART OF TEST WRITING

Let's put ourselves in the place of the GMAT test writer who wrote this question. He has just finished his sentence and he has his correct answer, but he isn't finished yet. He still has to write four other answer choices. It's actually kind of difficult to come up with four answer choices that seem plausible but are wrong. If the test writer makes the incorrect choices too obviously wrong, Joe Bloggs might be able to pick the correct answer without having really understood the rule of English involved. If the test writer makes the incorrect answer choices too subtle, Joe Bloggs won't find one that seems right to him, and therefore might guess at random. The test writer does *not* want Joe to guess at random. If Joe guesses at random, he might actually pick the right answer.

ONE DOWN, FOUR TO GO

Selecting the correct answer was easy for our test writer—after all, *he* wrote the question. He will probably spend much more time on the incorrect answer choices.

Answer Choice (A)

Coming up with the first wrong answer choice also is easy for our test writer; answer choice (A) always repeats the underlined part of the original sentence. This is the choice to select if you think the sentence is correct as written. Two down, three to go.

IF YOU CAN'T SELL A LEMON, REPACKAGE IT

To see whether Joe has spotted the error of the sentence, the ETS test writer will include the *same error* in at least one, usually two, of the other answer choices. If Joe didn't like the error in the original sentence, maybe he'll like it better surrounded by different words. Look at the same sentence again, this time with two incorrect answer choices that both include the same error found in the original sentence:

> Registered brokerage firms have been required to record details of all computerized program trades made in the past year so that government agencies <u>will be able to decide if they should be banned</u>.
>
> (A)
> (B) should be able to decide if they should be banned
> (C) should be able to decide if they can be banned
> (D)
> (E)

Joe Bloggs has no idea what point of grammar is being tested in this question. He picks answers because they sound good. Our test writer is hoping that one of these answer choices will sound better to Joe than the correct answer. Both choices change the sentence in different ways, but both still contain the ambiguous "they," and both are still wrong.

The GMAT on the GMAT:

"The GMAT has two primary limitations: (1) it cannot and does not measure all the qualities important for graduate study in management and other pursuits; (2) there are psychometric limitations to the test—for example, only score differences of certain magnitudes are reliable indicators of real differences in performance. Such limits should be taken into consideration as GMAT scores are used."

ALMOST RIGHT

Our test writer has one more kind of trap to insert into his question. This time the trap isn't for Joe Bloggs; it's for the person who has spotted the error in the sentence but is in too big a hurry to make fine distinctions.

Usually one of the incorrect answer choices will actually fix the original error—*but will create some new error in the process.*

Spotting the original error is all well and good, but our test writer wants to make sure you really "deserve" to get this one right. So he'll include an answer choice that's almost right. It will be a close variation of the "best" answer; it will correct the mistake in the original sentence; it will be *wrong.*

Here's the same sentence with an answer choice that fixes the original mistake but creates a new one:

> Registered brokerage firms have been required to record details of all computerized program trades made in the past year so that government agencies <u>will be able to decide if they should be banned</u>.
>
> (A)
> (B)
> (C)
> (D) will be able to decide if program trades should
>   be able to be banned
> (E)

Answer choice (D) fixes the original problem; there is no longer an ambiguous "they" in the sentence. Our test writer is hoping that anyone who has spotted the original error will read just far enough to see that answer choice (D) fixes it, but not far enough to see that there is something else wrong. What's wrong? On the GMAT, only animate objects are "able" to do anything.

THREE DOWN, TWO TO GO

Let's look at the entire problem, now that our test writer has finished it, and count our blessings.

> Registered brokerage firms have been required to record details of all computerized program trades made in the past year so that government agencies <u>will be able to decide if they should be banned</u>.
>
> (A) will be able to decide if they should be banned
> (B) should be able to decide if they should be
>   banned
> (C) should be able to decide if they can be banned
> (D) will be able to decide if program trades should
>   be able to be banned
> (E) will be able to decide if program trades should
>   be banned

Here's how to crack it

By spotting what was wrong in the original sentence, we could have eliminated three of the five answer choices. Choice (A) merely repeated the original sentence word for word. Choices (B) and (C) contained the same error found in the original sentence.

We're down to choice (D) or (E). Both fix the original error. What's the difference between them? Three words. If you don't see it, don't soul-search. Just pick one and move on. The correct answer is choice (E).

OUR BASIC APPROACH

To use POE, you must be able to spot the errors in the original sentences. Fortunately, ETS leans heavily on only a few major types of errors. Just recognizing these errors should enable you to answer many of the twenty-two problems in a Sentence Correction section—once you've learned one other important concept:

THE MOST COMMON ERROR IS *NO* ERROR

About one-fifth of the Sentence Correction sentences are fine just the way they are. If a sentence is correct as is, the "best" answer is answer choice (A), which repeats the original sentence. There are usually about five (A)s in every Sentence Correction section.

How do you tell when there is nothing wrong with a sentence?

You can tell that a sentence is correct by the *absence* of any of the other types of errors that we are going to show you how to look for. Try not to use your ear—at least not at first. As you read each sentence, you'll be marking off a mental checklist of likely ETS errors. If you come to the end of the list without having found an error in the sentence, chances are very good that there was none.

When in doubt, leave the question blank and come back to it after you've finished the other questions. Now count the number of (A)s you've already chosen. If you've marked down fewer than five (A)s, the odds are even greater that there was nothing wrong with the original sentence. If you've already chosen more than five (A)s, you haven't scoured carefully enough. Go back over this question, and any other (A)s you weren't completely sure about, and take a harder look.

We'll come back to (A)s later in the chapter, after you've learned how to spot the major errors.

BEFORE WE START, SOME BASIC TERMINOLOGY

You won't be asked to *name* the parts of speech on the GMAT. However, an acquaintance with some of these terms is necessary to understand the techniques we're about to show you.

- A *noun* is a word used to name a person, place, thing, or idea.

- A *verb* is a word that expresses action.

Here is a very basic sentence:

Sue opened the box.

In this sentence, *Sue* and *box* are both nouns, and *opened* is a verb. *Sue* is considered the subject of this sentence because it is the person, place, or thing about which something is being said. *Box* is considered the object of the sentence because it receives the action of the verb.

- An *adverb* is a word that modifies a verb.

- An *adjective* is a word that modifies a noun.

- A *preposition* is a word that notes the relation of a noun to an action or a thing.

- A *phrase* is a group of words acting as a single part of speech. A phrase is missing either a subject or a verb or both.

- A *prepositional phrase* is a group of words beginning with a preposition. Like any *phrase*, a prepositional phrase does not contain both a subject and a verb.

Here's a more complicated version of the same sentence.

Sue quickly opened the big box of chocolates.

In this sentence, *quickly* is an adverb modifying the verb *opened*. *Big* is an adjective modifying the noun *box*. *Of* is a preposition because it shows a relation between *box* and *chocolates*. *Of chocolates* is a prepositional phrase that acts like an adjective by modifying *box*.

- A *pronoun* is a word that takes the place of a noun.

- A *clause* is a group of words containing a subject and a verb.

Here's an even more complicated version of the same sentence:

Because she was famished, Sue quickly opened the big box of chocolates.

There are two clauses in this sentence. *Sue quickly opened the big box of chocolates* is considered an independent clause because it contains the main idea of the sentence, and could stand by itself. *Because she was famished* is also a clause (it contains a subject and a verb) but it cannot stand by itself. This is known as a dependent clause. The word *she* is a pronoun referring to the noun *Sue*.

THE MAJOR ERRORS OF GMAT ENGLISH

1. PRONOUN ERRORS

There are two main types of pronoun errors. The first is called *pronoun reference*. You saw an example of this in the sentence about program trading above. Take a look at a simple example:

> *Samantha and Jane went shopping, but she couldn't find anything she liked.*

This type of mistake used to drive Harold Ross, the founding editor of *The New Yorker*, crazy. He was famous for his scrawled "Who he?" in the margins of writers' manuscripts. It is supposed to be absolutely clear who is being referred to by a pronoun. In the example above, the pronoun "she" could refer to either Samantha or Jane. The pronoun is ambiguous and must be fixed. You can do this in three different ways:

> *Samantha and Jane went shopping, but Samantha couldn't find anything she liked.*

> *Samantha and Jane went shopping, but Jane couldn't find anything she liked.*

> *Samantha and Jane went shopping, but they couldn't find anything they liked.*

The second type of pronoun error is called *pronoun case*. Here is a simple example:

> *The average male moviegoer expects to see at least one scene of violence per film, and they are seldom disappointed.*

In this case, the pronoun "they" clearly refers to the average male moviegoer, so there is no ambiguity of reference. However, "the average male moviegoer" is *singular*. "They" cannot be used to take the place of a singular noun. There is really only one way to fix this sentence.

> *The average male moviegoer expects to see at least one scene of violence per film, and he is seldom disappointed.*

ETS is very fond of both of these types of errors, and routinely makes use of them several times during a test. By the way, as we mentioned earlier, you don't have to memorize any of the terminology we use. You simply have to recognize a GMAT English error when you see it.

Where Did the 1000 Top CEOs Go to College?	
Yale	32
Princeton	31
Harvard	22
U. of Mich.	18
U. Penn.	17
Northwestern	17
Stanford	16
Cornell	16

Source: *Business Week*, 1992

Which leaves 831 unaccounted for.

How Do You Spot a Pronoun Error?

That's easy. Look for pronouns.

A pronoun is a word that replaces a noun. Here's a list of common pronouns. (You don't need to memorize these—just be able to recognize them.)

B-School Lingo

Net Net: end result

Singular	Plural	Can Be Singular or Plural
I, me	we, us	none
he, him	they, them	any
she, her	both	you
you	some	who
it	these	which
each	those	what
another		theirs
either		that
neither		
one		
other		
such		
mine		
yours		
his, hers		
ours		
this		

Every single time you spot a pronoun, you should immediately ask yourself the following two questions:

- ◆ Is it completely clear, not just to me but to a pedantic ETS test writer, who or what the pronoun is referring to?

- ◆ Does the pronoun agree in number with the noun it is referring to?

Let's look at an example:

> While Brussels has smashed all Western European tourism revenue records <u>this year, they still lag well behind in exports</u>.
>
> (A) this year, they still lag well behind in exports
> (B) in the past year, they still lag well behind in exports
> (C) in the past year, it lags still well behind in exports
> (D) this year, they lag still well behind in exports
> (E) this year, it still lags well behind in exports

Here's how to crack it

As you read the sentence for the first time, look to see if there is a pronoun. There is: "they." Let's make sure the pronoun is being used correctly. Who is the "they" supposed to refer to? Brussels. Is Brussels plural? No, place names are always singular. We have a pronoun case problem here.

Now that you've spotted the problem, go through the answer choices. Any answer choice with the pronoun "they" in it has to be wrong. You can cross off answer choices (A), (B), and (D). You're down to answer choices (C) or (E).

Both of the remaining answer choices fix the original problem. Read them both carefully. If you aren't sure, take a fifty-fifty guess. If you said answer choice (E), you were right. The adverb "still" in answer choice (C) must go in front of the verb.

Q: What is the easiest way to spot a pronoun error?

2. MISPLACED MODIFIERS

Misplaced modifiers come in several forms, but ETS's favorite looks like this:

> *Coming out of the department store, John's wallet was stolen.*

When a sentence begins with a participial phrase (just a fancy term for a phrase that starts with a verb ending in *ing*), that phrase is supposed to modify the noun or pronoun immediately following it.

Was the "wallet" coming out of the department store? No.

There are two ways to fix this sentence.

First, we could change the second half of the sentence so that the noun or pronoun that comes after the participial phrase is actually what the phrase is supposed to refer to:

> Coming out of the department store, *John was robbed of his wallet.*

Or, we could change the first half of the sentence into an adverbial clause (which contains its own subject) so that it is no longer necessary for the first half of the sentence to modify the noun that follows it:

> As *John was* coming out of the department store, his wallet was stolen.

Other forms of misplaced modifiers:

   A. Participial phrases preceded by a preposition:

> *On leaving the department store, John's wallet was stolen.*

(Corrected version: On leaving the department store, John was robbed of his wallet.)

   B. Adjectives:

> *Frail and weak, the heavy wagon could not be budged by the old horse.*

(Corrected version: Frail and weak, the old horse could not budge the heavy wagon.)

C. Adjectival phrases:

> *An organization long devoted to the cause of justice, the mayor
> awarded a medal to the American Civil Liberties Union.*

(Corrected version: An organization long devoted to the cause of justice, the American Civil Liberties Union was awarded a medal by the mayor.)

A: Look for pronouns!

In each of these examples, the modifying phrase modified the wrong noun or pronoun.

HOW DO YOU SPOT A MISPLACED MODIFIER?

That's easy. *Whenever a sentence begins with a modifying phrase followed by a comma, the noun or pronoun right after the comma should be what the phrase is talking about.* Every single time you see a sentence that begins with a modifying phrase, check to make sure it modifies the right noun or pronoun. If it doesn't, you've spotted the error in the sentence.

The correct answer choice will either change the noun that follows the modifying phrase (the preferred method) or change the phrase itself into an adverbial clause so that it no longer needs to modify the noun.

Let's look at two examples:

> Originally written in 1961, Joseph Heller scored a
> literary hit with his comedic first novel, *Catch-22*.

(A) Originally written in 1961, Joseph Heller scored a literary hit with his comedic first novel, *Catch-22*.

(B) Originally written in 1961, Joseph Heller scored a literary hit with *Catch-22*, his comedic first novel.

(C) Originally written in 1961, *Catch-22*, the comedic first novel by Joseph Heller, was a literary hit.

(D) *Catch-22*, which was originally written in 1961 by Joseph Heller, scored a literary hit with his comedic first novel.

(E) *Catch-22*, the comedic first novel, scored a literary hit for Joseph Heller by its being written in 1961.

Here's how to crack it

As you read the sentence for the first time, go through your checklist. Is there a pronoun error in the sentence? No. Does the sentence begin with a modifying phrase? Yes. Now we're getting somewhere. Let's check to see if the modifying phrase actually modifies what it is *supposed to*. Does it? No. "Joseph Heller" is not what was written in 1961. This is a misplaced modifier.

Now that you've spotted the error, look through the other answer choices and eliminate any that contain the same error. Choice (B) contained the same error. Get rid of it. You're down to choices (C), (D), or (E).

Now, there are really only two ways to fix this kind of error, as you know. Do any of the answer choices change the noun that follows the modifying phrase? Yes. Answer choice (C). This is probably the right answer. Read through the other two choices just to make sure there's nothing better. Choices (D) and (E) contain awkward constructions. Choice (C) is the "best" answer.

<u>Although not quite as liquid an investment as</u> a money-market account, financial experts recommend a certificate of deposit for its high yield.

(A) Although not quite as liquid an investment as
(B) Although it is not quite as liquid an investment as
(C) While not being quite as liquid an investment as
(D) While it is not quite as liquid as an investment
(E) Although not quite liquid an investment as

Here's how to crack it

Go through your checklist. Is there a pronoun in this sentence? Yes, the third to last word of the sentence is a pronoun, but it clearly refers back to the certificate of deposit. False alarm. Does the sentence begin with a modifying phrase? Yes. Now we're getting warmer. Check to see whether the modifying phrase modifies what it's supposed to modify. Does "although not quite as liquid an investment . . ." refer to financial experts? No. This is a misplaced modifier.

The clearest way to fix this sentence would be to change the noun that follows the modifying phrase:

> *Although not quite as liquid an investment as a money-market account, a certificate of deposit is recommended by financial experts for its high yield.*

However, you can't fix *this* sentence that way for the very good reason that only the first phrase of the sentence was underlined. This time, you'll have to find a way to fix the modifying phrase itself. Look for an answer choice that changes the modifying phrase into an adverbial clause with its own subject and verb.

Choices (A), (C), and (E) do not have subjects and can therefore be eliminated immediately. Choices (B) and (D) each have a subject—in both cases, the word "it"—turning the modifying phrases into adverbial clauses. However choice (D) contains a new error: the word "as" has been moved, leaving "money-market" stranded in the middle of the sentence with no function. While it sounds atrocious, choice (B) is the "best" answer.

A close relative of a misplaced modifier is a *dangling modifier*. You can spot both errors in exactly the same way. Here's a simple example:

> *Before designing a park, the public must be considered.*

Again, this sentence starts with a modifying phrase followed by a comma. The noun following the comma is what the modifying phrase is supposed to modify. Is it? No! "The public" didn't design the park. A dangling modifier differs from a misplaced modifier in that a dangling modifier doesn't just modify the wrong word. There *is* no word for it to modify.

To fix this sentence, we would have to insert whoever is designing the park into the sentence:

> *Before designing a park, the architect must consider the public.*

3. PARALLEL CONSTRUCTION

There are two kinds of ETS sentences that test parallel construction. The first is a sentence that contains a list, or has a series of actions set off from one another by commas. Here's an example:

> *Among the reasons cited for the city councilwoman's decision not to run for reelection were the high cost of a campaign, the lack of support from her party, and desiring to spend more time with her family.*

When a main verb controls several phrases that follow it, each of those phrases has to be set up in the same way. In the sentence above, three reasons were listed. The three reasons *were* (main verb):

> the high cost of a campaign
> the lack of support from her party
> and
> desiring to spend more time with her family

The construction for each of the three reasons is supposed to be parallel. The first two items on the list are phrases that are essentially functioning as nouns: the high *cost* (of a campaign); the *lack* (of support from her party). However, the third item on the list seems more like a verb than a noun. How could we change the word "desiring" to a more noun-like state? If you said, "the desire," you were absolutely correct. It should read:

> the high cost of a campaign
> the lack of support from her party
> and
> *the desire* to spend more time with her family.

The second kind of ETS sentence that tests parallel construction is a sentence that is divided into two parts. Here's an example:

> *To say that the song patterns of the common robin are less complex than those of the indigo bunting is doing a great disservice to both birds.*

If the first half of a sentence is constructed in a particular way, the second half must be constructed in the same way. The first half of this sentence begins, "To...," therefore the second half has to begin the same way:

To say that the song patterns of the common robin are less complex than those of the indigo bunting is to do a great disservice to both birds.

How Do You Spot Parallel Construction?

That's easy. Every time you read a Sentence Correction problem, look to see if you can find a series of actions, a list of three things, or a sentence that is divided into two parts.

Q: What is a tip-off to a misplaced modifier error?

Here's an example:

> In a recent survey, the Gallup poll discovered that the average American speaks 1.3 languages, buys a new car every 5.2 years, <u>drinks 14 gallons of alcoholic beverages every year, and forgot to pay at least one bill per quarter</u>.
>
> (A) drinks 14 gallons of alcoholic beverages every year, and forgot to pay at least one bill per quarter
> (B) drinks 14 gallons of alcoholic beverages every year, and forgets to pay at least one bill per quarter
> (C) can drink 14 gallons of alcoholic beverages every quarter and forgot to pay at least one bill per quarter
> (D) drinks 14 gallons of alcoholic beverages every year, and forgets at least to pay one bill per quarter
> (E) drank 14 gallons of alcoholic beverages every year, and forgets to pay at least one bill per quarter

Here's how to crack it

As you read the sentence for the first time, run through your checklist. Is there a pronoun? No. Does the sentence begin with a modifying phrase? Yes, but the word after the phrase is what is supposed to be modified, so this is not a misplaced modifier. Is there a list of three things or a series of actions? Yes. Let's see if all the actions are parallel. The average American . . .

> speaks (1.3 languages)
> buys (a new car . . .)
> drinks (14 gallons . . .)
> and
> forgot (to pay . . .)

The first three verbs are all in the same tense, but the fourth one isn't. The problem in this sentence is a lack of parallel construction.

Now that you know what the error is, go through the answer choices. Any choice that contains the word "forgot" is wrong. We can eliminate choices (A) and (C). Choice (E), even though it fixes the parallel construction of the fourth verb, changes the parallel construction of the third verb. Eliminate.

Choices (B) and (D) have perfect parallel construction. If you aren't sure which one is correct, guess and move on. If you picked choice (B), you were right. In choice (D), the adjectival phrase "at least" had to be in front of "one bill."

4. TENSE

On the GMAT, tense problems are often just a matter of parallel construction. In general, if a sentence starts out in one tense, it should probably stay there. Let's look at an example:

> When he was younger he walked three miles every day and
> has lifted weights too.

The clause "when he was younger" puts the entire sentence firmly in the past. Thus the two verbs that follow should be in the past tense as well. You may not have known the technical term for "has lifted" (the present perfect tense) but you probably noticed that it was inconsistent with "walked" (the simple past tense). The sentence should read:

> When he was younger he walked three miles every day and
> lifted *weights too.*

Here are the tenses that come up on the GMAT:

Tense	Example
present	He *walks* three miles a day.
simple past	When he was younger, he *walked* three miles a day.
present perfect	He *has walked* three miles a day for the last several years.
past perfect	He *had walked* three miles a day until he bought his motorcycle.
future	He *will walk* three miles a day, starting tomorrow.

It isn't important that you know the names of these tenses, as long as you understand how they're used. As we said before, a sentence that begins in one tense should generally stay in the same tense. For example, a sentence that begins in the present perfect (which describes an action that has happened in the past, but is still potentially going on in the present as well) should stay in the present perfect.

> He has walked three miles a day for the last several years, and
> has never complained.

One exception to this rule is a sentence containing the past perfect (in which one action in the past happens before another action in the past). By definition, any action set in the past perfect must have another action coming after it set in the simple past.

A: A modifying phrase followed by a comma. To correct it, make sure that what comes after the comma is modified by what comes before it.

*He had ridden his motorcycle for two hours when it ran out
of gas.*

The only other exceptions to this rule come up when one action in a sentence
clearly precedes another:

> *The dinosaurs are extinct now, but they were once present on
> the earth in large numbers.*

In this case, the sentence is clearly referring to two different time periods:
"now," which requires the present tense, and a period long ago, which requires
the past tense.

How Do You Spot Tense Errors?

That's easy. Look for changes in verb tense *in the answer choices*. If the answer
choices give you several versions of a particular verb, then you should be
looking to see which one is correct. Here's an example.

> A doctor at the Amsterdam Clinic maintains that if
> children eat a diet high in vitamins and <u>took vitamin
> supplements, they will be less likely to catch</u> the
> common cold.
>
> (A) took vitamin supplements, they will be less
>   likely to catch
> (B) took vitamin supplements, they are less likely to
>   catch
> (C) take vitamin supplements, they were less likely
>   of catching
> (D) take vitamin supplements, they will be less
>   likely of catching
> (E) take vitamin supplements, they are less likely to
>   catch

Here's how to crack it

As you read the sentence, go through your checklist. There is one pronoun
("they") in the sentence, but in this case it clearly refers only to the children. Is
there a modifying phrase? No. Is there a list of things or a series of actions? Not
really. Are the verb tenses consistent? Look at the answer choices. Aha! (A) and
(B) offer us "took" while (C), (D), and (E) offer us "take." Let's see which is
correct.

Look at the dependent clause that is partially underlined.

> *...that if children* eat *a diet high in vitamins and* <u>took</u>
> <u>vitamin supplements</u>...

Obviously, one of these verbs is inconsistent with the other, and since only
one of them is underlined, that's the one that must be wrong. The correct
sentence must have a "take" in it, so we can eliminate choices (A) and (B). Choice
(C) puts the rest of the sentence in the past tense, so scratch (C). Choice (D) puts
the rest of the sentence in the future tense. This *might* be acceptable, but the

choice also uses the incorrect idiomatic expression "likely of catching." The correct answer to this question is Choice (E), which keeps the entire sentence in the present tense.

5. Subject–Verb Agreement Errors

A verb is supposed to agree with its subject. Let's look at an example:

> *The number of arrests of drunken drivers are increasing every year.*

ETS likes to separate the subject of a sentence from its verb with several prepositional phrases, so that by the time you get to the verb you've forgotten whether the subject was singular or plural.

The subject of the sentence above is "number," which is singular. The phrase "of arrests of drunken drivers" modifies the subject. The verb of this sentence is "are," which is plural. If we set off the prepositional phrases with parentheses, this is what the sentence looks like:

> *The number (of arrests of drunken drivers) are . . .*

To fix this sentence we need to make the verb agree with the subject:

> *The number (of arrests of drunken drivers) is increasing every year.*

How to Spot Subject–Verb Agreement Errors

Cover up the prepositional phrases between the subject and the verb of each clause of the sentence so you can see whether there is an agreement problem. You should also be on the lookout for nouns that sound plural but are in fact singular:

Some nouns that are generally singular

The Netherlands	(the name of any city, state, or country)
Tom or John	(any two singular nouns connected by an "or")
the family	
the audience	
politics	
measles	
the number	
the amount	

You are already on the lookout for pronouns since they're first on your checklist. Sometimes pronouns can be the subject of a sentence, in which case the verb has to agree with the pronoun. There are some pronouns that people tend to think are plural when they are in fact singular:

Singular pronouns
either
neither
each
everyone
everybody
nobody

Let's look at an example of a subject–verb error as it might appear on the GMAT:

> Many political insiders now believe that the dissension in Congress over health issues <u>decrease the likelihood for significant action being</u> taken this year to combat the rising costs of healthcare.
>
> (A) decrease the likelihood for significant action being
> (B) decrease the likelihood that significant action will be
> (C) decrease the likelihood of significant action to be
> (D) decreases the likelihood for significant action being
> (E) decreases the likelihood that significant action will be

Here's how to crack it

As you read the sentence for the first time, run through your mental checklist. Is there a pronoun, or a modifying phrase, or a list of several things, or a series of parallel actions, or a change in tense? Not this time. Let's check for subject-verb agreement. The subject of the independent clause is "insiders" and the correct verb, "believe," follows almost immediately, so there's no problem in the main clause.

However, let's look at the dependent clause that follows: "That the dissension over health issues decrease the likelihood…"

In this clause, the subject is "dissension," not "health issues." Remember to put parentheses around any prepositional phrases. It should look like this:

…the dissension (over health issues) decrease…

Is this correct? No, the singular "dissension" needs the singular verb "decreases." Looking at the answers, we can immediately eliminate choices (A), (B), and (C). Now let's examine choices (D) and (E). Both fix the subject-verb error, but choice (D) uses the unidiomatic expression "likelihood for." The correct answer is choice (E).

6. APPLES AND ORANGES

Another error that ETS likes to include is what we call apples and oranges. Here's a simple example:

The people in my office are smarter than other offices.

Taken literally, this sentence compares "the people in my office" with "other offices." This is what we call an apples-and-oranges sentence. It compares two dissimilar things (in this case, "people" and "offices.") To fix this sentence, we need to make the comparison clear. There are two ways to do this:

The people in my office are smarter than *the people* in other offices.
or
The people in my office are smarter than *those* in other offices.

We hope that you recognized "those" as a pronoun taking the place of "the people." The correct answer to an apples-and-oranges question on the GMAT almost invariably uses a pronoun ("that" or "those") rather than a repetition of the noun.

Apples-and-oranges problems also come up when you compare two actions:

Synthetic oils burn less efficiently than natural oils.

In this case, what is being compared is not the two types of oil, but how well each type of oil *burns*. You could fix this by changing the sentence to read,

Synthetic oils burn less efficiently than natural oils burn.

However, ETS would rather that you fix it by replacing the second verb (in this case, "burn") with a replacement verb ("do" or "does.") Here is how ETS would like to see this sentence rewritten:

Synthetic oils burn less efficiently than do natural oils.

HOW DO YOU SPOT APPLES AND ORANGES?

Look for sentences that make comparisons. These sentences often include words such as "than," "as," "similar to," and "like." When you find one of these comparison words, check to see whether the two things being compared are really comparable.

Let's look at an example.

> Doctors sometimes have difficulty diagnosing viral pneumonia because the early symptoms of this potentially deadly illness <u>are often quite similar to the common cold</u>.
>
> (A) are often quite similar to the common cold
> (B) often resemble that of the common cold
> (C) are often quite similar to those of the common cold
> (D) are often quite similar to the common cold's symptom
> (E) quite often are, like the common cold, similar

Here's how to crack it

Go through your checklist; do you see any suspicious pronouns, misplaced modifiers, unparallel constructions, needless shifts in tense, or subject-verb problems? Good. There aren't any. Do you see any comparison words? Yes, the sentence uses "are similar to." Let's see exactly what is being compared. The symptoms of one illness are being compared directly to . . . another illness. Aha! This is an apples-and-oranges error. To make this sentence correct, we need to compare the *symptoms* of one illness to the *symptoms* of the other, and the way ETS would prefer that we do it is to use a replacement pronoun.

Q: What is an indication of an apples-and-oranges error?

If we look at the answer choices, we can eliminate choices (A) and (E) because neither makes any attempt to compare symptoms to symptoms. Choice (B) looks promising because it uses the replacement pronoun "that"; however, "symptoms" is plural, and therefore can't be replaced by the singular "that." Choice (D) seems promising because it seems to be trying to compare symptoms to symptoms—but if you look closer, you'll notice that the last word of choice (D) is "symptom," which is singular. The correct answer is choice (C).

7. QUANTITY WORDS

ETS likes to see if you know how to indicate quantity. Here's an example.

> On the flight to Los Angeles, Nancy had to choose *among* two dinner entrees.

If there were more than two items being compared, then "among" would be correct. However, if there are only two choices available, the correct quantity word should be "between."

> On the flight to Los Angeles, Nancy had to choose *between* two dinner entrees.

Here are the comparison quantity words that come up on the GMAT most frequently:

if two items	if more than two items
between	among
more	most
better	best
less	least

A: A comparison could indicate an A & O error. Check that the two things being compared are comparable.

Another type of quantity word that shows up on the GMAT from time to time involves things that can be counted as opposed to things that can't. For example, if you were standing in line at a buffet, and you didn't want as big a serving of soup as the person in front of you received, which of the following would be correct?

> Could I have *fewer* soup, please?
> or
> Could I have *less* soup, please?

If an item can't be counted, the correct adjective would be "less." However, if we were talking about french fries (which can be counted) the correct adjective would be "fewer."

Singular Pronouns
either
neither
each
everyone
everybody
nobody
no one

countable Items	not-countable items
fewer	less
number	amount, quantity
many	much

HOW DO YOU SPOT QUANTITY WORD ERRORS?

That's easy. Look for quantity words. Whenever you see a "between," check to see if there are only two items being discussed in the sentence. (If there are more, you'll need an "among.") Whenever you see an "amount," make sure that whatever is being discussed cannot be counted. (If the sentence is talking about the "amount" of people, then you'll need to change it to "number.")

Here's what a quantity word error might look like on the GMAT:

> Of the many decisions facing the energy commission as it meets to decide on new directions for the next century, the question of the future of nuclear energy <u>is for certain the more perplexing</u>.
>
> (A) is for certain the more perplexing
> (B) is certainly the most perplexing
> (C) it seems certain, is the most perplexed
> (D) is certainly the more perplexing
> (E) it seems certain, is perplexing the most

Here's how to crack it

If your checklist includes quantity words, the word "more" will set off red flags as you read the sentence. If there were two decisions facing the energy commission, then "the more perplexing" would be correct. However, the sentence says there are "many" decisions. Therefore the sentence must read, "the most perplexing."

This lets us eliminate choices (A) and (D) immediately. Choice (C) gives the impression that it is the *question* that is perplexed. Eliminate. Choice (E) incorrectly positions "the most" after the word it is supposed to modify. The correct answer is choice (B).

8. IDIOM

ETS likes to test certain idiomatic expressions. Here's an easy example:

Q: A parallel construction error can be recognized by what giveaways?

> *There is little doubt that large corporations are indebted for the small companies that broke new ground in laser optics.*

It is incorrect to say you are indebted *for* someone.

> *There is little doubt that large corporations are indebted to the small companies that broke new ground in laser optics.*

Idiomatic errors are difficult to spot in that there is no single giveaway to look for. In fact, there are really no rules. Each idiom has its own particular usage. There is no real reason why an idiomatic expression is correct. It is simply a matter of custom.

However, you haven't been speaking English for the past twenty years for nothing. The main similarity between GMAT English and American English is that they both use the same idiomatic expressions.

You already know them.

HOW DO YOU SPOT IDIOMATIC ERRORS?

If you've gone through the first seven items on your checklist—pronouns, misplaced modifiers, parallel construction, tense, subject-verb agreement, apples and oranges, and quantity words—and still haven't found an error, try pulling idiomatic expressions out of the sentence so you can see whether they're correct.

Then make up your own sentence using the suspect idiom:

> *I am indebted for my parents for offering to help pay for graduate school.*

Does that sound right? Of course not. I am indebted *to* my parents. Usually if you take the expression out of the long and awkward sentence and use it in an everyday sentence, the error (if there is one) will be obvious. Here's what an idiom question might look like on the GMAT:

> The administration of a small daily dose of aspirin has not only been shown to lower the risk of heart attack, <u>and it has also been shown to help</u> relieve the suffering of arthritis.
>
> (A) and it has also been shown to help
> (B) and it has also been shown helpful to
> (C) but it has also been shown to help
> (D) but it has been shown helpful in addition for
> (E) in addition it has also been shown helping

Here's how to crack it

As always, run through your checklist. Is there a pronoun in the sentence? Yes, but if you check the answer choices, you'll discover that the same pronoun appears in each one. Obviously, pronoun error is *not* what is being tested this time. Is there a modifying phrase? No. So much for misplaced modifiers. Is there a list of things or a series of actions? No. To be sure that there really is no parallel construction problem we should look at the two halves of the sentence as well. The first half, " . . . has been shown," matches the second half, " . . . has also been shown," and both are in the same tense, so there is no problem with either parallel construction or tense. There are no comparison words either, so we don't have to worry about apples and oranges. Could there be something wrong with an idiomatic expression in the original sentence? Let's try a sentence of our own.

> *Not only is he nasty . . .*

How would you finish this sentence? If you said something like " . . . *but he is also disgusting*," you would be absolutely correct. In GMAT English, "not only. . ." is always followed somewhere in the same sentence by "but . . . also." Let's look at the answer choices to see which can be eliminated. (A), (B) and (E) all use some other conjunction instead of "but," which means that the only possible answers are (C) and (D). Choice (D) uses "in addition" instead of "also." This *might* not be fatal, but then keep reading after the underlining: "<u>helpful in addition for</u> relieve the suffering of arthritis." If the word "for" seems to stick out, it is because we need to form the infinitive case of "relieve" by using "to." Thus, the correct answer is (C).

THE IDIOMS MOST COMMONLY TESTED ON THE GMAT

There are, of course, thousands of idiomatic expressions that ETS could test on the GMAT. But here are a handful that seem to come up all the time.

not only . . . but also . . .	different from
not so much . . . as . . .	a consequence of
defined as	so . . . as to be . . .
regard as	so (adjective) that
neither . . . nor . . .	depicted as
modeled after	as great as
based on	as good as, or better than
a result of	distinguish from
to result in	attribute to
a debate over	credited with
a responsibility to	
responsible for	

ONE LAST EXAMPLE:

The foresight <u>that was evident in the court's selection of an independent trustee</u> to oversee the provisions of the agreement will probably go unremarked by the press.

(A) that was evident in the court's selection of an independent trustee

(B) that was evident by the court's selection of an independent trustee

(C) evidenced with the court's selection of an independent trustee

(D) evidenced of the court's selection of an independent trustee

(E) that was evident of the court's selection of an independent trustee

Q: What is the rule when looking for tense errors?

Here's how to crack it

As you read the sentence, go through your checklist. Is there a pronoun? No. Does the sentence begin with a modifying phrase? No. Is there a list of three things or a series of actions? No. Is there a tense error? No. Is there a subject-verb problem? No. Is there a comparison word such as "similar" or "than"? No. Are there any quantity words to check? No. Do any expressions in the sentence seem suspicious? No.

We have checked off all the items on our list. Maybe nothing is wrong with this sentence. Mark down choice (A) provisionally. When you've finished with the entire section, count the (A)s you've chosen. If you have too many, go back to this problem and take a closer look. If you have five or fewer, however, you were probably right in the first place. The "best" answer to this question is choice (A).

IF YOU'RE REALLY GUNG HO

You can expand your checklist to include as many types of errors as you like. Obviously the more types of errors you can identify, the more prepared you'll be to take the test. But you should bear in mind that while there are other types of errors that we haven't discussed, these errors don't come up very often on the GMAT. For example, a sentence with redundant words has appeared on the test from time to time, but not even as often as once per test. If you're seriously gunning to get every Sentence Correction question correct, you should dig out your old grammar book from high school and study it carefully. You should also take as many of the real ETS Sentence Correction sections in the *Official Guide for GMAT Review* as you can; pay special attention to the idiomatic expressions that come up in these sections since these are sometimes repeated.

What Happens If I Know There's Something Wrong but I Can't Figure out What It Is?

You've just finished reading a sentence and there's obviously something wrong with it. You go through your checklist, but either this is an error that isn't on your list or you just aren't seeing it. What should you do?

A: Keep the same tense throughout the sentence.

Go straight to the answer choices to look for clues. Here's a set of answer choices from one of the previous examples:

(A) decrease the likelihood for significant action
being
(B) decrease the likelihood that significant action
will be
(C) decrease the likelihood of significant action to
be
(D) decreases the likelihood for significant action
being
(E) decreases the likelihood that significant action
will be

Forget about the original sentence entirely for a moment. Just looking at these answer choices, do you see anything that strikes you?

By examining the first few words of each of the answer choices, you will often find an excellent hint as to what kind of error you might be looking for in the original sentence. For example, in the answers above, ETS is offering you a choice of "decrease" or "decreases." What kind of error might this mean? Bingo: subject-verb agreement.

Even if the first few words of the answer choices do not provide a clue, all is not lost. Remember how our ETS test writer constructs wrong answer choices: the test writer likes to throw in one or more answer choices that fix the original error but create new errors in the process. You may not have been able to spot the original error, but you'll probably see the *new* errors in the bogus answer choices.

As you read the remaining answer choices, look for differences. Sometimes the realization that one answer choice is exactly the same as another with the exception of a couple of words will enable you to choose between them.

When you've eliminated everything you can, guess and move on. Remember: If you can eliminate one or more answer choices, you'll be most likely to gain points by guessing.

SUMMARY

1. GMAT English is different from American English. You have to learn the rules.

2. Fortunately, the Sentence Correction section tests only a handful of rules. Once you learn them, you will be able to score quite well on this section.

3. Make a checklist of errors to look for when you read a Sentence Correction section. The major errors you should look for in a Sentence Correction problem are:

    A. *Pronouns*: If a sentence contains a pronoun, check to see whether the pronoun clearly refers to the noun it is replacing; also check to see whether the pronoun agrees in number with the noun to which it refers.

    B. *Misplaced modifiers:* If the sentence begins with a modifying phrase, check to make sure the noun it modifies comes directly after the modifying phrase.

    C. *Parallel construction:* If a sentence contains a list of three things, or a series of actions, or is broken up into two halves, check to make sure the parts of the sentence are parallel.

    D. *Tense:* If the answer choices contain different verb tenses, make sure the tense of the verb or verbs in the original sentence is correct. For the most part, verb tense should stay consistent throughout a sentence.

    E. *Subject-verb agreement:* ETS sometimes puts extraneous prepositional phrases between the subject and the verb. Cover up these phrases so you can see whether the subject and the verb of each clause in the sentence agree with each other.

    F. *Apples and oranges:* When a sentence makes a comparison, check to see whether the two things being compared are comparable.

    G. *Quantity Words:* Whenever you see a quantity word (countable vs. uncountable; two vs. three or more) check to see if it is being used correctly.

    H. *Idiom:* If a sentence contains an idiomatic expression that seems wrong to you, try taking the expression out of the sentence and creating a sentence of your own with the suspect expression.

4. If you've spotted the error, go through the answer choices and eliminate any that contain the same error. Then look at the remaining answer choices and find the one that fixes the sentence.

5. If you can't find the error, first look to the answer choices for clues. Then consider the possibility that there might not be an error.

6. About one-fifth of the sentences are correct as they are. When a sentence is correct, the answer is choice (A), which simply repeats the sentence word for word.

7. Once you've gained confidence in your ability to spot the major errors, you should expand your checklist to include other types of errors.

Reading Comprehension

7

The Reading Comprehension section of the GMAT contains three reading passages, each ranging from 200 to 350 words in length. Each passage is followed by from four to seven questions, for a total of 18 questions.

Before we begin, take a moment to read the following set of instructions, which is a close approximation of the instructions you will find on the real GMAT.

> Directions: In this section, there are three reading passages, each followed by questions about the content of the passages. You should answer the questions based on your knowledge of what has been directly said in the passage or what can be inferred from it. Answer each question by choosing the best response.

Be sure you know and understand these instructions before you take the GMAT. If you learn them ahead of time, you won't have to waste valuable seconds reading them on the day you take the test.

GMAT READING COMPREHENSION: CRACKING THE SYSTEM

It's important to know the instructions printed before each group of Reading Comprehension passages on the GMAT, but it's much more important to understand what these instructions mean. ETS's instructions don't tell you everything you need to know about GMAT Reading Comprehension passages. The rest of the chapter will teach you what you do need to know.

Our techniques will enable you to

1. gain points on the test by skipping (in some cases) one of the reading passages entirely

2. read quickly in a way that will allow you to understand the main idea of the passage

3. eliminate answer choices that could not possibly be correct

4. take advantage of outside knowledge

5. take advantage of inside information (about the way ETS's test writers think)

6. find answers in some cases *without reading the passages*

BASIC PASSAGE TYPES

There are only three types of passages on the GMAT, and a reading comprehension section generally has one of each:

1. *The social science passage*: This usually concerns a social or historical issue. For example, you might see a passage about world food shortages or the history of a civil rights movement.

2. *The science passage*: This might describe a scientific phenomenon, such as gravitation or plate tectonics.

3. *The business passage*: This usually discusses a business-related topic. For example, you might see a passage about the privatization of state-owned industries, or the causes of inflation.

The three passages can appear in any order.

ORDER OF DIFFICULTY

In the Reading Comprehension section, neither the questions nor the passages are presented in order of difficulty. Thus, it is important for you to figure out your *own* order of difficulty.

CHOOSING THE ORDER IN WHICH YOU DO THE PASSAGES

When the proctor tells you to begin the Reading Comprehension section, your first impulse will be to launch straight into the first passage—but you will be infinitely better off if you pause for a moment to reconnoiter. Take a few seconds to look at the first few words of each of the three passages

There are several factors to bear in mind in making your decision:

◆ *Familiarity with the subject matter*: You may have just finished reading a newspaper article about the number of women CEOs in the United States, or perhaps in college you wrote a paper on continental drift. If the topic is at all familiar to you, you will feel much more comfortable answering questions about it.

◆ *Which type of passage you generally prefer*: After they've done a few timed sections, most people find they have a favorite type of passage. Don't be surprised if your favorite runs counter to your normal choice of reading matter. Even if you never read science articles in real life, you may find that on the GMAT you like the science passages best.

◆ *Which of the three passages is the "minority passage."* Invariably, the subject matter for one of the passages on each test will concern a minority group. There can sometimes be certain advantages to doing this passage. We'll tell you more about this later in the chapter.

◆ *The structure of the passage*: Many of the passages on the GMAT fall into a few key structure types. We'll be showing you how to recognize these later in the chapter, but here are two quick examples: if a passage begins, "The new economic climate provides opportunities as well as risks . . ." it is pretty clear how the rest of the passage will be organized (first, some examples of the opportunities, and then some examples of the risks); if a passage begins, "There are three main classes of stars," again, the organization of the passage should be fairly clear right away.

Sentence Correction Review

Q: How do you know if there is a quantity word mistake?

◆ *The length of the passages.* Several recent experimental GMAT Reading Comprehension sections have included two short passages (250 words) with seven questions each, and one longer passage (350 words) with four questions. Obviously, if you find two short passages and a long passage—other things being equal—it would make sense to start with the two shorter passages.

Deciding on your own order should take no more than a few seconds. In general, start with the passage that is easiest for you. Then do the second easiest. If you are going to run out of time, it might as well be on the passage you find the most difficult.

It May Even Make Sense for You to Skip One Reading Comprehension Passage Entirely— If You Read Normally

Some people find that by the time they've finished reading a passage carefully, there is little time left to answer the questions. If you insist on reading GMAT passages the way you *normally* read—carefully, word-by-word—you may be able to increase your score by skipping one entire passage and the questions based on that passage. Rather than invest the time to read three passages and answer all the questions hastily, you may be better off concentrating on two of the passages and the questions related to those passages. Skipping an entire passage and its questions is in some ways more efficient than skipping a few questions on each passage, because you spend less time reading.

On the Other Hand, Normal Reading Doesn't Make Any Sense on the GMAT

GMAT reading has nothing to do with normal reading. For one thing, no one in his right mind would ever read one of these passages of his own free will. They are almost always boring.

How to Succeed in Business

GMAT reading has even less to do with business reading. If your boss asked you to analyze a quarterly report and make a presentation of all the points it raised, you would go home and spend hours going over it. You would look for important information, anticipate questions, and memorize statistics.

Business reading is a careful, painstaking process.

How to Succeed on the GMAT

If you try to read GMAT passages the way you read quarterly reports, you'll never have time for the questions. Worse, you'll have spent a lot of time absorbing information that you don't need to know.

READING COMPREHENSION QUESTIONS COVER ONLY ONE-THIRD OF THE MATERIAL IN THE PASSAGE

Each reading passage is followed by as many as seven questions. You've probably assumed that to answer these questions correctly you'll need to know all the information contained in the passage. But this isn't true. The questions cover only a small portion of the passage. We're going to teach you how to identify the important part and ignore most of the rest. The less time you spend reading the passage, the more time you'll have for earning points.

There are two types of questions in Reading Comprehension, and neither requires you to memorize specific information:

1. *General questions*: To answer these, you need to have an understanding of the main idea and, perhaps, the *structure* of the passage.

2. *Specific questions*: Since you'll be asked about only a few specific pieces of information, it's silly to try to remember all the specific information contained in a passage. It makes much more sense to have a vague idea of where specific information is located in the passage. That way you'll know where to look if you need it.

GMAT READING: THE PRINCETON REVIEW METHOD

Think of a GMAT reading passage as a house. The main idea of the passage is like the overall plan of the house; the main idea of each paragraph is like the plan of each room. Reading the passage is like walking quickly through the house. You don't want to waste time memorizing every detail of every room; you want to develop a general sense of the layout of the house.

Later, when ETS asks you what was sitting on the table beside the chair in the master bedroom, you won't know the answer off the top of your head, but you will know exactly where to look for it. And you'll be able to answer more questions in less time than someone who has tried to memorize every detail.

STEP ONE: READ FOR THE MAIN IDEA

Take a look at the first paragraph of a sample GMAT passage:

> Biologists have long known that some types of electromagnetic radiation such as X rays and gamma rays can be dangerous to human beings. Operating at a frequency of 10^{18} through 10^{22}, these rays, which are well above the visible light spectrum, were first detected in the early years of the 20th century.

Here's how to crack it

The first sentence of a paragraph should always be read carefully since it is so often the key to understanding the entire paragraph. This first sentence was no exception: the paragraph is about two types of radiation and their danger to humans. Many students find that it helps to jot down a couple of key words in the margin next to the paragraph to encapsulate the main idea.

However, once you've got that main idea, it isn't necessary to pay a lot of attention to the other sentences in the paragraph. For example, if you've already read the second sentence of this paragraph, you probably noticed that while the sentence included some specific facts, it added nothing to our understanding of the main point of the paragraph. Later, if ETS asks you a specific question about line 5, you can go back and find out the answer; it will still be there.

Sentence Correction Review

A: Be familiar with the list on page 60!

THINK OF THIS AS *VARIABLE* SPEED READING

Until you know what the main idea of a paragraph is, you want to read very carefully. However, as soon as you've got a handle on what is going on, you can speed up. Let your eyes glaze over when you get to the small details. Until ETS asks you about them, who cares?

The goal is to spend no more than two minutes "reading" the entire passage. Impossible? Sure, if you're going to insist on reading the way you normally do. Just remember that you don't get any points for reading the passages; when you take the real GMAT the proctor will *not* be walking around the test room awarding extra points for great reading technique. You get points for *answering questions*.

Try reading the second paragraph in the way we've suggested above:

> However, until now, no one has ever suggested that microwave radiation might also be harmful. In preliminary laboratory results, Cleary and Milham have found elevated growth rates in cancer cells exposed to low doses of microwaves. Cleary exposed cancer cells to levels of radiation that are commonly found in microwave ovens and found that the abnormal cells grew 30 percent faster than did unexposed cells. Milham's study focused on ham radio operators who are commonly exposed to levels of radiation slightly higher than those emitted by cellular telephones. He discovered elevated levels of myeloid leukemia.

Here's how to crack it

Reading the first sentence carefully, we realize that this paragraph is going off on a tangent thought. In fact, the passage is *not* going to be about the dangers of X-rays or gamma rays; it is going to be about the possible dangers of microwaves. Now that we have the main idea, we can afford to skim or skip over the rest of the paragraph. If ETS asks us later about Cleary or Milham, we'll know where to find them, but until then, we can let this part of the passage pass in a blur.

Now try reading the last paragraph of the passage:

> The methodology of Cleary and Milham has been questioned by other scientists in the field. However, no one seriously disputes that their preliminary findings must be taken seriously or that new studies should be set up to try to duplicate their results.

Although federal guidelines for how much electromagnetic energy can be allowed to enter the work and home environment have been made more stringent since they were first implemented in 1982, the recent studies pose troubling questions about the safety of microwaves.

Here's how to crack it

The first word of the second sentence ("however") let us know that the author was going to come back to the original point: microwaves may be dangerous. Was this a conclusion? You bet.

In retrospect, the organization of the passage is pretty clear.

- The *first* paragraph states the dangers of other types of waves.

- The *second* paragraph talks about the dangers of microwaves as shown by two studies.

- The *third* qualifies the two studies, but decides that, on balance, microwaves may indeed be dangerous.

STEP 2: AS YOU READ, LOOK FOR STRUCTURAL SIGNPOSTS

Certain words instantly tell you a lot about the structure of a passage. For example, if you were reading a paragraph that began, "There are three reasons why the Grand Canyon should be strip-mined," at some point in the paragraph you would expect to find three reasons listed. If a sentence begins, "on the one hand," you would expect to find an "on the other hand" later in the sentence. These structural signposts show an alert reader what's going to happen later in a passage. Here are some structural signposts to look out for on the GMAT.

TRIGGER WORDS

The second paragraph you just read began with a word which probably automatically clued you in that a change was on the way: the word was "however."

Trigger words (such as "however" and "but") always signal a change in the direction of a passage. Here's a simple example:

First paragraph: Most economists believe that the
                           budget deficit will take years to
                           remedy. . .

Second paragraph: HOWEVER (trigger word), some
                           economists believe there may a
                           fast solution to the problem.

In this example the trigger word signals that the second paragraph will modify or qualify what has gone before. A trigger word at the beginning of any paragraph is a sure sign that this paragraph will disagree with what was stated in the preceding one.

Number of Women at the Top

1980—10 out of 6,400 executive officers and directors in the United States were women.
1990—19 out of 4000 executive officers and directors in the United States were women.
Source: *Fortune*, 1990

Trigger words are important even if they do not appear at the beginning of a paragraph; they always signal a change of meaning, even if it is only within a sentence. Here are the trigger words that often appear on the GMAT:

but
although (even though)
however
yet
despite (in spite of)
nevertheless
nonetheless
notwithstanding
except
while
unless
on the other hand

CONTINUING-THE-SAME-TRAIN-OF-THOUGHT WORDS

Some structural signposts let you know that there will be no contradiction, no change in path. If you see a "first of all" it stands to reason that there will be a "second of all" and perhaps a "third." Other signs of continuation:

in addition
by the same token
likewise
similarly
this (implies a reference to preceding sentence)
thus (implies a conclusion)

One other continuing structural element that appears on the GMAT is not a word. Sentences that appear inside *parentheses* often contain information you'll need to answer a question. You should circle any sentence that is enclosed within parentheses.

YIN-YANG WORDS

One of ETS's all-time favorite types of passage contrasts two opposing viewpoints, and certain words immediately give this away. See if you can supply the second half of the following sentences:

> The *traditional view* of the causes of global warming focuses on the burning of fossil fuel . . .

(Second half: however, the *new* view is that there is some other cause.)

> *Until recently*, it was thought that the Mayan civilization was destroyed as a result of drought . . .

(Second half: however, *now* we believe that they were destroyed by space invaders.)

The *classical* model of laissez-faire capitalism does not even admit the possibility of government intervention . . .

(Second half: but the *rock and roll* version of laissez-faire capitalism says, "Let me just get my checkbook.")

Before 1960, it was commonly assumed that the atom was the smallest particle in the universe . . .

(Second half: however, *after 1960* scientists began to suspect that there was something even smaller.)

Whenever you spot a "yin" word, you should realize that there is a "yang" on the way. Some other yin-yang words:

Yin	Yang
generally	(however, this time . . .)
the old view	(however, the new view . . .)
the widespread belief	(but the in-crowd believes . . .)
most scientists think	(but Doctor Spleegle thinks . . .)
on the one hand	(on the other hand . . .)

GETTING THROUGH THE PASSAGE FASTER

Structural elements like these can help you to understand a passage faster, with less "reading" and less wear and tear on your brain. When you spot one of these signposts, circle it. A structural signpost is usually more important to your understanding of a passage than any individual fact within that passage.

STEP 3: ATTACK THE QUESTIONS

Once you've grasped the main ideas of the paragraphs, you can attack the questions aggressively. As we noted earlier, each passage is followed by up to 7 questions of varying levels of difficulty. These questions *generally* follow the organization of the passage. In other words, a question about the first paragraph will probably come before a question about the second paragraph.

Some people believe it's a good idea to look at the questions before reading the passage. According to their reasoning, reading the questions first allows you to determine what's important in the passage. We might agree if there weren't as many as seven of them. It's impossible to keep that many questions in your head and read a complicated passage at the same time. By approaching the passages the way we've suggested, you'll get the general questions through an understanding of the main idea, and you'll know just where to look to find the answers to specific questions.

GENERAL QUESTIONS

- ◆ "What is the primary purpose of this passage?"
- ◆ "What is the author's tone?"
- ◆ "Which of the following best describes the structure of the passage?"

Each of the questions above is a general question. A two-minute "read" using the techniques we've shown you over the last few pages is generally enough to answer the general questions—without going back to the passage. In our courses, we encourage students to do the general questions first, then go to the specific questions. Always try to answer a general question in your own words *before* you look at the answer choices.

USING POE TO ELIMINATE WRONG ANSWERS ON GENERAL QUESTIONS

Once you have your *own* idea of what the answer should be, it's time to use POE to zero in on *ETS*'s answer. In the chapter on Sentence Correction, you learned that it's often easier to eliminate incorrect answers than to select the correct answers. The Process of Elimination is just as useful on Reading Comprehension questions. How can you use POE to eliminate answers to general questions?

General questions have general answers. Thus, we can eliminate any answer to a general question that focuses on only one part of the passage or is too specific. We can also eliminate answers which are not in the passage at all. For example, here's a question based on the passage you have already read:

> The main topic of the passage is
>
> (A) the health hazards of X rays and gamma rays on humans
> (B) the overly severe federal guidelines on radiation
> (C) the potential dangers of microwaves
> (D) to compare and contrast the work of Cleary and Milham
> (E) the limits of study methodology in science

Here's how to crack it

In spite of the fact that X-rays and gamma rays were mentioned in the first sentence, we know that this was just an introductory thought to get to the real idea of the passage—the danger of microwaves. So eliminate choice (A). The federal guidelines in choice (B) were mentioned in the passage, but only at the very end. Could this be the main idea of the entire passage? No way. Choice (C) is the correct answer, and exactly what we would have been expecting from our fast "read." While Cleary and Milham are discussed several times, they are never compared, so we can eliminate choice (D). And while the passage mentions that the methodologies of the two scientists have been questioned, this is not the main idea, so we can eliminate choice (E) as well.

SPECIFIC QUESTIONS

- "The passage suggests which of the following about the laboratory results on microwaves mentioned in line 12?"

- "According to the passage, a study of ham radio operators might be expected to find which of the following?"

Sentence Correction Review: Quantity Comparison Words

comparing two items
between
more
better
less

comparing more than two items
among
most
best
least

Each of the questions above is a specific question. Specific questions have specific answers which you'll now need to find. Naturally, your 2-minute "read" has not equipped you to know the answers to these questions off the top of your head, but every specific question gives you a clue about where to look for the answer.

LINE NUMBERS

How do you find the answer to the following question?

> "The passage suggests which of the following about the federal guidelines on microwaves mentioned in line 12?"

That's easy: it has a line number. All you have to do is go back to the cited line or lines and read starting a little above the indicated place and finishing a little below.

LEAD WORDS

How do you find the answer to *this* question?

> "According to the passage, a study of ham radio operators might be expected to find which of the following?"

When a question seems to be specific but has no line number, look for a catchy word or phrase in the question. For example, in this question, there's a very clear specific reference: "ham radio operators." We call this a **lead** phrase. Now that you know what you're looking for, run your finger down the passage until you see your lead word or phrase. When you find it, you will have almost certainly found your answer.

Try this technique out right now by running your finger down the passage below until you find "ham radio operators." Don't read; just look:

> Biologists have long known that some types of
> electromagnetic radiation such as X rays and gamma
> rays can be dangerous to human beings. Operating at
> *Line*   a frequency of 10^{18} through 10^{22}, these rays, which are
> (5)   well above the visible light spectrum, were first
> detected in the early years of the 20th century.
>   However, until now, no one has ever suggested that
> microwave radiation might also be harmful. In
> preliminary laboratory results, Cleary and Milham
> (10)   have found elevated growth rates in cancer cells
> exposed to low doses of microwaves. Cleary exposed
> cancer cells to levels of radiation that are commonly
> found in microwave ovens and found that the
> abnormal cells grew 30 percent faster than did
> (15)   unexposed cells. Milham's study focused on ham
> radio operators who are commonly exposed to levels
> of radiation slightly higher than those emitted by
> cellular telephones. He discovered elevated levels of
> myeloid leukemia.

Q: What should be the very first thing you do when you come to a Reading Comprehension section?

A: Order the passages: find the longest passage with the least number of questions and save for last.

(20)   The methodology of Cleary and Milham has been questioned by other scientists in the field. However, no one seriously disputes that their preliminary findings must be taken seriously or that new studies should be set up to try to duplicate their results.

(25)   Although federal guidelines for how much electromagnetic energy can be allowed to enter the work and home environment have been made more stringent since they were first implemented in 1982, the recent studies pose troubling questions about the safety of microwaves.

USING POE TO ELIMINATE WRONG ANSWERS ON SPECIFIC QUESTIONS

Specific questions have very specific answers. Before you even go to the answer choices, you should usually be able to point to the exact spot in the passage where the answer to the question is to be found.

Once you go to the answer choices, you'll probably be able to eliminate several right away. However, if you are down to two possibilities, don't try to prove one of the answers right. Look for something in the passage that will make one of the answers *wrong*. It's often easier to find the flaw in the incorrect answer. For example, here's a question (complete with answer choices) based on the passage you have already read:

> According to the passage, a study of ham radio operators might be expected to find which of the following?
>
> (A) The presence of X rays and gamma rays
> (B) Unusual cells growing 30% faster than normal
> (C) A level of radiation exposure similar to that found in users of microwave ovens
> (D) Higher levels present of a particular type of leukemia
> (E) Levels of radiation identical to those emitted by cellular phones

Here's how to crack it

The lead words, "ham radio operators" led us to the second half of the second paragraph. If you haven't already, read the relevant sentences and get an idea of what you might expect the answer to be.

Now, go to the answer choices. Would a study of ham radio operators find the presence of X rays and gamma rays? Well, neither are mentioned in *this* paragraph. The *first* paragraph did mention these rays—but only to introduce the dangers of microwaves. So much for choice (A).

Both choices (B) and (C) were mentioned in this paragraph, but only in connection with *Cleary's* work—which had nothing to do with ham radio operators.

You might have been torn between choices (D) and (E) since both come from the right place in the passage. Don't try to decide which is correct. Look for a reason why one of them is *wrong*. Let's attack choice (E). It says that ham operators were exposed to levels of radiation identical to those emitted by cellular phones. Is that *exactly* what the passage said? Well, no. According to the passage, ham radio operators were exposed to slightly *higher* levels. Choice (E) is history. The correct answer must be choice (D).

INFERENCE QUESTIONS

- ◆ "Which of the following can be inferred from the passage about the level of radiation from cellular telephones?"

Although this question asks you to draw an inference, you'll find that ETS's idea of an inference will be much more timid than yours. GMAT inferences go at most a *tiny* bit further than the passage itself. If your thinking on this type of question becomes too subtle, you'll get it wrong. Here's an example:

> Which of the following can be inferred from the passage about the studies conducted by Cleary and Milham?
>
> (A) Cleary's results were better documented than Milham's.
> (B) Neither study is scientifically valid.
> (C) Both studies indicated that microwaves were more harmful than X rays.
> (D) The final results were not in at the time the article was written.
> (E) The results of both studies were based on the same scientific data.

Here's how to crack it

The passage never said that one study was better than the other, so eliminate answer choice (A). While both studies were questioned in the third paragraph, it would be inferring far too far to say that neither was scientifically valid. Eliminate choice (B). The passage never said that microwaves were more harmful than X rays. It seems likely that they are less harmful. Eliminate choice (C). The results of both studies were called "preliminary" in paragraph two. Thus, choice (D) seems so obvious that you might almost hesitate to call it an inference. This is exactly the kind of inference ETS feels comfortable making. Choice (E) was not just *not* stated. It is likely to be false. Cleary concentrated on cancerous cells exposed to levels of radiation equivalent to microwave ovens. Milham studied ham radio operators. The correct answer was (D).

ADVANCED POE: ATTACKING DISPUTABLE ANSWER CHOICES

You've eliminated two answer choices on a Reading Comprehension question, but you can't decide which of the remaining three choices is best. All three seem to be saying the same thing. How do you choose between them? The test writers at ETS want their correct answers to be indisputable so that no one will ever be able to complain.

Here are three statements. Which of them is indisputable?

(A) Shaw was the greatest dramatist of his time.

(B) Shaw's genius was never understood.

(C) Shaw was a great dramatist, although some critics disagree.

When you read a Reading Comprehension question, determine whether it is general or specific. To answer general questions, you need to have an understanding of the main idea and the structure of the passage. To answer specific questions, you need to have a vague sense of where information is in the passage and to be able to go back and locate it when asked.

Shaw's status as a playwright will always be a matter of opinion. If ETS made statement (A) the correct answer to a Reading Comprehension question, people who got the question wrong might argue that not everyone considers Shaw the greatest dramatist of his time.

If ETS made statement (B) the correct answer to a Reading Comprehension question, people who got the question wrong could argue that someone, somewhere in the world, must have understood poor old Shaw.

Statement (C), by contrast, is indisputable. Most critics would agree that Shaw was *a* great dramatist. If there are any critics who do not, ETS covers itself with its little disclaimer: "although some critics disagree." Statement (C) is so vague that no one could possibly argue with it.

In general: An answer choice that is highly specific and unequivocal is *disputable* and is therefore usually not the correct answer.

An answer choice that is general and vague is *indisputable* and is therefore often the correct answer.

How to Pick an Indisputable Answer Choice

Certain words make a statement so vague that it is almost impossible to dispute. Here are some of these words:

usually
sometimes
may
can
some
most

If a statement says that Shaw is *sometimes* considered to be the greatest dramatist ever, who can dispute that?

How to Avoid a Disputable Answer Choice

Certain words make a statement so specific that it is easy to dispute. Here are some of these words:

always
must
everybody
all
complete
never

If a statement says that Shaw is *always* considered to be the greatest dramatist ever, who couldn't dispute that?

WHAT DOES WALLY WANT TO PICK?

The GMAT was created in 1954. Although some of the question types have changed, the philosophical outlook of the test has remained pretty much the same. Every year the same information is tested in pretty much the same way. The GMAT is frozen in time. It harks back to a more innocent era—a time when there were answers to every question, and America was always right, and all our problems were on the way to being solved. ETS reading passages are still largely written from that perspective.

Q: What is the purpose of skimming the passage?

It is a perspective you may not understand, since you probably weren't around in the 1950s. But we've all experienced that era indirectly, in the form of 1950s television sitcoms. Think of the GMAT as the test Wally Cleaver would have had to take if he'd decided to go to business school.

Whenever you're in doubt about an answer, it always helps to ask yourself whether Wally would have felt comfortable selecting that answer.

RESPECT FOR PROFESSIONALS

ETS has tremendous respect for all professionals—doctors, scientists, economists, writers, and artists. After all, Dr. Kildare never got sued for malpractice, and Wally would feel very uncomfortable selecting an answer choice that implied that any professional was a terrible person.

By the same token, it would be unusual to find a correct answer choice that took any but the lightest digs at America. Our country is pretty much beyond ETS's reproach.

MODERATE EMOTION

ETS avoids strong emotions on the GMAT. If Wally took the GMAT, he would never pick an answer choice that took too strong a position about anything. The author's tone might be "slightly critical," but it will not be "scornful and envious." The author's tone might be "admiring," but it will never be "wildly enthusiastic."

THE MINORITY PASSAGE

For many years minority groups have complained—justifiably—that ETS tests discriminate against them. ETS responded to this criticism by adding a minority passage to many of its tests. One of the reading passages on the GMAT you take will almost certainly be about some minority group—blacks, Chicanos, women (for some reason, they consider women to be a minority group), etc.

Designed to answer charges that ETS tests are biased, the minority passage is invariably positive in tone. This doesn't make the test any fairer to minorities, but it does sometimes make the test easier to beat. Any answer choice that expresses negative views of the minority in question is almost certainly wrong.

Try the following example:

The author considers women's literature to be

(A) derivative
(B) lacking in imagination
(C) full of promise and hope
(D) much better than the literature being written by
    men today
(E) uninteresting

A: To allow a basic familiarity
    with the topic and to sum up
    each paragraph.
    Devote only about two
    minutes to skimming; do
    not get caught up in details
    or difficult concepts.
    Remember, you get points
    for answering the ques-
    tions, not reading the
    passage.

Here's how to crack it

You don't need to see the passage to answer this question. The whole purpose of the minority passage is to illustrate to everyone how broad-minded and unbiased the GMAT really is. *Derivative, lacking in imagination,* and *uninteresting* all express negative opinions of literature written by (what ETS considers to be) a minority group. Wally would never have picked choices (A), (B), or (E).

Answer choice (D) goes too far in the other direction. As far as Wally and ETS are concerned, women's literature is just as good as, but no better than, anyone else's. The answer must be choice (C).

PUTTING ALL THIS TO WORK

Now that you know something about how to tackle GMAT passages, and what to look for, try the sample passage below. Find the main idea of each paragraph (and if you like, jot down a few key words about each in the margin); look for structural signposts along the way (and circle them when you find them).

Try to spend no more than two minutes "reading." Remember, you only get points for answering questions. Don't feel you have to do the questions in the order in which they are presented. As we've said, if you've understood the main idea of the passage, it makes sense to do the general questions first. Leave for last any specific questions that don't seem to have an obvious reference place in the passage. (At the end of this chapter you will find the same passage repeated with all the handwritten markings one of our teachers made when she "read" the passage.)

Until recently, corporate ideology in the United
States has held that bigger is better. This traditional
view of the primacy of big, centralized companies is
Line now being challenged as some of the giants of
(5) American business are being outperformed by a new
generation of smaller, streamlined businesses. If it
was the industrial revolution that spawned the era of
massive industrialized companies, then perhaps it is
the information revolution of the 1990s that is
(10) spawning the era of the small company.
    For most of this century, big companies dominated
an American business scene that seemed to thrive on
its own grandness of scale. The expansion westward,
the growth of the railroad and steel industries, an
(15) almost limitless supply of cheap raw materials, plus a

population boom that provided an ever-increasing demand for new products (if not always a cheap source of labor) all coincided to encourage the growth of large companies.

(20)   But rapid developments in the marketplace have begun to change the accepted rules of business, and have underscored the need for fast reaction times. Small companies, without huge overhead and inventory, can respond quickly to a technologically

(25)   advanced age in which new products and technologies can become outmoded within a year of their being brought to market.

Of course, successful emerging small companies face a potential dilemma in that their very success will

(30)   tend to turn them into copies of the large corporate dinosaurs they are now supplanting. To avoid this trap, small companies may look to the example of several CEOs of large corporations who have broken down their sprawling organizations into small, semi-

(35)   independent divisions capable of making the leap into the next century.

1. The primary purpose of the passage is to

   (A) present evidence that resolves a contradiction
         in business theory
   (B) discuss reasons why an accepted business
         pattern is changing
   (C) describe a theoretical model and a method
         whereby that model can be tested
   (D) argue that a traditional ideology deserves new
         attention
   (E) resolve two conflicting explanations for a
         phenomenon

2. According to the passage, all of the following are
    examples of developments that helped promote the
    growth of large companies earlier in this century
    EXCEPT

   (A) the growth of the railroad industry
   (B) America's westward expansion
   (C) an almost inexhaustible source of raw materials
   (D) the existence of an inexpensive source of labor
   (E) the development of an industry to produce steel

3. The author's attitude toward the traditional view
    expressed in lines 1-4 can best be described as

   (A) scornful and denunciatory
   (B) dispirited and morose
   (C) critical but respectful
   (D) admiring and deferential
   (E) uncertain but interested

Reading Comprehension trigger words that signal a change in meaning:
• but
• although (even though)
• however
• yet
• despite (in spite of)
• nevertheless
• nonetheless
• notwithstanding
• except
• while
• unless
• on the other hand

4. It can be inferred from the passage that which of the following actions would be most consistent with the traditional ideology described in the passage?

(A) Splitting a manufacturing company into several smaller divisions.

(B) Bringing a new product to market within a year.

(C) Creating a department to utilize new emerging technologies.

(D) Expanding an existing company in anticipation of growing demand.

(E) Cutting inventory and decreasing overhead.

5. According to the passage, to avoid the trap posed by "the potential dilemma" mentioned in line 29, emerging successful small companies will have to do which of the following?

(A) Turn for advice to the industry analysts who earlier predicted the problems of large companies.

(B) Avoid taking paths that will make them too successful.

(C) Learn to embrace the traditional ideology of large corporations.

(D) Create small interconnected divisions rather than expanding in traditional ways.

(E) Hire successful CEOs from other firms.

6. Which of the following best describes the organization of the first paragraph of the passage?

(A) A conventional model is dismissed and an alternative introduced.

(B) An assertion is made and a general supporting example is given.

(C) Two contradictory points of view are presented and evaluated.

(D) A historical overview is given to explain a phenomenon.

(E) A new theory is described and then qualified.

7. It can be inferred from the passage that small companies are better able to adapt to the new business climate due to which of the following factors?

    I. low overhead and inventory
    II. the ability to predict when new products will become outmoded
    III. the capacity to change quickly to meet new challenges

    (A) I only
    (B) II only
    (C) III only
    (D) I and III only
    (E) I, II, and III

ATTACKING THE QUESTIONS

1. The primary purpose of the passage is to

    (A) present evidence that resolves a contradiction in business theory
    (B) discuss reasons why an accepted business pattern is changing
    (C) describe a theoretical model and a method whereby that model can be tested
    (D) argue that a traditional ideology deserves new attention
    (E) resolve two conflicting explanations for a phenomenon

Here's how to crack it

This is a general question, and general questions always reflect the structure of the passage. The first words of the passage were "until recently." We hope you recognized right away that this was "yin-yang" terminology, as was "this traditional view." Obviously this passage was about to present a *new* view.

The old view, according to the passage, was that in America large companies were always better off than small companies. Of course, the new view is that smaller companies are now doing better than big companies. This was probably enough for you to answer all the general questions in this section, but lets look quickly at the rest of the passage: paragraph two gave historical reasons why bigger used to be better; paragraph three explained why this was no longer true today; and paragraph five concludes by talking about how small companies can stay successful as they inevitably get bigger. Let's look at the answer choices.

(A) In yin-yang passages, new is virtually always better than old. There is really no contradiction here, and besides, how could a 250-word passage "resolve" anything definitively? Eliminate.

(B) This is the correct answer. It mirrors the yin-yang structure of the passage—the accepted pattern of almost a century is now changing.

(C) If you picked this one, you were thinking too hard. Perhaps you thought the primacy of the small company was the new theoretical model, about to be tested. However, the passage seems to imply that the decline of large companies and the ascendancy of small companies started before anyone even realized what was happening, let alone came up with some smart theory about it.

(D) Was the author arguing that in fact the traditional view that "bigger is better" is actually correct after all? Nope. Eliminate.

(E) GMAT passages virtually never "resolve" anything. How could you hope to resolve a complex issue in 250 words? While there are two conflicting elements in this passage, they are not conflicting explanations for a single phenomenon.

2. According to the passage, all of the following are examples of developments that helped promote the growth of large companies earlier in this century EXCEPT

(A) the growth of the railroad industry
(B) America's westward expansion
(C) an almost inexhaustible source of raw materials
(D) the existence of an inexpensive source of labor
(E) the development of an industry to produce steel

Here's how to crack it

This is a specific question without a line number, but you probably knew just where to look. Which paragraph gave historical background on the growth of large companies? If you said paragraph two, you are absolutely correct.

The first time you "read" this passage, you may have skipped over the specifics in this paragraph since they weren't necessary to understand the purpose of the paragraph. Now, of course, you are interested. But even if you had spent twenty minutes you didn't really have memorizing the entire passage, wouldn't you still have wanted to peek back at this paragraph just to make sure you remembered it correctly? Since you were going to have to look back anyway, it made sense to skip over the details the first time around. Remember, there was no guarantee that there would even be a question about this information. It is not unusual to find GMAT passages whose questions completely ignore whole paragraphs at a time.

This is an "except" question, which means that every answer choice is correct but one. The answer to this question was buried inside the parentheses in line 17–18: ("If not always a cheap source of labor.") The answer to this question is choice (D).

3. The author's attitude toward the traditional view expressed in lines 1-4 can best be described as

(A) scornful and denunciatory
(B) dispirited and morose
(C) critical but respectful
(D) admiring and deferential
(E) uncertain but interested

Here's how to crack it

You could eliminate two of these answer choices without even reading the passage. Wally would never have chosen an answer that described an attitude toward the ideology of companies like General Motors in terms like "scornful and denunciatory" or "dispirited and morose." As far as the passage is concerned, the traditional ideology no longer works, so we can pretty much rule out choice (D), admiring and deferential. Choice (E) is a little too vague. Both choices (A) and (B) are so strong and out in left field that we can safely eliminate them. The only possible answer is choice (C).

Need to take the GMAT, but allergic to paper?

No problem, just wait to take the test until October 1997. From that time onward, according to ETS, the GMAT will be available only in computerized form.

4. It can be inferred from the passage that which of the following actions would be most consistent with the traditional ideology described in the passage ?
   - (A) Splitting a manufacturing company into several smaller divisions.
   - (B) Bringing a new product to market within a year.
   - (C) Creating a department to utilize new emerging technologies.
   - (D) Expanding an existing company in anticipation of growing demand.
   - (E) Cutting inventory and decreasing overhead.

Here's how to crack it

The trick in inference questions is to infer as little as possible. The traditional ideology is that bigger is better. Which of the answer choices shows a situation getting bigger? The correct answer is choice (D). Choices (A) and (E) both illustrate the process of downsizing as described in the passage. Choices (B) and (C) illustrate the lean-and-mean tactics attributed in the passage to small companies.

5. According to the passage, to avoid the trap posed by "the potential dilemma" mentioned in line 29, emerging successful small companies will have to do which of the following?
   - (A) Turn for advice to the industry analysts who earlier predicted the problems of large companies.
   - (B) Avoid taking paths that will make them too successful.
   - (C) Learn to embrace the traditional ideology of large corporations.
   - (D) Create small interconnected divisions rather than expanding in traditional ways.
   - (E) Hire successful CEOs from other firms.

Here's how to crack it

Whenever you see a specific question with line numbers, always remember to read a little above and a little below the cited line. In this case, we are not interested so much in the "dilemma" as in how to avoid the trap posed by the dilemma. The answer to this question is in the last three lines of the passage.

Let's look at the answer choices:

(A) is an interesting idea, but it is not said in the passage, so we can eliminate it.

(B) has the right idea, but takes it too far. It is practically un-American to think that a company would try not to become too successful.

(C) The traditional ideology is what got the big companies into trouble. Eliminate.

(D) This is the correct answer, and a nice paraphrase of what was said in the last three lines of the passage.

(E) The passage suggests that small companies could learn from these CEOs, but does not suggest that the small companies *hire* the CEOs.

6. Which of the following best describes the organization of the first paragraph of the passage?

(A) A conventional model is dismissed and an alternative introduced.
(B) An assertion is made and a general supporting example is given.
(C) Two contradictory points of view are presented and evaluated.
(D) A historical overview is given to explain a phenomenon.
(E) A new theory is described and then qualified.

Here's how to crack it

This is a structure question pure and simple. Let's look at the answers:

(A) correctly describes this yin-yang paragraph.

(B) ignores the structure of the passage.

(C) is close, but fails to show that one point of view is considered superior to the other.

(D) describes paragraph two instead of paragraph one.

(E) The word "qualified" means "limited." The author seems to like the idea of the small company, and certainly doesn't qualify it in the first paragraph.

7. It can be inferred from the passage that small companies are better able to adapt to the new business climate due to which of the following factors?

    I. low overhead and inventory
   II. the ability to predict when new products will become outmoded
  III. the capacity to change quickly to meet new challenges

    (A) I only
    (B) II only
    (C) III only
    (D) I and III only
    (E) I, II, and III

B-School Lingo

Quant Jock: a mathematical athlete who is happiest crunching numbers

Quick and Dirty: an abbreviated analysis, often involving numbers

Here's how to crack it

I, II, III questions are nasty because you have to answer three questions in order to get one right. It is often a good idea to leave these for last. Where in the passage were small companies actually described? If you said paragraph three, you were absolutely correct. Since this is an inference question, we need to make sure we don't infer too far. Let's look at statement I. Can we infer that small companies are better able to adapt because of low inventory? Sure. On lines 23–24 the passage reads, "Small companies, without huge overhead and inventory…"

Since we know that statement I works, we can cross off choices (B) and (C); why? Because neither includes statement I. Let's look at statement II. While it seems likely that the ability to predict ahead of time which products are going to become outmoded would help small companies adapt faster, there is no indication in the passage that anyone has the ability to predict ahead. If you aren't sure about statement II, you can skip it and go on to statement III. This statement is definitely true. It is a paraphrase of line 24. The correct answer is choice (D).

HERE'S WHAT A READING PASSAGE SHOULD LOOK LIKE AFTER YOU'VE FINISHED READING IT

trad. view: bigger better

new view: small is better

hist. reasons for big companies' early success

Until recently, corporate ideology in the United States has held that bigger is better. This traditional view of the primacy of big, centralized companies is now being challenged as some of the giants of American business are being outperformed by a new generation of smaller, streamlined businesses. If it was the industrial revolution that spawned the era of massive industrialized companies, then perhaps it is information revolution of the 1990s that is spawning the era of the small company.

For most of this century, big companies dominated an American business scene that seemed to thrive on its own grandness of scale. The expansion westward, the growth of the railroad and steel industries, an almost limitless supply of cheap raw materials, plus a

Line (5)

(10)

(15)

population boom that provided an ever-increasing demand for new products (if not always a cheap source of labor) all coincided to encourage the growth of large companies.

(20)   But rapid developments in the marketplace have begun to change the accepted rules of business, and have underscored the need for fast reaction times. Small companies, without huge overhead and inventory, can respond quickly to a technologically
(25)   advanced age in which new products and technologies can become outmoded within a year of their being brought to market.

Of course, successful emerging small companies face a potential dilemma in that their very success will
(30)   tend to turn them into copies of the large corporate dinosaurs they are now supplanting. To avoid this trap, small companies may look to the example of several CEOs of large corporations who have broken down their sprawling organizations into small, semi-
(35)   independent divisions capable of making the leap into the next century.

reasons for small companies' recent success

danger for small companies: getting too big

B-School Lingo

Run the Numbers: analyze quantitatively

SUMMARY

1. A GMAT Reading Comprehension section contains three passages. Each passage is followed by up to 7 questions, for a total of 18 questions. The three types of passages that may appear on the test are social science, science, and business.

2. Neither Reading Comprehension questions nor passages are presented in any order of difficulty. It is generally a more effective strategy to decide on your *own* order in which to do the passages.

3. If you insist on reading these passages the way you normally read, it might make sense to skip one entire passage and the questions based on that passage, in order to have enough time to read the other two thoroughly. However, if you can make the transition to GMAT reading, you may find that even if reading comprehension is not your strength, you have time to do all three passages well, perhaps skipping one or two difficult questions from each passage.

4. GMAT reading has nothing to do with reading, and even less to do with business reading. GMAT passages contain many more pieces of information than you'll be tested on. Trying to remember all this useless information is silly.

5. Read a passage for its main idea. This will enable you to answer the general questions, and give you a good idea of where to look for the answers to specific questions. Specific facts are unimportant at this stage. Let your eyes glaze over them. Write notes in the margin.

6. Structural signposts can help you see how a passage is organized. Look for trigger words, continuing-the-same-train-of-thought words, and yin-yang constructions.

7. Attack general questions first, based on the main idea of the passage.

8. Answers to specific questions can be found either through **line numbers** or **lead words**. When line references are given, read a little above and a little below the cited lines.

9. Attack answer choices that are disputable. Specific, strong statements are often wrong. Vague, wimpy statements are often correct.

10. The tone of a minority passage is invariably positive. This can sometimes help you to answer questions even if you haven't had time to read the entire passage.

11. If the Beaver's older brother, Wally, wouldn't have liked a particular answer, there's a good chance it's wrong. Wally wouldn't have liked answers that

   A) are disrespectful to professionals
   B) are too strong
   C) condone prejudicial attitudes

12. I, II, III questions are best tackled by POE. If they're taking too much time, leave them for last.

Critical Reasoning

The Critical Reasoning section of the GMAT consists of very short reading passages (typically twenty to 100 words). Each of these passages is followed by one or two questions, giving a total of sixteen questions. These questions are supposed to test your ability to think clearly. ETS says that "no knowledge of the terminology and of the conventions of formal logic is presupposed." Nevertheless, you'll find that while it may not be presupposed, some knowledge of the rudiments of formal logic—as applied by The Princeton Review—can substantially increase your score.

THE HISTORY OF CRITICAL REASONING

Over the years ETS has tried several different formats in an attempt to test reasoning ability.

The original GMAT contained a section called Best Arguments. In 1961, ETS replaced this section ("in part because research indicated that [doing so] would increase the predictive effectiveness of the test") with something called Organization of Ideas. In 1966, this section was also phased out, and for six years reasoning ability went unmeasured by ETS. In 1972, ETS tried again, with a section called Analysis of Situations. Finally, on the October 1988 version of the GMAT, ETS unveiled Critical Reasoning for the first time.

WELL, NOT EXACTLY THE *FIRST* TIME

In fact, Critical Reasoning looks a lot like Best Arguments. ETS has used this type of question for years on the LSAT and the GRE—respectively, the Law School Admission Test and the Graduate Record Exam.

Before we begin, take a moment to read a close approximation of the instructions at the beginning of each Critical Reasoning section:

> Directions: After reading each question, pick the
> best answer among the choices that follow.

Obviously you won't need to read these instructions again.

HOW TO ATTACK THE CRITICAL REASONING SECTION

The terseness of ETS's instructions implies that all you need on this section is common sense. Common sense will certainly help, but you should also understand a bit about the formal logic on which Critical Reasoning is based.

Like the other types of questions found on the GMAT, Critical Reasoning questions tend to be predictable. There are only a few question types, and as you learn how the test writers use their smattering of formal logic to write Critical Reasoning questions, you'll be able to anticipate the answers to certain of those questions.

Most Common Causes of Death in the Workplace

	% of all worker deaths
Assaults	21%
Highway accidents	20%
Falls	10%
Caught in, under, between objects	10%
Struck by objects	9%
Electrocutions	5%
Airplane crashes	4%
Explosions	3%

Source: *Monthly Labor Review,* 1994

In this chapter we'll teach you how to:

1. use clues in the questions to anticipate the kind of answer you're looking for in a passage

2. analyze and attack the passages in an organized fashion

3. understand the basic structure of the passages

4. use Process of Elimination to eliminate wrong choices

A WORD ABOUT GMAT LOGIC

GMAT logic is different from the formal logic you may have studied in college. Our review of GMAT logic is not intended to be representative of logic as a whole. We don't intend to teach you logic. We're going to teach you *GMAT* logic.

THE PASSAGE

Most of the passages in the Critical Reasoning section are in the form of *arguments* in which the writer tries to convince the reader of something. Here's an example:

> In the past 10 years, advertising revenues for the magazine *True Investor* have fallen by 30%. The magazine has failed to attract new subscribers, and newsstand sales are down to an all-time low. Thus, sweeping editorial changes will be necessary if the magazine is to survive.

There are three main parts to an argument.

The Conclusion: This is what the author is trying to convince us of.

The Premises: These are the pieces of evidence the author gives to support the conclusion.

The Assumptions: These are unstated ideas or evidence without which the entire conclusion might be invalid.

In the passage above, the author's *conclusion* is found in the last line:

> *Thus, sweeping editorial changes will be necessary if the magazine is to survive.*

To support this, the author gives three pieces of evidence, or *premises*: Advertising revenue is down; there are no new subscribers; and very few people are buying the newspaper at the newsstand.

Are there any *assumptions* here? Well, not in the passage itself. Assumptions are never stated by the author. They are parts of the argument that have been left

Reading Comprehension Review

Q: What should you keep in mind with inference questions?

out. Even the best thought-out argument has assumptions. In this case one important assumption the author seems to be making is that it was the old editorial policy that caused the problems the magazine is now encountering. Another assumption is that editorial changes alone will be enough to restore the magazine's financial health.

A Critical Reasoning passage is not necessarily made up of only these three parts. The passage might contain other information as well—extraneous ideas, perhaps, or statements of an opposing point of view. It's also possible for some important part of an argument to be missing—its conclusion, for example. Sometimes ETS will ask *you* to supply the conclusion.

THIS IS NOT LIKE READING COMPREHENSION

Reading Comprehension passages are long and filled with useless facts. By now you've gotten used to reading these passages for their structure, letting your eyes skip over factual data you probably won't be tested on anyway.

By contrast, Critical Reasoning passages are quite short, and every single word should be considered carefully. Shades of meaning are very important in this section.

THE QUESTION

Immediately after the passage, there will be a question. There is usually only one question per passage. In the chapter on Reading Comprehension, we told you that it was a waste of time to try to read Reading Comprehension questions *before* you read the passage; after all, each Reading Comprehension passage is followed by 6 or 7 questions. It is impossible to keep that many questions in your head. In Critical Reasoning, however, since there is usually only one question per passage, it is essential that you

always read the question first.

The question contains important clues that will tell you what to look for as you read the passage.

THERE ARE SEVEN QUESTION TYPES

Here are examples of the seven question types you'll see (we'll go into much greater detail later in the chapter):

1. What is the conclusion in the passage above?

As you read the passage, you'll be looking to identify and separate the premises from the conclusion.

2. What conclusion is best supported by the passage above?

The passage connected to this type of question will simply be a list of premises. You will have to supply your own conclusion.

3. The passage above assumes that . . .

As you read the passage in question, you will be looking for an unstated premise on which the argument depends.

4. Which of the following, if true, would most strengthen the conclusion drawn above?

This type of question is like an assumption question in that it is asking you to find an unstated premise on which the argument depends, and then bolster it.

5. Which of the following, if true, would most seriously weaken the conclusion of the passage above?

This type of question, like an assumption question, is asking you to find an unstated premise of the argument and poke holes in it.

6. Which of the following can best be inferred from the passage above?

This question, like inference questions in the Reading Comprehension section, is at most asking you to go a tiny, tiny bit further than the passage does.

7. Which of the following most resembles the method used by the author to make the point above?

This type of question asks you to find an argument in the answer choices that mimics the original argument.

While the wording of the questions may vary, these are the question types you'll see—there are only seven. Each type of question has its own strategy.

The Answer Choices

As you read through this chapter you will notice that certain sentences keep coming up again and again in our discussions of how to eliminate wrong answers.

"This answer choice goes too far."

"That choice is out of the scope of the argument."

Scope

Scope is the single most valuable tool to eliminate answer choices in Critical Reasoning questions. It takes a little practice to figure out how scope works. We'll give you an introduction to the concept here, but you'll need to work through the entire chapter (and perhaps do some timed sections in the *Official*

Guide for GMAT Review) to understand it completely.

Here's an example:

Reading Comprehension Review

Reading Comprehension trigger words that signal a conclusion:

therefore

thus

so

hence

implies

indicates

In an effort to save money, a country's government is considering reducing its military spending. However, without military contracts, crucial industries in that country face bankruptcy, which could disrupt the economy. Thus, the same government that is reducing its military spending will eventually have to provide these industries with money for peacetime research and development.

Which of the following states the conclusion of the passage above?

(A) The necessity of providing money to keep crucial industries from going bankrupt will discourage the government from reducing its military budget.

(B) If the government decreases its military budget, it will eventually be forced to increase its military budget to its former level.

(C) The industries that receive research and development money will be successful in their efforts to convert to peacetime manufacturing.

(D) In the event of war, this country would be unprepared for military conflict.

(E) Reducing military spending to save money will result in some increases in other types of spending.

We will be discussing how to do this type of question (find-the-conclusion) very shortly, but for now we're going to summarize the argument and skip right to the answer choices in order to illustrate how to use scope as an elimination technique. The argument states that a country wants to save money by decreasing its military budget; however, in order to keep the industries that depend on military contracts from collapsing, the country will have to *spend* some additional money as well.

ETS REWARDS NARROW MINDS

In critical reasoning it is easy to think too much. Answer choice (A) might look very tempting at first, because it seems to take the argument to its logical conclusion: "Hey, if cutting military spending is going to end up *costing* the country money, they may as well not do it." But the ETS test writers consider answer choice (A) to be outside the scope of this argument. In fact, if you think about it, we have no idea whether the government will be discouraged or not, or even whether the costs of supplying R and D money will be greater than the savings in military spending. This answer goes much further than the argument itself.

Choice (B) goes too far as well. Perhaps cutting military spending will turn out to be a bad idea, but even if that is true, how do we know that the country will then eventually decide to increase military spending? What might happen in the future is well outside the scope of this argument.

We can eliminate choice (C) for the same reason, since it merely goes off on a tangent to speculate as to the ultimate fate of the industries mentioned in the passage. Whether these industries succeed in making the transition to peacetime manufacturing is not crucial to this argument.

If you are tempted by choice (D), you're still thinking too much. When a country reduces its military spending, you could argue that it might be less prepared for war—but that is way outside the scope of this passage. Be careful not to impose your own value judgments or thought processes on these questions.

Choice (E) may have seemed simplistic when you first read it. You might even have thought that it wasn't really a conclusion at all, that it was more like a summary. However, this is the answer the ETS test writer would choose. And remember, *he's* the one who makes up the answer key. Choice (E) stayed within the scope of the argument.

LOGICAL REASONING

Before we get into specific strategies for dealing with Critical Reasoning questions, it's helpful to understand two major types of reasoning used in logic: **deduction** and **induction**.

Deduction is the process of finding a conclusion that *must* follow from the premises that are given. Here's an example:

> *All Marx Brothers movies are comedies.* Duck Soup *is a Marx Brothers movie. Therefore,* Duck Soup *is a comedy.*

In this example we are given two premises and a conclusion that must follow from these premises. There is no way to argue with this logic. As long as the premises are correct, the conclusion must be valid. This particular kind of deductive reasoning is called a *syllogism*. Make one up on your own—it's easy:

> *Warren Beatty always sleeps with his costars. This year he is costarring in a movie with Roseanne. Therefore, Warren Beatty will sleep with Roseanne.*

The chances of seeing a syllogism on the GMAT are pretty slim, but it *is* likely that you'll see one type of question that uses deductive reasoning—a question that will give you a list of premises and then ask for a conclusion that *must* follow logically.

GMAT test writers don't use deductive logic very often. For one thing, since deductive logic must be true, it's hard to come up with four enticing wrong answers. In addition, there's very little deductive logic to be found in real life. Most of the everyday logic we use is based on inductive reasoning. In a deductive argument, as long as the premises are true, the conclusion must be true.

In an *inductive* argument, even if the premises are true, the best we can say about the conclusion is that it *may* be true. In other words, the conclusion does not necessarily have to follow from the premises. In an inductive argument a

Q: What is the very first thing you should do when starting a critical reasoning passage?

conclusion is often predicted to be true based on the fact that a similar statement is true, or has been true in the past.

There are three types of inductive reasoning that appear on the GMAT: statistical arguments, arguments by analogy, and causal arguments.

STATISTICAL ARGUMENTS

A: Read the questions! This will allow you to focus on the questions when you read the passage.

A statistical argument uses statistics to "prove" its point. Remember what Mark Twain said: "There are lies, damned lies, and statistics."

> *Four out of five doctors agree: The pain reliever in Sinutol is the most effective analgesic on the market today. You should try Sinutol.*

The conclusion (you should try Sinutol) is based on the premise that four out of five doctors found the pain reliever in Sinutol to be the most effective. However, a literal reading of the passage tells us that the statistic that the author uses in support of his conclusion is only based on the opinions of five doctors (all of whom may be on the board of directors of Sinutol). The author's conclusion is based on the *assumption* that four out of *every* five doctors will find Sinutol to be wonderful. This may be correct, but we do not know for sure. Therefore, the most we can say about the conclusion is that it may be true.

Whenever you see statistics in an argument, always be sure to ask yourself the following question: Are the statistics representative?

ARGUMENTS BY ANALOGY

An argument by analogy compares one situation to another, ignoring the question of whether the two situations are comparable.

> *Studies indicate that use of this product causes cancer in laboratory animals. Therefore, you should stop using this product.*

The author's conclusion (you should stop using the product) is based on the premise that the product causes cancer in laboratory animals. This argument is not really complete. It relies on the *assumption* that since this product causes cancer in laboratory animals, it will also cause cancer in humans.

Whenever you see a comparison in a Critical Reasoning passage, you should ask yourself: Are these two situations really comparable?

CAUSAL ARGUMENTS

Causal arguments take an effect and suggest a cause for it:

> *Every time I wear my green suit, people like me. Therefore, it is my green suit that makes people like me.*

The author's conclusion (it is the green suit that makes people like him) is based on the premise that every time he wears it, he has observed that effect. But this argument relies on the *assumption* that there is no other possible cause for people liking him. Perhaps he always wears a red tie with his green suit, and it's really the tie that people like.

Whenever you spot a cause being suggested for an effect, ask yourself whether there might be an alternative cause.

You've now seen all the logic you'll need to attack Critical Reasoning. Let's apply your knowledge to the question types.

FIND-THE-CONCLUSION QUESTIONS

Here's a typical find-the-conclusion question. Remember, always read the question first.

1. When young students first look at modernist abstract painting, their eyes are assailed by a seemingly meaningless mass of squiggles. It is only after a study of the history of art and the forces which led up to abstraction that it is possible to appreciate the intellectual sophistication of modern art. Thus, a high-school study of modern art should always begin with a study of the history of art.

   Which of the following is the main point of the passage above?

   (A) To understand the history of art, it is necessary to study modern art.
   (B) Young students are unable to appreciate fully the complexities of modern art.
   (C) An understanding of the history of art is essential to an understanding of modern art.
   (D) To understand abstract art, students must first study the history of art.
   (E) A high-school study of modern art will have little relevance to students who lack a historical perspective.

Since you read the question first, you knew that as you began reading the passage you would need to separate the conclusion of the argument from its premises. Before you start analyzing the passage, here are a few pointers:

HOW TO FIND THE CONCLUSION IF IT IS STATED IN THE PASSAGE

- ◆ Look for conclusions at the beginning and end of a passage. Most arguments follow one of two common structures:

  Premise, premise, premise, conclusion
  or
  conclusion, premise, premise, premise.

Therefore the conclusion can often be found in the first or last sentence of the passage.

- ◆ Look for the same kinds of structural signposts we showed you in the Reading Comprehension chapter. Words like

therefore	hence
thus	implies
so	indicates that

often signal that a conclusion is about to be made.

- ◆ Look for a statement that cannot stand alone; in other words, a statement that needs to be supported by premises.

- ◆ If you can't find the conclusion, look for the premises instead. These are the parts of the argument that support the conclusion.

Premises are often preceded by another kind of signpost. Words like

because	in view of
since	given that

signal that evidence is about to be given to support a conclusion.

NOW LET'S ANALYZE THE PASSAGE

1. When young students first look at modernist abstract painting, their eyes are assailed by a seemingly meaningless mass of squiggles. It is only after a study of the history of art and the forces which led up to abstraction that it is possible to appreciate the intellectual sophistication of modern art. Thus, a high-school study of modern art should always begin with a study of the history of art.

Which of the following is the main point of the passage above?

(A) To understand the history of art, it is necessary to study modern art.

(B) Young students are unable to appreciate fully the complexities of modern art.

(C) An understanding of the history of art is essential to an understanding of modern art.

(D) To understand abstract art, students must first study the history of art.

(E) A high-school study of modern art will have little relevance to students who lack a historical perspective.

Here's how to crack it

Look at the first sentence of the passage. If this is the conclusion, it must be supported by other statements in the passage. Does the second sentence, for example, support the first? No, it goes on to make another point. The first sentence is probably not the conclusion. Look at the last sentence. This seems more like a conclusion. It follows the word "thus"—conclusion signpost—and makes a statement that cannot stand alone. Furthermore, the rest of the passage seems to be leading up to this sentence. We've found our conclusion. The passage can be broken down as follows:

Q: Most arguments can be divided into what three parts?

1. Students don't understand modern art. (premise)

2. To understand modern art, it is necessary to study art history. (premise)

3. Therefore, students who study modern art should first study art history. (conclusion)

Let's look at the answer choices:

> (A) To understand the history of art, it is necessary to study modern art.

This statement actually reverses the second premise. Not only is it not the conclusion, it's not even a premise. Eliminate.

> (B) Young students are unable to appreciate fully the complexities of modern art.

This statement is the first premise, not the conclusion. Eliminate.

> (C) An understanding of the history of art is essential to an understanding of modern art.

This is a correct statement of the second premise, but, again, it is not the conclusion.

> (D) To understand abstract art, students must first study the history of art.

This looks pretty good. It's a restatement of the last sentence of the passage. Note that the Reading Comprehension strategy of avoiding words taken directly from the passage does not work in Critical Reasoning questions where you are being asked to identify a part of an argument that has already been stated in the passage. In these cases an answer choice that takes a quotation from the passage may well be correct.

> (E) A high-school study of modern art will have little relevance to students who lack a historical perspective.

Choice (E) may seem a little tempting at first. To be sure, it is *a* conclusion—and it begins with the same words found in the last sentence of the passage. The question you must ask yourself is whether this statement encapsulates the conclusion found in the passage. The conclusion in the passage states that a high-school study of art should begin with art history. Answer choice (E) does not restate the conclusion—it goes further to explain why students need art history. In other words, it is outside the scope of the argument.

A: Conclusion, premise (evidence), and assumptions (unstated evidence).

SUPPLY-YOUR-OWN-CONCLUSION QUESTIONS

Supply-your-own-conclusion questions are much more common than find-the-conclusion questions. The passage gives you a list of premises. You will have to decide which of the answer choices is the best conclusion to the passage. There are two basic types: questions that require you to reason deductively and passages that test your ability to reason inductively.

A DEDUCTIVE SUPPLY-THE-CONCLUSION QUESTION

2. Fred is taller than Phil.
   Jane is taller than Phil.
   Susan is taller than Jane.
   Tom is taller than Fred.

   If the information above is true, which of the following statements must also be true?

   (A) Fred is taller than Jane.
   (B) Tom is taller than Phil.
   (C) Susan is shorter than Tom.
   (D) Fred is shorter than Jane.
   (E) Phil is taller than Jane.

Here's how to crack it

The question asks which of the statements *must* be true. You're being asked to make a conclusion based on the premises listed in the passage. You may have noticed that you're also being asked to reason deductively. The only type of reasoning that allows you to know that a conclusion *must* be true is deductive reasoning.

The best way to keep all the premises straight is to draw a diagram, or a series of diagrams:

Be sure to distinguish what you *know* to be true from things that merely *could* be true. Now let's attack the answer choices:

(A) Fred is taller than Jane.

From the diagram you can see that while both Fred and Jane are taller than Phil, we do not know the exact relationship between the heights of Fred and Jane. Fred *could* be taller than Jane, but we do not know for certain. Eliminate.

(B) Tom is taller than Phil.

We know from the diagram that Tom is taller than Fred. Since we also know that Fred is taller than Phil, it follows that Tom is, in fact, taller than Phil. This must be the answer. All the same, you should always look at the other answer choices.

(C) Susan is shorter than Tom.

We know that Tom is taller than Fred, who is also taller than Phil. We know that Susan is taller than Jane, who is also taller than Phil. The only thing we know for certain is that both Susan and Tom are taller than Phil. The exact relationship between their heights is unknown. Eliminate.

(D) Fred is shorter than Jane.

Note that answer choice (D) is the exact opposite of answer choice (A). Since we could not tell who was taller in answer choice (A), we can eliminate choice (D) for the same reason.

(E) Phil is taller than Jane.

This one's easy. One of the premises directly contradicts this statement. Eliminate.

AN INDUCTIVE SUPPLY-THE-CONCLUSION QUESTION

3. Fewer elected officials are supporting environmental legislation this year than at any time in the last decade. In a study of thirty elected officials, only five were actively campaigning for new environmental legislation. This comes at a time when the public's concern for the environment is growing by leaps and bounds.

Which of the following conclusions is best supported by the passage above?

(A) More elected officials are needed to support environmental legislation.
(B) Elected officials have lost touch with the concerns of the public.
(C) The five elected officials who actively campaigned for new environmental legislation should be congratulated.
(D) If the environment is to be saved, elected officials must support environmental legislation.
(E) If elected officials are truly to represent their constituents, many of them must increase their support of environmental legislation.

Q: What are the three types of inductive reasoning that continually pop up in critical reasoning passages?

Here's how to crack it

By reading the question, you can deduce two things: First, this is a supply-the-conclusion passage. Second, since the question does not ask you to supply a conclusion that *must* be true, the reasoning in this passage will be inductive. Here are some guidelines for spotting conclusions among the answer choices:

A: Statistical (using numbers to support an argument), analogy (using a comparison), and causal (presenting cause and effect). Learn to recognize the reasoning of an argument: it will help you answer the question.

- ◆ Conclusions are supported by *all* the evidence in the passage. As you look at each answer choice, check to see whether the potential conclusion is supported not by some of the premises but by all of them. A statement that follows from only one of the premises will not be the conclusion.

- ◆ Because the conclusion in this type of question is not in the passage, the answer cannot be just a restatement of a sentence from the passage.

- ◆ Several answer choices will be obviously wrong. Eliminate these first, then decide which of the remaining answers follows most clearly from the premises.

- ◆ Be wary of answer choices that go further than the scope of the original argument. For example, if the passage has given you several noncontroversial facts about advertising, do not select an answer choice that says advertising is a waste of time.

Let's attack the answer choices:

> (A) More elected officials are needed to support environmental legislation.

This statement ignores the last premise of the passage—that the *public* is becoming more and more concerned about the environment. A conclusion must be supported by all its premises. Eliminate.

> (B) Elected officials have lost touch with the concerns of the public.

This is *a* conclusion, but it goes beyond the scope of the argument and ignores parts of the first two premises that relate to the environment.

> (C) The five elected officials who actively campaigned for new environmental legislation should be congratulated.

This statement, while consistent with the sentiments of the author, again does not deal with the last premise, relating to the concerns of the public.

(D) If the environment is to be saved, elected officials must support environmental legislation.

This answer choice again ignores the last premise in the passage. The correct conclusion to this passage must support all of its premises. Eliminate.

Q: What are some helpful approaches to finding the conclusion?

(E) If elected officials are truly to represent their constituents, many of them must increase their support of environmental legislation.

Bingo. This conclusion is supported by all the premises, and it does not go beyond the scope of the argument.

ASSUMPTION QUESTIONS

An assumption question asks you to identify an unstated premise of the passage from among the answer choices. Remember that if an argument depends on one or more unstated premises, it must be based on inductive reasoning. As you read the passage, watch for the three kinds of inductive reasoning we've classified.

You should also remember that in an inductive argument, the conclusion does not *have* to be true, although it *may* be true. Assumptions plug holes in the argument and help make a conclusion true. Here are some guidelines for spotting assumptions among the answer choices:

◆ Assumptions are never stated in the passage. If you see an answer choice that comes straight from the passage, it is not correct.

◆ Assumptions support the conclusion of the passage. Find the conclusion in the passage, then try out each answer choice to see whether it makes the conclusion stronger.

◆ Assumptions frequently trade on the gaps inherent in inductive reasoning. If the argument uses statistics, you should probably ask yourself whether the statistics involved are representative. If the argument offers an analogy, you should ask yourself whether the two situations are analogous. If the argument proposes a cause for an effect, you should ask yourself whether there might be some other cause.

CRITICAL REASONING ◆ 105

Now Let's Try the Passage

A: Look at the beginning or end of the passage and be familiar with conclusion flag words (see list on page 100).

4. Many people believe that gold and platinum are the most valuable commodities. To the true entrepreneur, however, gold and platinum are less valuable than opportunities that can enable him to further enrich himself. Therefore, in the world of high finance, information is the most valuable commodity.

The author of the passage above makes which of the following assumptions?

(A) Gold and platinum are not the most valuable commodities.
(B) Entrepreneurs are not like most people.
(C) The value of information is incalculably high.
(D) Information about business opportunities is accurate and will lead to increased wealth.
(E) Only entrepreneurs feel that information is the most valuable commodity.

Here's how to crack it

The question tells you that you are looking for an assumption, which means you can assume that the reasoning of the passage is inductive. You'll be looking for a hole in the argument.

Since an assumption supports the conclusion, it's a good idea to know what the conclusion is. Can you identify it? It was in the last sentence, preceded by "therefore": "In the world of high finance, information is the most valuable commodity."

As you read the passage, keep your eyes open for potential holes in the argument. For example, as you read it might occur to you that the author is assuming that there is no such thing as bad information. Anyone who has ever taken a stock tip knows the error in that assumption.

Don't be upset if you can't find a hole in the argument as you read. The answer choices will give you a clue.

Let's attack the answer choices:

(A) Gold and platinum are not the most valuable commodities.

Does this support the conclusion? In a way, it does. If information is supposed to be the most valuable commodity, it might help to know that gold and platinum are *not* the most valuable commodities.

However, saying that gold and platinum are *not* the most valuable commodities does not necessarily mean that information *is* the most valuable commodity.

(B) Entrepreneurs are not like most people.

If most people find gold and platinum to be the most valuable commodities, while entrepreneurs prefer information, then it *could* be inferred that entrepreneurs are not like most people. Does this support the conclusion, though? Not really. Remember, ETS rewards narrow thinking.

Reading Comprehension Review

Q: Where do you find the answers to all the questions?

> (C) The value of information is incalculably high.

This answer seems to restate the conclusion. Remember, an assumption is an *unstated* premise. In addition, it goes beyond the scope of the argument. To say that information is valuable does not mean that its value is "incalculable."

> (D) Information about business opportunities is accurate and will lead to increased wealth.

This is the correct answer. If the business information is not accurate, it could not possibly be valuable. Therefore this statement supports the conclusion by plugging a dangerous hole in the argument.

> (E) Only entrepreneurs feel that information is the most valuable commodity.

Does this statement strengthen the conclusion? Actually, it might weaken it. The conclusion states that "in the world of high finance, information is the most valuable commodity." Presumably the world of high finance is not composed exclusively of entrepreneurs. If only entrepreneurs believe information to be the most valuable commodity, then not everyone in the world of high finance would feel the same way.

STRENGTHEN-THE-ARGUMENT QUESTIONS

If a question asks you to strengthen an argument, it is saying that the argument can be strengthened; in other words, again, you're going to be dealing with an inductive passage. The argument won't be complete by itself. The conclusion *may* be true, but it doesn't have to be.

Like assumption questions, strengthen-the-argument questions are really asking you to find a hole in the argument and to fix it with additional information. Here are some guidelines for spotting strengthen-the-argument statements among the answer choices:

◆ The correct answer will strengthen the argument with *new* information. If you see an answer choice that comes straight from the passage, it's wrong.

◆ The new information you're looking for will support the conclusion of the passage. Find the conclusion in the passage, then try out each answer choice to see whether it makes the conclusion stronger.

- Strengthen-the-argument questions frequently trade on the gaps inherent in inductive reasoning. If the argument uses statistics, you should probably ask yourself whether the statistics involved are representative. If the argument offers an analogy, you should ask yourself whether the two situations are analogous. If the argument proposes a cause for an effect, you should ask yourself whether there might be some other cause.

Reading Comprehension Review

A: In the passage! Do not use any outside information to answer a question.

NOW LET'S TRY THE PASSAGE

5. It has recently been proposed that we adopt an all-volunteer army. This policy was tried on a limited basis several years ago, and was a miserable failure. The level of education of the volunteers was unacceptably low, while levels of drug use and crime soared among army personnel. Can we trust our national defense to a volunteer army? The answer is clearly "No."

Which of the following statements, if true, most strengthens the author's claim that an all-volunteer army should not be implemented?

(A) The general level of education has risen since the first time an all-volunteer army was tried.

(B) The proposal was made by an organization called Citizens for Peace.

(C) The first attempt to create a volunteer army was carried out according to the same plan now under proposal and under the same conditions as those that exist today.

(D) A volunteer army would be less expensive than an army that relies on the draft.

(E) The size of the army needed today is smaller than that needed when a volunteer army was first tried.

Here's how to crack it

You know from reading the question that you're expected to fix a flaw in the argument. Even better, the question itself tells you the conclusion of the passage: "An all-volunteer army should not be implemented."

Since the reasoning in a strengthen-the-argument question has to be inductive, it pays to see whether the argument is statistical, causal, or analogous. You may have noticed that the argument *does*, in fact, use an analogy. The author is basing his conclusion on the results of one previous experience. In effect he is saying, "The idea didn't work then, so it won't work now." This is the potential flaw in the argument.

If you didn't spot the argument by analogy, don't worry. You would probably have seen it when you started attacking the answer choices:

(A) The general level of education has risen since
the first time an all-volunteer army was tried.

Does this support the author's conclusion? Actually, it may weaken the conclusion. If the general level of education has risen, it could be argued that the level of education of army volunteers is also higher. This would remove one of the author's objections to a volunteer army. Eliminate.

(B) The proposal was made by an organization
called Citizens for Peace.

This is irrelevant to the author's conclusion. You might have wondered whether a group called Citizens for Peace was the right organization to make suggestions about the army. Attacking the reputation of a person in order to cast doubt on that person's ideas is a very old pastime. There's even a name for it: an ad hominem fallacy. An ad hominem statement does not strengthen an argument. Eliminate.

(C) The first attempt to create a volunteer army
was carried out according to the same plan
now under proposal and under the same
conditions as those that exist today.

This is the correct answer. The passage as it stands is potentially flawed because we cannot know that a new attempt to institute an all-volunteer army would turn out the same way it did before. Answer choice (C) provides new information that suggests that the two situations *are* analogous.

(D) A volunteer army would be less expensive than
an army that relies on the draft.

Does this support the conclusion? No. In fact, it makes a case *for* a volunteer army. Eliminate.

(E) The size of the army needed today is smaller
than that needed when a volunteer army was
first tried.

Like answer choice (D), this answer contradicts the conclusion of the passage. If we need a smaller army today, maybe we would be able to find enough smart and honest volunteers to make a volunteer army work. Eliminate.

WEAKEN-THE-ARGUMENT QUESTIONS

If a question asks you to weaken an argument, it implies that the argument can be weakened; in other words, once again you're going to be dealing with an inductive argument. The argument won't be complete by itself. The conclusion *may* be true, but it doesn't have to be.

Always stick to the passage. The easiest way to strengthen an argument is to strengthen the conclusion. You can do this by presenting new evidence to strengthen the conclusion. Therefore, to find the answer which best strengthens the argument, look for new evidence. Any answer choice that comes from the passage will probably be wrong. Also, look for assumptions that strengthen the conclusion. New evidence or assumptions, whether statistical, analogy, or causal, must support the conclusion.

Like assumption questions and strengthen-the-argument questions, weaken-the-argument questions are really asking you to find a hole in the argument. This time, however, you don't need to fix the hole. All you have to do is expose it. Here are some guidelines for finding weaken-the-argument statements among the answer choices:

Assumption Guidelines

(1) Assumptions are never stated in the passage.
(2) An assumption must support the conclusion; eliminate answer choices which do not strengthen the conclusion.
(3) Assumptions frequently work to fill in gaps in the reasoning of the argument. Look to see if the assumption, whether it is statistical, analogy, or casual, links the evidence to the conclusion.

♦ The statement you'll be looking for should weaken the *conclusion* of the passage. Find the conclusion in the passage, then try out each answer choice to see whether it makes the conclusion less tenable.

♦ Weaken-the-argument questions frequently trade on the gaps inherent in inductive reasoning. If the argument uses statistics, ask yourself whether the statistics involved are representative. If the argument offers an analogy, ask yourself whether the two situations are analogous. If the argument proposes a cause for an effect, ask yourself whether there might be some other cause.

NOW LET'S TRY THE PASSAGE

6. The recent turnaround of the LEX Corporation is a splendid example of how an astute chief executive officer can rechannel a company's assets toward profitability. With the new CEO at the helm, LEX has gone, in only three business quarters, from a 10 million dollar operating loss to a 22 million dollar operating gain.

   A major flaw in the reasoning of the passage above is that

   (A) the passage assumes that the new CEO was the only factor that affected the corporation's recent success
   (B) the recent success of the corporation may be only temporary
   (C) the chief executive officer may be drawing a salary and bonus that will set a damaging precedent for this and other corporations
   (D) the author does not define "profitability"
   (E) rechanneling assets is only a short-term solution

Here's how to crack it

You know from reading the question that you'll need to find a flaw in the reasoning of the argument. As you read the passage, look for the conclusion. The correct answer choice will weaken this conclusion. In this passage the conclusion is in the first sentence: "The recent turnaround of the LEX Corporation is a splendid example of how an astute chief executive officer can rechannel a company's assets toward profitability."

Because this is a weaken-the-argument question that uses inductive reasoning, you should look to see whether the argument is statistical, causal, or analogical. In this case the argument is causal. The passage implies that the sole cause of the LEX Corporation's turnaround is the new CEO. While this *may* be true, it is also possible that there are other causes. If you didn't spot the causal argument, don't worry. You would probably have seen it when you attacked the answer choices. Let's do that now:

Q: What is the most effective way to eliminate answer choices?

    (A) the passage assumes that the new CEO was the only factor that affected the corporation's recent success

This is the correct answer. The new chief executive officer may not have been the cause of the turnaround—there may have been some other cause we don't know about.

    (B) the recent success of the corporation may be only temporary

It may be hasty to crown LEX with laurels after only three economic quarters, but this statement doesn't point out a flaw in the *reasoning* of the passage. Eliminate.

    (C) the chief executive officer may be drawing a salary and bonus that will set a damaging precedent for this and other corporations

This answer choice may seem tempting because it's not in favor of the new CEO. But this alone doesn't represent a major flaw in the reasoning of the passage. Eliminate.

    (D) the author does not define "profitability"

An author can't define every word he uses. Profitability seems a common enough word, and a change in the balance sheet from minus 10 million to plus 22 million seems to qualify. Eliminate.

    (E) rechanneling assets is only a short-term solution

Like answer choice (B), this statement implies that all the votes aren't in yet. This does not affect the reasoning of the argument, however. Eliminate.

INFERENCE QUESTIONS

Like inference questions in the Reading Comprehension section, Critical Reasoning inference questions do not really ask you to make an inference. In fact, you will often find that the answer to a Critical Reasoning inference question is so basic that you won't believe it could be correct the first time you read it. Inference questions often have little to do with the conclusion of the passage; instead they might ask you to make inferences about one or more of the premises.

7. In film and videotape, it is possible to induce viewers to project their feelings onto characters on the screen. In one study, when a camera shot of a woman's face was preceded by a shot of a baby in a crib, the audience thought the woman's face was registering happiness. When the same shot of the woman's face was preceded by a shot of a lion running toward the camera, the audience thought the woman's face was registering fear. Television news teams must be careful to avoid such manipulation of their viewers.

Which of the following can be inferred from the passage?

(A) Television news teams have abused their position of trust in the past.
(B) The expression on the woman's face was, in actuality, blank.
(C) A camera shot of a baby in a crib provoked feelings of happiness in the audience.
(D) Audiences should strive to be less gullible.
(E) The technique for manipulating audiences described in the passage would work with film or videotape.

Here's how to crack it

This is an inference question. ETS is probably not interested in the conclusion of the passage. You'll be looking for a statement that seems so obvious that it almost doesn't need saying. Let's attack the answer choices:

(A) Television news teams have abused their position of trust in the past.

If you chose this answer, you inferred too much. The passage doesn't say that news teams have ever abused their position of trust. Eliminate.

(B) The expression on the woman's face was, in actuality, blank.

The audience had no idea what the expression on the woman's face was, and neither do we. It would make sense for the woman's face to be blank, but we don't know whether this is so. This answer goes too far.

(C) A camera shot of a baby in a crib provoked feelings of happiness in the audience.

This is the correct answer. The passage says that the audience projects its own feelings onto characters on the screen. If the audience believes the woman's face reflects happiness, then that must have been their own reaction.

(D) Audiences should strive to be less gullible.

This statement goes way beyond the intent of the passage. Eliminate.

    (E) The technique for manipulating audiences
         described in the passage would work with
         film or videotape.

Again, this statement goes too far to be the correct answer to an inference
question. Eliminate.

Q: How would you tackle an
assumption question?

MIMIC-THE-REASONING QUESTIONS

Mimic-the-reasoning questions ask you to recognize the method of reasoning
used in a passage and then identify the same line of reasoning in one of the
answer choices. The best way to understand the passage associated with a
reasoning question is to simplify the terms. Here's an example: "If it rains, I will
stay home today." We could simplify this by saying, "If A, then B."

8. World-class marathon runners do not run more than
six miles a day when they are training. Therefore, if
you run more than six miles a day, you are not
world-class.

Which of the following statements supports its
conclusion in the same manner as the argument
above?

(A) Sprinters always run in the morning. If it is
morning, and you see someone running, it
will not be a sprinter.

(B) Paint never dries in less than three hours. If it
dries in less than three hours, it is not paint.

(C) Little League games are more fun for the
parents than for the children who actually
play. Therefore, the parents should be made
to play.

(D) If a car starts in the morning, chances are it
will start again that evening. Our car always
starts in the morning, and it always starts in
the evening as well.

(E) If you sleep less than four hours a night, you
may be doing yourself a disservice. Studies
have shown that the most valuable sleep
occurs in the fifth hour.

Here's how to crack it

First, simplify the argument in the passage. World-class marathon runners do
not run more than six miles a day when they are training. (If A, then B.)
Therefore, if you run more than six miles a day, you are not world-class. (If not
B, then not A.)

CRITICAL REASONING ◆ 113

Now let's attack the answer choices:

> (A) Sprinters always run in the morning. If it is
> morning, and you see someone running, it
> will not be a sprinter.

A: Because assumptions are unstated, eliminate any answer choices which are stated in the passage. Also, look for the three types of reasoning—statistical, analogical, and causal—which may be used as an assumption.

Just because this answer choice is also about running doesn't mean the reasoning will be the same. In fact, it is unlikely that ETS would use the same subject matter for the correct answer. If we simplify this argument, we get: If A, then B. If B, then not A. Is this the same reasoning used in the passage? No. Eliminate.

> (B) Paint never dries in less than three hours. If it
> dries in less than three hours, it is not paint.

If we simplify this argument, we get: If A, then B. If not B, then not A. This is the correct answer.

> (C) Little League games are more fun for the
> parents than for the children who actually
> play. Therefore, the parents should be made
> to play.

Simplifying this argument, we get . . . not much. The reasoning here is totally different. Also, note that the subject matter here is still about sports. Eliminate.

> (D) If a car starts in the morning, chances are it
> will start again that evening. Our car always
> starts in the morning, and it always starts in
> the evening as well.

If we simplify this argument, we get: If A, then B. If always A, then always B. That doesn't sound right. Eliminate.

> (E) If you sleep less than four hours a night, you
> may be doing yourself a disservice. Studies
> have shown that the most valuable sleep
> occurs in the fifth hour.

Simplifying this argument, we get . . . again, not much. The reasoning in this answer choice is very different from the reasoning in the passage. Eliminate.

RESOLVE-THE-PARADOX QUESTIONS

Some GMAT questions ask you to resolve an apparent paradox or explain a possible discrepancy. In these questions, the passage will present you with two seemingly contradictory facts. Your job is to find the answer choice that allows both of the facts from the passage to be true.

Here's an example:

> In 1994, the TipTop airline reported an increase in the total number of passengers it carried from the year before, but a *decrease* in total revenues—even though prices for its tickets on all routes remained unchanged during the two-year period.

> Which of the following, if true, best reconciles the apparent paradox described above?
>
> (A) TipTop Airlines was a victim of a mild recession in 1994.
> (B) Total passenger miles were up in 1994.
> (C) Fuel costs remained constant during the two-year period.
> (D) Passengers traveled shorter (and thus less expensive) distances in 1994.
> (E) TipTop did not buy any new airplanes or equipment in 1994.

Q: How would you approach a strengthening- or weakening-the-argument question?

Here's how to crack it

First, restate the contradiction in your own words.

"TipTop's profits went down even though they flew more passengers."

Now, let's see which of the answer choices makes both of the facts in the argument true.

> (A) TipTop Airlines was a victim of a mild recession in 1994.

(A) If TipTop was affected by a recession, that might explain a loss of revenues. But since ticket prices remained the same, it would not explain how the number of passengers could have increased at the same time. Eliminate.

> (B) Total passenger miles were up in 1994.

(B) If total passenger miles were up, and prices remained the same, there is no way that there could have been a loss of revenues. We can eliminate this choice as well.

> (C) Fuel costs remained constant during the two year period.

(C) If fuel costs had *not* remained constant, the company's profits might have fallen. An increase in fuel prices could have increased their costs and cut into profits. But it would not have cut into total *revenues*, which is what we are concerned with in this passage. Of course, since choice (C) told us that the costs remained constant, this choice has no bearing on the argument at all. Eliminate.

(D) Passengers traveled shorter (and thus less expensive) distances in 1994.

(D) Bingo! If passengers traveled on short, inexpensive flights, then they paid less money. In spite of the increase in number of passengers, the money they paid could have added up to less than that of the year before. This was the best answer, but always remember to read all the choices anyway.

(E) TipTop did not buy any new airplanes or equipment in 1994.

(E) This answer is much like choice (C). If TipTop *had* bought new planes, it might have cut into its profits, but it would not have had any bearing on revenues. Of course, since choice (E) told us that TipTop did not buy any planes, there is no relevance at all. Eliminate.

A: Expose the assumption and build it up to strengthen it or tear it down to weaken it.

SUMMARY

1. Critical Reasoning is made up of short passages. Each of these passages is followed by one or two questions, for a total of sixteen questions.

2. ETS says that no formal logic is required to answer these questions, but in fact some knowledge of the rudiments of GMAT logic *will* increase your score.

3. There are three parts to an argument:

   A. the conclusion
   B. the premises
   C. assumptions

4. This section is not like Reading Comprehension in that

   A. you should never skim; each word is important
   B. you should always read the question first
   C. most of the Reading Comprehension techniques we have shown you are inappropriate in this section

5. Always read the question first because it will contain clues that will help you to find the answer as you read the passage.

6. In Critical Reasoning, the most important POE technique is eliminating answers that are outside the scope of the argument.

7. There are two main types of reasoning: *deductive* and *inductive*. In deductive logic the conclusion *must* follow from the premises. In inductive logic the conclusion may be true, but it does not have to be. Three popular kinds of inductive logic are

   A. statistical arguments—ask yourself whether the statistics are representative
   B. arguments by analogy—ask yourself whether the two situations are analogous
   C. causal arguments—ask yourself whether there might be an alternative cause

   These three kinds of inductive logic are very important in assumption questions, weaken-the-argument questions, and strengthen-the-argument questions.

8. There are seven question types. Each type has its own strategy.

   A. *Find-the-Conclusion Questions*
   Break the argument down into its parts and look for signposts. A conclusion must be supported by its premises.

   B. *Supply-the-Conclusion Questions*

   ◆ If the question asks which conclusion *must* follow, the reasoning will be deductive. This type of question can usually be diagramed.
   ◆ All other supply-the-conclusion passages will be inductive. The correct answer will be supported by *all* the premises.

   C. *Assumption Questions*

   Assumptions are unstated premises that support the conclusion. Assumption questions always involve inductive logic. Look for a flaw in the argument that is fixed by the assumption.

   D. *Strengthen-the-Argument Questions*

   These are also based on inductive logic. Look for answer choices that support the conclusion with new information.

   E. *Weaken-the-Argument Questions*

   Also based on inductive logic, these questions ask you to find answers that point out flaws in the reasoning of passages.

   F. *Inference Questions*

   Like Reading Comprehension inference questions, these questions do not actually want you to infer. Unlike most Critical Reasoning questions, these questions will concern the *premises*, not the conclusion.

   G. *Mimic-the-Reasoning Questions*

   This type of question asks you to find an argument in one of the answer choices that mimics the method of reasoning used in the original argument. Most of these questions can be answered by simplifying (if A, then B).

PART ◆ III

How to Crack the
Writing Assessment

9 Writing Assessment

The GMAT begins with a one-hour Analytical Writing Assessment during which you'll be asked to write two essays. You won't know the essay topics in advance, nor will you be given a choice of topics. The AWA is scored separately from the rest of the GMAT.

WHY ADD ESSAYS TO THE GMAT?

The business schools themselves asked ETS to make the addition. Recent studies have indicated that verbal skills are more important to success in business (and in business school) than had been previously thought.

The business schools have also had to contend with a huge increase in the number of applicants from overseas. Admissions officers at the business schools were finding that the application essays they received from outside the United States did not always accurately reflect the abilities of the students who were supposed to have written them. To put it more bluntly, some of these applicants were paying native English speakers to write their essays for them.

The GMAT writing assessment is thus at least partly a check on the writing ability of foreign applicants who now make up more than one-third of all applicants to American business schools.

At the business schools' request, all schools to which you apply now receive, in addition to your writing assessment score, a photocopy of the actual essays you wrote.

HOW DO THE SCHOOLS USE THE WRITING ASSESSMENT?

If you are a citizen of a non-English-speaking country you can expect the schools to look quite closely both at the score you receive on the essays you write, and at the essays themselves. If you are a native English speaker with reasonable verbal scores and English grades in college then the writing assessment is not likely to be a crucial part of your package.

On the other hand, if your verbal skills are *not* adequately reflected by your grades in college, or in the other sections of the GMAT, then a strong performance on the writing assessment could be extremely helpful.

HOW WILL THE ESSAYS BE SCORED?

When you get your GMAT score back from ETS, you will also receive a separate score for the writing assessment. Each essay is read by two readers, each of whom will assign your writing a grade from 1-6, in half-point increments (6 being the highest score possible). If the two scores are within a point of each other, they will be averaged. If there is a more than one-point spread, the essays will be read by a third reader, and scores will be adjusted to reflect the third scorer's evaluation.

ETS uses the "holistic" scoring method to grade essays; your writing will be judged not on small details but rather on its overall impact. The ETS essay-readers are supposed to ignore penmanship and small errors of grammar and spelling. Considering that these poor readers are going to have to plow through over 600,000 essays each year, this is probably just as well.

WHO ARE THESE PEOPLE ANYWAY?

We'll put this in the form of a multiple choice question:

Your essays will be read by

(A) captains of industry

(B) leading business school professors

(C) college TAs working part time

If you guessed (C) you're doing just fine.

HOW MUCH TIME DO THEY GET TO GRADE EACH ESSAY?

Two minutes, tops. Essays are graded in eight-hour marathon sessions (nine to five, with an hour off for lunch). The essay readers are each required to read thirty essays per hour.

Obviously, these poor graders do not have time for an in-depth reading of your essay. They probably aren't going to notice how carefully you thought out your ideas, or how clever your analysis was. Under pressure to meet their quota, they are simply going to be giving it a fast skim.

By the time your reader gets to your essay, she will probably already have seen over a hundred—and no matter how ingenious you were in coming up with original ideas, many of those hundred essays will almost certainly have used some of the same points yours is about to make.

SO HOW DO YOU SCORE HIGH ON THE GMAT ESSAYS?

On the face of it, you might think it would be pretty difficult to impress these jaded readers, but it turns out that there are some very specific ways to persuade them of your superior writing skills.

WHAT ETS DOESN'T WANT YOU TO KNOW

In a 1982 internal study, two ETS researchers analyzed a group of essays written by actual test takers and the grades that those essays received. The most successful essays had one thing in common. Which of the following characteristics do you think it was?

- ◆ Good Organization
- ◆ Proper Diction
- ◆ Noteworthy Ideas
- ◆ Good Vocabulary
- ◆ Sentence Variety
- ◆ Length
- ◆ Number of Paragraphs

What Your Essay Needs in Order to *Look* Like a Successful Essay

The ETS researchers discovered that the essays that received the highest grades from ETS essay graders had one single factor in common.

Length.

To go a long way toward assuring a good grade on the writing assessment, you need to take one simple step: *write as much as you possibly can*. Each essay should include at least four indented paragraphs.

Does Handwriting Count?

Officially, no. ETS essay readers are supposed to ignore handwriting completely. However, they wouldn't be human if they didn't subconsciously give a sigh of relief when they pick up an essay with neat penmanship. If your handwriting is so tiny or messy that your essay is illegible, then the readers may not be able to get beyond that.

In addition, you should try to be neat about any cross-outs or edits that you make. Which of the following paragraphs would you rather read?

> *I agree with the statement "No pain, no gain." In this competitive society, an individual cannot be expected to ~~know exactly what expect~~ to accomplish all of his or her goals without suffering first.*

> *I agree with the statement "No pain, no gain." In this competitive society, an individual cannot be expected to ~~know exactly what expect to~~ accomplish all of his or her goals without suffering first.*

No one can be expected to write an essay under timed conditions without any edits or cross-outs whatever. However, by making these as neat and inconspicuous as possible (like the second paragraph above) you will give the essay-reader the impression that you are in command.

What Will the Essay Topics Look Like?

There are two types of essay topics: Analysis of an Issue and Analysis of an Argument. Here's an example of each:

Analysis of an Issue

> *Reacting to statistics of increased crime and violence, some advocates have argued that it is necessary for the entertainment industry to police itself by censoring television programs and popular music lyrics. However, civil liberties advocates argue that it has not been demonstrated that watching television violence or listening to violent lyrics in songs leads to real violence.*

The ETS booklet describes an "outstanding" Analysis of an Issue essay as one that: "explores ideas and develops a position on the issue with insightful reasons and/or persuasive examples, is clearly well organized, demonstrates superior control of language, including diction and syntactic variety, demonstrates superior facility with the conventions of standard written English . . ."

Which do you find more compelling, the call for censorship of entertainment media or civil libertarians' response to it? Explain your position, using relevant reasons and/or examples drawn from your own experience, observations, or reading.

Analysis of an Argument

A new medical test that allows the early detection of a particular disease will prevent the deaths of people all over the world who would otherwise die from the disease. The test has been extremely effective in allowing doctors to diagnose the disease 6 months to a year before it would have been spotted by conventional means.

Discuss how logically convincing you find this argument. In explaining your point of view, be sure to analyze the line of reasoning and the use of evidence in the argument. Also discuss what, if anything, would make the argument more sound and persuasive, or would help you to better evaluate its conclusion.

You will have to write one essay on each topic.

THE WRITING ASSESSMENT: BASIC PRINCIPLES

You might think that there is really no way to prepare for the writing assessment (other than by practicing writing over a long period of time.) After all, you won't find out the topic of the essay they'll ask you to write until you get there, and there is no way to plan your essays in advance.

OH YES, YOU CAN *TOO* PLAN YOUR ESSAYS IN ADVANCE

In fact, there are some very specific ways to prepare for the GMAT essays that go beyond length and good penmanship. Of course, if all you had to worry about was the ETS graders, these techniques might not be necessary. However, your GMAT essays are being sent to the schools to which you are applying. Just in case the admissions officers decide to read them, you want them to be good.

So how can you prepare ahead of time?

CREATING A TEMPLATE

When a builder builds a house, the first thing he does is construct a frame. The frame supports the entire house. After the frame is completed, he can nail the walls and windows to the frame. We're going to show you how to build the frame for the perfect GMAT essay. Of course, you won't know the exact topic of the essay until you get there (just as the builder may not know what color his client is going to paint the living room), but you will have an all-purpose frame on which to construct a great essay no matter what the topic is.

We call this frame the *template*.

PRECONSTRUCTION

In addition, a builder can also pre-build certain parts of his house, so they can just be nailed into place when he is ready for them. Just as a builder can construct the windows of a house in his workshop weeks before he arrives to install them, so can you pre-build certain elements of your essay.

We call all this *preconstruction*.

In the rest of this chapter we'll show you how to prepare *ahead of time* to write essays on two topics you won't see until you open your test booklet. Let's begin with the Analysis of an Issue essay.

ANALYSIS OF AN ISSUE

Writing the Analysis of an Issue essay requires a series of steps.

Step 1: Read the topic.

Step 2: Decide the general position you are going to take—for or against the position.

Step 3: Brainstorm. Come up with a bunch of supporting ideas or examples. It helps to write these down on a piece of scrap paper. These supporting statements are supposed to help convince the reader that your main thesis is correct.

Step 4: Look over your supporting ideas, and throw out the weakest ones. There should be three to five left over.

Step 5: Write the essay, using all the preconstruction and template tools you're going to be learning in this chapter.

Step 6: Read over the essay and do some editing. The GMAT readers will not take away points for small additions written in the margin or cross-outs to correct spelling or grammar mistakes.

WHAT THE READERS ARE LOOKING FOR

The essay topic for the Analysis of an Issue will ask you to choose a side on an issue and develop coherent reasons or examples in defense of your position. You aren't required to know any more about the subject than would any normal person. As far as ETS is concerned, it doesn't even matter which side of the argument you take—as long as your essay is well written. So what constitutes a well-written essay?

The essay readers will be looking for four characteristics as they skim at the speed of light through your Analysis of an Issue essay. According to a booklet prepared by ETS, "an outstanding essay . . .

- explores ideas and develops a position on the issue with insightful reasons and/or persuasive examples,

- is clearly well organized,

- demonstrates superior control of language, including diction and syntactic variety,

- demonstrates superior facility with the conventions of standard written English, but may have minor flaws."

To put it more simply, they're looking for good organization, good supporting examples for whatever position you've taken, and a reasonable use of the English language. Let's start with good organization, and the easiest way to accomplish it—the template.

A SAMPLE TEMPLATE

You will want to come up with your own template, but here is an elementary example just to get you started:

Paragraph 1:

The issue of _____

_____ is a controversial one. On the one hand,

_____ .

On the other hand, _____

_____ .

However, in the final analysis, I believe that _____

_____ .

Paragraph 2:

One reason for my belief is that _____

_____

_____

_____ .

Paragraph 3:

Another reason for my belief is _____

_____

_____

_____ .

Paragraph 4:

Perhaps the best reason is _____

_____

_____

_____ .

Paragraph 5:

For all these reasons, I therefore believe that _____

_____

_____

_____ .

Let's try fitting the Analysis of an Issue topic we've already seen into this organizational structure.

Essay topic 1:

> *Reacting to statistics of increased crime and violence, some advocates have argued that it is necessary for the entertainment industry to police itself by censoring television programs and popular music lyrics. However, civil liberties advocates argue that it has not been demonstrated that watching television violence or listening to violent lyrics in songs leads to real violence.*
>
> *Which do you find more compelling, the call for censorship of entertainment media or civil libertarians' response to it? Explain your position, using relevant reasons and/or examples drawn from your own experience, observations, or reading.*

How would this topic fit into the first paragraph of our template? Take a look.

> The issue of <u>censorship of popular TV programs and music lyrics</u> is a controversial one. On the one hand, <u>increased crime and violence are causing a disintegration of the framework of our society</u>. On the other hand, <u>free speech is one of our most important freedoms, guaranteed by the constitution</u>. However, in the final analysis, I believe that <u>the dangers of subjecting impressionable young minds to questionable values makes self-censorship by the entertainment industry a viable alternative.</u>

If we were writing the rest of this essay, we would start giving supporting examples and reasons for our position, but for now, let's concentrate on the first paragraph. Could we have used this template to take the other side of the argument? Sure. Here's how that would look:

> The issue of <u>censorship of popular TV programs and music lyrics</u> is a controversial one. On the one hand, <u>free speech is one of our most important freedoms, guaranteed by the constitution</u>. On the other hand, <u>increased crime and violence are causing a disintegration of the framework of our society</u>. However, in the final analysis, I believe that <u>the principle of free speech is too precious to allow censorship in any form</u>.

OKAY, IT WORKS WITH THAT TOPIC, BUT WILL IT WORK WITH ANOTHER?

Of course. Let's try the same template with another topic.

Essay topic 2:

> *Everyone agrees that countries need governing, and yet the cost of government seems to increase every year. Government bureaucracy is often blamed for these increases and while some people feel that these increasing costs are only to be expected, others have argued that our federal bureaucracy needs to be overhauled.*
>
> *Which do you find more compelling, the acceptance of the increasing cost of government, or the call for an overhaul of federal bureaucracy? Explain your position, using relevant reasons and/or examples drawn from your own experience, observations, or reading.*

> The issue of <u>the overhaul of our federal bureaucracy</u> is a controversial one. On the one hand, <u>federal jobs employ a huge number of Americans, making any attempt to prune the federal payroll both difficult and painful</u>. On the other hand, <u>the percentage of our tax-dollars spent simply on the upkeep of this huge bureaucratic juggernaut is rising at an alarming rate</u>. However, in the final analysis, I believe that <u>the political and financial price of bureaucratic reform would be too high</u>.

As you can see, this template will fit practically any situation. To prove it, let's try it out on one of the great philosophical arguments of our time.

Tastes Great/Less Filling

Essay topic X:

Some people say that they drink light beer because it tastes great. Others say it's less filling.

Which reason for drinking light beer do you find more compelling? Explain your position, using relevant reasons and/or examples drawn from your own experience, observations, or reading.

The issue of <u>whether light beer is so popular because of its taste or because of its lack of calories</u> is a controversial one. On the one hand, <u>light beer does have a pleasingly mild taste</u>. On the other hand, <u>light beer also offers a sharply reduced number of calories</u>. However, in the final analysis, I believe that <u>light beer is so popular because of its great taste</u>.

Now You Try It

Read the following topic carefully. Decide which side of the argument you want to be on, and then fill in the blanks of the first paragraph of this template.

You may have noticed in the previous examples that to make this particular template work most effectively, the first "on the one hand" should introduce the argument that you are ultimately going to support. The "on the other hand" should be the argument you are going to disprove. The sentence beginning "however, in the final analysis" will return to the point of view that you believe in.

Essay topic 3:

One of the primary reasons cited by doctors for rising fees to patients is the increasing cost to the doctors themselves of malpractice insurance. These doctors say that a cap on monetary awards in malpractice cases would result in lower costs for health care. Patient groups contend, however, that some malpractice is so heinous that there should be no limit set on the financial award.

Which do you find more compelling, the call for a cap on medical malpractice awards or the response to it? Explain your position, using relevant reasons and/or examples drawn from your own experience, observations, or reading.

The issue of _____

_____ is a controversial one. On the one hand,

_____

_____ .

On the other hand, _____

_____ .

However, in the final analysis, I believe that _____

_____ .

If you were completing the entire essay, now you would write paragraphs giving support to your belief, but for right now let's concentrate on that first paragraph. Here's one way Topic 3 could have gone:

> The issue of <u>capping malpractice awards</u> is a controversial one. On the one hand, <u>health care costs are rising so quickly that drastic measures are needed to contain them</u>. On the other hand, <u>when an individual's life is ruined as a result of a doctor's negligence , that individual deserves fair recompense</u>. However, in the final analysis, I believe that <u>by capping the awards at a reasonable amount we can both lower the cost of health care and protect the rights of victims of malpractice</u>.

ARE THERE OTHER TEMPLATES?

There are many ways to organize an Analysis of an Issue essay, and we'll be showing you a few variations, but the important thing is that you bring with you to the exam a template you have practiced and are comfortable with. Whatever the topic of the essay, and whatever your personal mood that day, you don't want to have to think for a second about how your essay will be organized. By deciding on a template in advance you will already have your organizational structure down before you get there.

That said, it's important that you develop your *own* template, based on your own preferences and your own personality. Of course, yours may have some similarities to one of ours, but it should not mimic ours exactly—for one thing, because it's pretty likely that when this edition of our book comes out, the folks who write the GMAT will read it, and they might take a dim view of anyone who blatantly copies one of our templates word-for-word.

B-School Lingo

Three Cs: three primary business forces—Customer, Competition, Company

Total Quality Management: the Edward Demming method of management that caught on with the Japanese and is currently hot in American business—managing the quality of service, process, people, and objectives

Customizing Your Template

Your organizational structure may vary in some ways, but it will always include the following elements: *the first paragraph* should illustrate to the reader that you have understood the topic, and that you have chosen a position. To do this, first restate the topic, then say how you feel about it. The first paragraph does not have to be more than a couple of sentences.

In the *second, third, and fourth paragraphs* you will develop examples and ideas to support your thesis. *The last paragraph* should sum up your position on the topic, using slightly different wording from the first paragraph.

Here are some alternate ways of organizing your essay.

Variation 1:

1st paragraph: state both sides of the argument briefly before announcing what side you are on.

2nd paragraph: support your argument

3rd paragraph: further support

4th paragraph: further support

5th paragraph: conclusion

Variation 2:

1st paragraph: state your position.

2nd paragraph: acknowledge the arguments in favor of the *other* side.

3rd paragraph: rebut each of those arguments.

4th paragraph: conclusion

Variation 3:

1st paragraph: state the position you will eventually contradict, i.e. "Many people believe that . . ."

2nd paragraph: contradict that first position, i.e. "However, I believe that . . ."

3rd paragraph: support your position

4th paragraph: further support

5th paragraph: conclusion

So Much For Organization. Now, What About Support?

We've shown you how templates and structure words can be used to help the organization of your essay. However, organization is not the only important item on the essay reader's checklist. You will also be graded on how you support your main idea.

THE KEY TO GOOD SUPPORT: BRAINSTORMING

Learning to use the structural words we've just been discussing is in fact a way to bring pre-built elements into the GMAT examination room with you. Along with a template, they will enable you to concentrate on your ideas without worrying about making up a structure from scratch. But what about the ideas themselves?

After reading the essay topic, you should take a couple of minutes to plan out your essay. First, decide which side of the issue you're going to take. Then, begin brainstorming. On a piece of scrap paper, write down all the reasons and persuasive examples you can think of in support of your essay. Don't stop to edit yourself; just let them flow out. Then, go through what you've written down to decide on the order in which you want to make your points. You may decide, on reflection, to skip several of your brainstorms—or you may have one or two new ones as you organize.

Here's an example of what some brainstorming might produce in the way of support for Analysis of an Issue Topic #1:

Main Idea: Censorship of television programs and popular music lyrics would be a mistake.

Support:

1. Freedom of speech was one of the founding principles of this country. It has been too hard won for us to give it up.

2. Who would perform this censorship, and how would we ensure that there was no political agenda attached to it?

3. Once started, censorship of violent content is hard to stop or to curb. Where would we draw the line? *Hamlet*? *Bambi*?

4. So far, the evidence of different studies is conflicted. The causative link between violence on television and real violence has not yet been convincingly proven.

5. While upsetting to many, the lyrics of such entertainers as Snoop Doggy Dogg continue a long tradition of protest of social conditions that has stretched over the centuries and has included such artists as Bob Dylan and Woody Guthrie.

After you've finished brainstorming, look over your supporting ideas and throw out the weakest ones. There should be three to five ideas left over. Plan the order in which you want to present these ideas. You should start with one of your strongest ideas.

GETTING SPECIFIC

The GMAT readers are looking for supporting ideas or examples that are, in their words, "insightful" and persuasive." What do they mean? Suppose you asked your friend about a movie she saw yesterday, and she said,
"It was really cool."

The Analysis of an Issue Essay in Six Steps

Step One: Read the topic.

Step Two: Decide your position, for or against.

Step Three: Brainstorm for about two minutes.

Step Four: Select the strongest three to four supporting ideas.

Step Five: Write the essay, using preconstruction and template tools.

Step Six: About two minutes before time is up, read over your essay and neatly correct for spelling or grammar mistakes. Additions should be made neatly above the sentence. GMAT readers will not take away points for cross-outs.

Well, you'd know that she liked it, and that's good—but you wouldn't know much about the movie. Was it a comedy? An action adventure? Were the characters sexy? Did it make you cry?

The GMAT readers don't want to know that the movie was cool. They want to know that you liked it because:

"It traced the development of two childhood friends as they grew up and grew apart."

or because:

"It combined the physical comedy of the Three Stooges with the action adventure of *Raiders of the Lost Ark.* "

You want to make each example as precise and compelling as possible. After you have brainstormed a few supporting ideas, spend a couple of moments on each one making it as specific as possible. For example, let's say we are working on an essay supporting the idea that the United States should stay out of other countries' affairs.

Too vague: When the United States sent troops to Vietnam, things didn't work out too well. (*How* didn't they work out? What were the results?)

More specific: Look at the result when the United States sent troops to Vietnam. After more than a decade of fighting in support of a dubious political regime, American casualties numbered in the tens of thousands, and we may never know how many Vietnamese lost their lives as well.

ANALYSIS OF AN ISSUE: FINAL THOUGHTS

You've picked a position, you've brainstormed, you've brought with you a template and some structure words; brainstorming should have taken about three minutes. Now it's time to write your essay. Write as neatly as possible, indenting each of the four or five paragraphs. Use all the tools you've learned in this chapter. Remember to keep an eye on your watch. You don't want to spend more than half the allotted time on the first essay.

If you have a minute at the end, read over your essay and do any editing that's necessary. The GMAT readers will not take away points for small additions written in the margin, or cross-outs to correct spelling or grammar mistakes.

Then, with half your time remaining, you'll turn to the second essay topic.

THE SECOND TOPIC: ANALYSIS OF AN ARGUMENT

The Three Types of GMAT Logic

(1) Statistical
(2) Analogical
(3) Causal

You'll be able to use all the skills we've just been discussing on the second type of essay as well—with one major change. The Analysis of an Argument essay must initially be approached just like a logical argument in the Critical Reasoning section.

An Analysis of an Argument topic requires a series of steps.

Step One: Read the topic and separate out the conclusion from the premises.

Step Two: Since they're asking you to critique (read "weaken") the argument, concentrate on identifying its assumptions.

Brainstorm as many different assumptions as you can think of. It helps to write these out on a piece of scrap paper.

Step Three: Look at the premises. Do they actually help to prove the conclusion?

Step Four: Choose a template that allows you to attack the assumptions and premises in an organized way.

Step Five: At the end of the essay, remember to take a moment to illustrate how these same assumptions could be used to make the argument more compelling.

Step Six: Read over the essay and do some editing. The GMAT readers will not take away points for small additions written in the margin or cross-outs to correct spelling or grammar mistakes.

WHAT THE READERS ARE LOOKING FOR

An Analysis of an Argument topic presents you with an argument. Your job is to critique the argument's line of reasoning and the evidence supporting it, and suggest ways in which the argument could be strengthened. Again, you aren't required to know any more about the subject than would any normal person—but you must be able to spot logical weaknesses. If this is starting to remind you of Critical Reasoning, you are exactly right.

The essay readers will be looking for four things as they skim through your Analysis of an Argument essay at the speed of light. According to a booklet prepared by ETS, "an outstanding argument essay . . .

- clearly identifies and insightfully analyzes important features of the argument

- develops ideas cogently, organizes them logically, and connects them smoothly with clear transitions

- effectively supports the main points of the critique

- demonstrates superior control of language, including diction, syntactic variety, and the conventions of standard written English. There may be minor flaws."

To put it more simply, the readers will be looking for all the same things they were looking for in the Analysis of an Issue essay—plus one extra ingredient: a cursory knowledge of the rules of logic.

The ETS booklet describes an "outstanding" Analysis of an Argument essay as one that: "clearly identifies and insightfully analyzes important features of the argument, develops ideas cogently, organizes them logically, and connects them smoothly with clear transitions, effectively supports the main points of the critique, demonstrates superior control of language, including diction, syntactic variety, and the conventions of standard written English . . ."

CRITICAL REASONING IN ESSAY FORM

In any GMAT argument, the first thing to do is to separate the conclusion from the premises.

Let's see how this works with an actual essay topic. Here's the Analysis of an Argument topic you saw before:

Topic:

> *A new medical test that allows the early detection of a particular disease will prevent the deaths of people all over the world who would otherwise die from that disease. The test has been extremely effective in allowing doctors to diagnose the disease 6 months to a year before it would have been spotted by conventional means.*
>
> *Discuss how logically convincing you find this argument. In explaining your point of view, be sure to analyze the line of reasoning and the use of evidence in the argument. Also discuss what, if anything, would make the argument more sound and persuasive, or would help you to better evaluate its conclusion.*

The conclusion in this argument comes in the first line:

> *A new medical test that allows the early detection of a particular disease will prevent the deaths of people all over the world who would otherwise die from that disease.*

The premises are the evidence in support of this conclusion.

> *The test has been extremely effective in allowing doctors to diagnose the disease 6 months to a year before it would have been spotted by conventional means.*

The assumptions are the *unspoken* premises of the argument—without which the argument would fall apart. Remember, that assumptions are often causal, analogical, or statistical. What are some assumptions of *this* argument? Let's brainstorm.

BRAINSTORMING FOR ASSUMPTIONS

You can often find assumptions by looking for a gap in the reasoning:

medical test → early detection: According to the conclusion, the medical test leads to the early detection of the disease. There doesn't seem to be a gap here.

early detection → nonfatal: In turn, the early detection of the disease allows patients to survive the disease. Well, hold on a minute. Is this necessarily true? Let's brainstorm:

Fastest growing professions	
increase by year 2005	
Paralegal	85%
System analyst	79%
Physical therapist	76%
Psychologist	64%
Travel agent	62%
Corrections officer	61%
Flight attendant	60%
Computer programmer	56%
Management analyst	52%
Marketing/P.R.	47%
Doctor	34%
Lawyer	34%

Source: Bureau of Labor Statistics, 1993

1. First of all, do we know that early detection will necessarily lead to survival? We don't even know if this disease is *curable*. Early detection of an incurable disease is not going to help someone survive it.

2. Second, will the test be widely available, and cheap enough for general use? If the test is expensive or only available in certain parts of the world, people will continue to die from the disease.

3. Will doctors and patients interpret the tests correctly? The test may be fine, but if doctors misinterpret the results or if patients ignore the need for treatment, then the test will not save lives.

Q: What are the three most important aspects of writing a good Analysis of an Issue essay?

THE USE OF THE EVIDENCE

Okay, we've uncovered some assumptions. Now, ETS also wants to know what we thought of the argument's "use of evidence." In other words, did the premises help to prove the conclusion? Well, in fact, no, they didn't. The premises here (information to the effect that the test can *spot* the disease 6 months to a year earlier than conventional tests) does not really help to prove the conclusion that the test will save *lives*.

ORGANIZING THE ANALYSIS OF AN ARGUMENT ESSAY

We're ready to put this into a ready-made template. In any Analysis of an Argument essay, the template structure will always be pretty straightforward: you're simply going to reiterate the argument, attack the argument in three different ways (one to a paragraph), summarize what you've said and mention how the argument could be strengthened. From an organizational standpoint, this is pretty easy.

A SAMPLE TEMPLATE

Of course, you will want to develop your *own* template for the Analysis of an Argument essay, but to get you started, here's one possible structure:

The argument that _____(restatement of the conclusion)_____ is not

entirely logically convincing, since it omits certain crucial assump-

tions.

First, the argument assumes that _____

_____ .

Second, the argument never addresses, _____

_____ .

Finally, the argument omits _____

_____ .

Thus, the argument is not completely sound. The evidence in

support of the conclusion _____ .

Ultimately, the argument might have been strengthened by _____

_____ .

A: Make it look neat, write at least four or five paragraphs, and have it clearly organized (an introduction which explains the side you are taking, a middle with your points and examples, and a conclusion to sum up your position).

HOW WOULD OUR BRAINSTORMING FIT INTO THE TEMPLATE?

Here's how the assumptions we came up with for this argument would have fit into the template:

> The argument that <u>the new medical test will prevent deaths that would have occurred in the past</u> is not entirely logically convincing, since it omits certain crucial assumptions.
>
> First, the argument assumes that <u>early detection of the disease will lead to a reduced mortality rate. There are a number of reasons why this might not be true. For example, the disease might be incurable (etc. etc.).</u>
>
> Second, the argument never addresses <u>the point that the existence of this new test, even if totally effective, is not the same as the widespread use of the test (etc. etc.).</u>
>
> Finally, <u>even supposing the ability of early detection to save lives, and the widespread use of the test, the argument still depends on the doctors' correct interpretation of the test and the patients' willingness to undergo treatment. (etc. etc.)</u>
>
> Thus, the argument is not completely sound. The evidence in support of the conclusion <u>(further information about the test itself) does little to prove the conclusion— that the test will save lives— since it does not address the assumptions I have already raised.</u> Ultimately, the argument might have been strengthened by <u>making it plain that the disease responds to early treatment, that the test will be widely available around the world, and that doctors and patients will make proper use of the test.</u>

CUSTOMIZING YOUR ANALYSIS OF AN ARGUMENT TEMPLATE

Your organizational structure may vary in some ways, but it will always include the following elements: *the first paragraph* should sum up the argument's conclusion. In the *second, third, and fourth paragraphs*, you'll attack the argument and the supporting evidence. In the last paragraph, you should summarize what you've said and mention how the argument could be strengthened. Here are some alternate ways of organizing your essay.

VARIATION 1:

1st paragraph: restate the argument

2nd paragraph: discuss the link (or lack of same) between the conclusion and the evidence presented in support of it

3rd paragraph: show three holes in the reasoning of the argument

4th paragraph: show how each of the three holes could be plugged up by explicitly stating the missing assumptions

The key to an Analysis of an Argument essay is how clearly you critique the argument. (You'll usually want to write a weaken-the-argument essay rather than a strengthen-the-argument essay.)

VARIATION 2:

1st paragraph: restate the argument and say it has three flaws

2nd paragraph: point out a flaw and show how it could be plugged up by explicitly stating the missing assumption

3rd paragraph: point out a second flaw and show how it could be plugged up by explicitly stating the missing assumption

4th paragraph: point out a third flaw and show how it could be plugged up by explicitly stating the missing assumption

5th paragraph: summarize your argument that because of these three flaws, the argument is weak

ANALYSIS OF AN ARGUMENT: FINAL THOUGHTS

You've separated the conclusion from the premises. You've brainstormed for the gaps that weaken the argument. You've noted how the premises support (or don't support) the conclusion. Now it's time to write your essay. Write as neatly as possible, indenting each of the four or five paragraphs. Use all the tools you've learned in this chapter. Remember to keep an eye on your watch. You don't want to run out of time.

Again, if you have a minute at the end, read over your essay and do any editing that's necessary. The GMAT readers will not take away points for small additions written in the margin, or cross-outs to correct spelling or grammar mistakes.

PRECONSTRUCTION

In both essays, the ETS readers will be looking for evidence of your facility with standard written English. This is where preconstruction comes in. It's amazing how a little elementary preparation can enhance an essay. We'll be looking at four tricks that almost instantly improve the appearance of a person's writing:

- ◆ Structure words
- ◆ Contrast words
- ◆ Short sentence/long sentence
- ◆ The impressive book reference

STRUCTURE WORDS

In chapter 7, we brought up a problem that most students encounter when they get to the reading comprehension section: There isn't time to read the passages carefully and still have enough time to answer all the questions. To get around this problem, we showed you some ways to spot the overall organization of a dense reading passage in order to understand the main idea and to find specific points quickly.

When you think about it, the ETS essay readers are facing almost the identical problem: They have less than two minutes to read your essay and figure out if it's any good. There's no time to appreciate the finer points of your argument. All they want to know is whether it's well organized and reasonably lucid—and to find out, they will be looking for the *same* structural clues you have learned to look for in the reading comprehension passages. Let's mention them again:

(A) When entire paragraphs contradict each other, there are some useful *pairs* of words that help to make this clear:

> *on the one hand* → *on the other hand*
>
> *the traditional view* → *the new view*

(B) If you have three points to make in a paragraph, it helps to point this out ahead of time:

> *There are three reasons why I believe that the Grand Canyon should be strip-mined. First . . . Second . . . Third . . .*

(C) If you want to clue the reader to the fact that you are about to support the main idea with examples or illustrations, the following words are useful:
for example
to illustrate
for instance
because

(D) To add yet another example or argument in support of your main idea, you can use one of the following words to make that clear:
furthermore
in addition
similarly

The Analysis of an Argument Essay in Six Steps

Step One: Read the topic. Isolate the conclusion and premises.
Step Two: Identify its assumptions. Brainstorm for two minutes.
Step Three: Look at the assumptions. Do they help to prove the conclusion?
Step Four: Choose a template that allows you to attack the assumptions in an organized way.
Step Five: Illustrate how these same assumptions could be used to make the argument more compelling.
Step Six: Do some editing. The GMAT readers will not take away points for neat additions or cross-outs to correct spelling or grammar mistakes.

just as
also
moreover

(E) To indicate that the idea you are about to bring up is important, special, or surprising in some way, you can use one of these words:
surely
truly
undoubtedly
clearly
certainly
indeed
as a matter of fact
in fact
most important

Q: What are the three most important aspects of writing a good Analysis of an Argument essay?

(F) To tell the reader that you are about to reach a conclusion, you might use one of these words:
therefore
in summary
consequently
hence
in conclusion
in short

How It Works

Here's a paragraph consisting of a main point and two supporting arguments:

> I believe he is wrong. He doesn't know the facts. He isn't thinking clearly.

Watch how a few structure words can class up this paragraph and make it clearer at the same time:

> I believe he is wrong. **For one thing**, he doesn't know the facts. **For another**, he isn't thinking clearly.

> I believe he is wrong. **Obviously**, he doesn't know the facts. **Moreover**, he isn't thinking clearly.

> I believe he is wrong **because, first**, he doesn't know the facts, and **second**, he isn't thinking clearly.

> **Certainly**, he doesn't know the facts, and he isn't thinking clearly **either**. **Consequently**, I believe he is wrong.

THE APPEARANCE OF DEPTH

You may have noticed that much of the structure we have been discussing thus far has been about contrasting viewpoints. Nothing will give your writing the *appearance* of depth faster than learning to use this technique. The idea is to set up your main idea by first introducing its opposite.

> *It is a favorite ploy of incoming presidents to blame the federal bureaucracy for the high cost of government, but I believe that bureaucratic waste is only a small part of the problem.*

You may have noticed that this sentence contained a "trigger word." In this case, the trigger word "but" tells us that what was expressed in the first half of the sentence is going to be contradicted in the second half. We discussed trigger words in the Reading Comprehension chapter of this book. Here they are again:

> but, however, on the contrary, although, yet, while, despite, in spite of, rather, nevertheless, instead

By using these words, you can instantly give your writing the appearance of depth.

Example:

> Main thought: *I believe television programs should be censored.*
>
> *While many people believe in the sanctity of free speech, I believe television programs should be censored.*
>
> *Most people believe in the sanctity of free speech, but I believe television programs should be censored.*

In addition to trigger words, here are a few other words or phrases you can use to introduce the view you are eventually going to decide *against*:

> admittedly, true, certainly, granted, obviously, of course, undoubtedly, to be sure, one cannot deny that, it could be argued that

CONTRASTING VIEWPOINTS WITHIN A PASSAGE

Trigger words can be used to signal the opposing viewpoints of entire paragraphs. Suppose you saw an essay that began

> *Many people believe that youth is wasted on the young. They point out that young people never seem to enjoy, or even think about, the great gifts they have been given but will not always have: physical dexterity, good hearing, good vision. However . . .*

A: Make it look neat, write at least four or five paragraphs, and have it clearly organized (an introduction where you state that you will analyze the reasoning of the topic, a middle to pick apart the argument by exposing assumptions, and a conclusion where you state how the argument could be strengthened and where you also sum up your position). Remember, this essay uses the same skills and approach you developed for the critical reasoning section of the test.

What do you think is going to happen in the second paragraph? That's right, the author is now going to disagree with the "many people" of the first paragraph.

Setting up one paragraph in opposition to another lets the reader know what's going on right away. The organization of the essay is immediately evident.

RHYTHM

Many people think good writing is a mysterious talent that you either have or don't have, like good rhythm. In fact, good writing has a kind of rhythm to it, but there is nothing mysterious about it. Good writing is a matter of mixing up the different kinds of raw materials that you have available to you—phrases, dependent and independent clauses, to build sentences that don't all sound the same.

SHORT SENTENCES, LONG SENTENCES

The ETS graders won't have time to savor your essay, but they know that effective writing mixes up short and long sentences for variety, and consequently they will be looking to see how you put sentences together. Here's an example of a passage in which all the sentences sound alike:

> Movies cost too much. Everyone agrees about that.
> Studios need to cut costs. No one is sure exactly how
> to do it. I have two simple solutions. They can cut
> costs by paying stars less. They can also cut costs by
> reducing overhead.

Why did all the sentences sound alike? Well, for one thing, they were all about the same length. For another thing, the sentences were all made up of independent clauses with the same exact setup: subject, verb, and sometimes object. There were no dependent clauses, almost no phrases, no structure words, and, frankly, no variety at all. Here's the same passage, but this time we varied the sentence length by combining some clauses, using conjunctions. We also threw in some structure words.

> Everyone agrees that movies cost too much.
> Clearly, studios need to cut costs, but no one is sure
> exactly how to do it. I have two simple solutions: they
> can cut costs by paying stars less and by reducing
> overhead.

THE IMPRESSIVE BOOK REFERENCE

In any kind of writing, it pays to remember who your audience will be. In this case, the essays are primarily going to be graded by college teaching assistants. They wouldn't be human if they didn't have a soft spot in their heart for someone who can refer to a well-known nonfiction book or a famous work of literature.

A significant part of receiving a high score on an essay is writing at least two pages in neat, readable handwriting and providing a basic structure for your essay. The structure should consist of an introduction, a body, and a conclusion.

Before beginning any essay, always brainstorm! Write your ideas out on scrap paper.

What book should you pick? Obviously it should be a book that you have actually read and liked. We do not advise picking a book if you've only seen the movie. Hollywood has a habit of changing the endings.

You might think that it would be impossible to pick a book to use as an example for an essay before you even know the topic of the essay, but it's actually pretty easy. Just to give you an idea of how it's done, let's pick a famous work of literature that most people have read at some point in their lives: Shakespeare's *Hamlet*.

Now let's take each of the topics we've been using in this chapter, and see how we could work in a reference to *Hamlet*.

Essay topic #1: Should television and song lyrics be censored in order to curb increasing crime and violence?

. . . Where would such censorship stop? In an attempt to prevent teen suicide, would an after-school version of Shakespeare's *Hamlet* be changed so that the soliloquy read, "To be, or . . . whatever"?

Essay topic #2: Is government bureaucracy to blame for the increased cost of government?

If you were to compare the United States government to Shakespeare's *Hamlet*, the poor bureaucrats would represent the forgotten and insignificant Rosencrantz and Guildenstern, not the scheming pretenders to the throne.

Essay topic #3: Should the maximum amount of a medical malpractice lawsuit be capped in the interest of lowering the cost of health care?

Malpractice awards are getting out of hand. If Shakespeare's era was reportedly the most litigious age in history, surely ours must come a close second. If he were writing today, you have the feeling Hamlet might have said, "Alas poor Yorick, he should have gotten a better malpractice lawyer."

You get the idea. Since your essays may be read by the admissions officers at the schools to which you are applying, you might think it would be better to cite a book by a well-regarded economist or business guru rather than that of a playwright or novelist. As long as your example feels like an organic addition to your essay, it won't matter too much who you cite. But you may find that these economic references are harder to work into your essay—and they will almost certainly go over the head of the essay *graders*.

THE AWA

It seems unlikely that anyone is going to be rejected by a business school based on these essays, so don't bother feeling intimidated. Think of it this way: The essays represent an *opportunity* if your verbal scores are low, or if English is your second language. For the rest of us, the essays are as good a way as any to warm up (and wake up) before the sections that count.

SUMMARY

1. The GMAT writing assessment will consist of two essays to be written in one hour. They will be scored from 1–6 in half-point increments.

2. The essays may be read by the schools to which you apply, but the essays will be *graded* by underpaid, overworked college instructors who have only two minutes to read each essay.

3. To score high on the writing assessment:

    a. Write as many words as possible.

    b. Use a pre-built template to organize your thoughts.

    c. Use structure words, contrast words, and a combination of short and long sentences to give the appearance of depth to your writing

    d. Refer to a well-known work of literature or nonfiction.

4. For the Analysis of an Issue topic:

    Step 1: Read the topic.

    Step 2: Decide the general position you are going to take—for or against the position.

    Step 3: Brainstorm. Come up with a bunch of supporting ideas or examples. It helps to write these down on a piece of scrap paper. These supporting statements are supposed to help convince the reader that your main thesis is correct.

    Step 4: Look over your supporting ideas, and throw out the weakest ones. There should be three to five left over.

    Step 5: Write the essay, using all the preconstruction and template tools you learned in this chapter.

    Step 6: Read over the essay and edit your work.

5. For the Analysis of an Argument topic:

    Step 1: Read the topic and separate out the conclusion from the premises.

    Step 2: Since they're asking you to critique (read "weaken") the argument, concentrate on identifying its assumptions. Brainstorm as many different assumptions as you can think of. It helps to write these out on a piece of scrap paper.

    Step 3: Look at the premises. Do they actually help to prove the conclusion?

Step 4: Choose a template that allows you to attack the assumptions and premises in an organized way.

Step 5: At the end of the essay, remember to take a moment to illustrate how these same assumptions could be used to make the argument more compelling.

Step 6: Read over the essay and edit your work.

PART IV

How to Crack the Math GMAT

GMAT Math:
Basic Principles

WHAT'S COVERED IN THE MATH SECTIONS

Of the six 25-minute multiple-choice sections that count on the GMAT, three will be math sections. One of these, called Data Sufficiency, has a peculiar format and will be covered in a later chapter. The other two math sections contain standard problem-solving questions. The two sections are identical in format. Each contains 16 problems that test your general knowledge of three subjects:

1. arithmetic
2. basic algebra
3. geometry

WHAT ISN'T COVERED IN THE MATH SECTIONS

The good news is that you won't need to know calculus, trigonometry, or any of the complicated parts of geometry. The bad news is that the specialized, business-type math you're probably good at isn't tested, either. There will be no questions on computing the profit on three ticks of a particular bond sale, no questions about amortizing a loan, no need to calculate the bottom line of a small business.

ANCIENT HISTORY

For the most part what you'll find on the GMAT is a kind of math you haven't had to think about in years: high-school math. The GMAT is more difficult than your old nemesis, the SAT, but the problem-solving on the GMAT tests the same general body of knowledge tested by the SAT. Since most people who apply to business school have been out of college for several years, high-school math may seem a bit like ancient history. In the next few chapters, we'll give you a fast review of the important concepts, as well as show you some powerful techniques for cracking the system.

ORDER OF DIFFICULTY

The questions in each of the problem-solving sections are arranged in order of difficulty:

1. The first third of the section is relatively easy.
2. The middle third of the section is of medium difficulty.
3. The final third of the section is difficult.

Of the sixteen questions in a problem solving section:

1 – 5	relatively easy
6 – 11	medium
12 – 16	difficult

B-School Lingo

Valuation: adds up projected future cash flow into current dollars

Value-Based Decision Making: applying values and ethics to the process of business

The only exception is when ETS gives you two questions based on the same information. For example, problems 7 and 8 might refer to one chart. In this case, problem 7 is easier than a normal problem 7, but problem 8 is *much* tougher than a normal problem 8.

THE PRINCETON REVIEW APPROACH

When it comes to the GMAT, most people solve the easy questions, get some of the medium questions right, and miss most of the difficult questions. In order to get a very good score it isn't necessary to get every question right. As we told you in chapter 3, you can do extremely well on this test by skipping a large number of questions.

Since each question is worth the same number of points, it makes sense to concentrate on the questions you know how to do. For the most part, that means you should do the easy questions first, then the medium questions, and, unless you're shooting for a very high score, skip most of the difficult questions. However, it may be that when you've finished this book some of the "difficult" questions won't seem difficult anymore.

EXTRA HELP

Although we'll show you which mathematical principles are most important for the GMAT, this book cannot take the place of a basic foundation in math. We find that most people, even if they don't remember much of high-school math, pick it up again quickly. Our drills and examples will refresh your memory if you've gotten rusty, but if you have serious difficulties with the following chapters, you should consider a more thorough review. This book will enable you to see where you need the most work. Always keep in mind, though, that if your purpose is to raise your GMAT score, it's a waste of time to learn math that won't be tested.

> Always keep in mind that if your purpose is to raise your GMAT score, it's a waste of time to learn math that won't be tested. Don't get us wrong, we think the derivation of π is fascinating, but . . .

BASIC INFORMATION

Try the following problem:

2. How many even integers are there between 17 and 27?

   (A) 9
   (B) 7
   (C) 5
   (D) 4
   (E) 3

This is a very easy question. You can tell by its number: It is question 2 out of 16 questions. Even so, if you don't know what an integer is, the question will be impossible to answer. Before moving on to arithmetic, you should be sure you're familiar with some basic terms and concepts. This material isn't difficult, but you must know it cold. (The answer, by the way, is C.)

INTEGERS

Integers are the numbers we think of when we think of numbers. They can be negative or positive. They do not include fractions. The positive integers are:

$$1, 2, 3, 4, 5, \text{etc.}$$

Ancient History 101

The GMAT will test your, probably rusty, knowledge of high-school math.

The negative integers are:

$$-1, -2, -3, -4, -5, \text{etc.}$$

Zero (0) is also an integer. It is neither positive nor negative.

Positive integers get bigger as they move away from 0; negative integers get smaller. Look at this number line:

2 is bigger than 1, but –2 is smaller than –1.

POSITIVE AND NEGATIVE

Positive numbers are to the right of the zero on the number line above. Negative numbers are to the left of zero on the number line above.

There are three rules regarding the multiplication of positive and negative numbers:

1. pos. times pos. = pos.

   $2 \times 3 = 6$

2. pos. times neg. = neg.

   $3 \times -4 = -12$

3. neg. times neg. = pos.

   $-2 \times -3 = 6$

If you add a positive number and a negative number, you're subtracting the number with the negative sign in front of it from the positive number.

$$4 + (-3) = 1$$

If you add two negative numbers, you add them as if they were positive, then put a negative sign in front of the sum.

$$-3 + -5 = -8$$

DIGITS

There are ten digits:

$$0, 1, 2, 3, 4, 5, 6, 7, 8, 9$$

All integers are made up of digits. In the integer 246, there are three digits—2, 4, and 6. Each of the digits has a different name:

> 6 is called the units digit
>
> 4 is called the tens digit
>
> 2 is called the hundreds digit

A number with decimal places is also composed of digits, although it is not an integer. In the decimal 27.63 there are four digits:

> 7 is the units digit
>
> 2 is the tens digit
>
> 6 is the tenths digit
>
> 3 is the hundredths digit

ODD OR EVEN

Even numbers are integers that can be divided evenly by 2. Here are some examples:

> – 4, –2, 0, 2, 4, etc.   (note that 0 is even)

Any integer, no matter how large, is even if its last digit can be divided evenly by 2. Thus 777,772 is even.

Odd numbers are integers that cannot be divided evenly by 2. Here are some examples:

> –5, –3, –1, 1, 3, 5, etc.   (note that 0 is not odd)

Any integer, no matter how large, is odd if its last digit cannot be divided evenly by 2. Thus 222,227 is odd.

There are several rules that always hold true with even and odd numbers:

> *even* × *even* = *even*
>
> *odd* × *odd* = *odd*
>
> *even* × *odd* = *even*
>
> *even* + *even* = *even*
>
> *odd* + *odd* = *even*
>
> *even* + *odd* = *odd*

It isn't necessary to memorize these, but you must know that the relationships always hold true. The individual rules can be derived in a second. If you need to know "even × even," just try 2 × 2. The answer in this case is even, as "even × even" always will be.

Q: 20,179.01792

In the number above, which of the following two digits are identical?

(A) the tens digit and the hundredths digit

(B) the ones digit and the thousandths digit

(C) the hundreds digit and the tenths digit

(D) the thousands digit and the tenths digit

(E) the thousands digit and the hundredths digit

REMAINDERS

If a number cannot be divided evenly by another number, the number that is left over at the end of division is called the remainder.

$$\begin{array}{r} 3\ \text{R}1 \\ 2\overline{)7} \end{array}$$

A: D. Both the thousands digit and tenths digit are 0.

CONSECUTIVE INTEGERS

Consecutive integers are integers listed in order of increasing size without any integers missing in between. For example, –3, –2, –1, 0, 1, 2, 3 are consecutive integers. The formula for consecutive integers is $n, n + 1, n + 2, n + 3$, etc., where n is an integer.

Some consecutive even integers: –2, 0, 2, 4, 6, 8, etc.
Some consecutive odd integers: –3, –1, 1, 3, 5, etc.

DISTINCT NUMBERS

If two numbers are distinct, they cannot be equal. For example, if x and y are distinct, then they must equal different values.

PRIME NUMBERS

A prime number is a number that can be divided evenly only by two numbers: itself and by 1. Thus 2, 3, 5, 7, 11, 13 are all prime numbers. The number 2 is the only even prime number. Neither 0 nor 1 is a prime number.

DIVISIBILITY RULES

If a number can be divided evenly by another number, it is said to be divisible by that number.

Some useful shortcuts:

- ♦ A number is divisible by 2 if its units digit can be divided evenly by 2. Thus 772 is divisible by 2.

- ♦ A number is divisible by 3 if the sum of its digits can be divided evenly by 3. We can instantly tell that 216 is divisible by 3, because the sum of the digits (2 + 1 + 6) is divisible by 3.

- ♦ A number is divisible by 5 if its final digit is either 0 or 5. Thus 60, 85, and 15 are all divisible by 5.

FACTORS AND MULTIPLES

A number is a *factor* of another number if it can be divided evenly into that number. Thus the factors of 15, for example, are 1, 3, 5, and 15.

A number x is considered to be a *multiple* of another number y if y times another integer = x. For example, 15 is a multiple of 3 (3×5); 12 is also a multiple of 3 (3×4).

Absolute Value

The *absolute value* of a number is the distance between that number and 0 on the number line. The absolute value of 6 is expressed as | 6 |.

$$| 6 | = 6$$
$$| -5 | = 5$$

STANDARD SYMBOLS

The following standard symbols are frequently used on the GMAT:

Symbol	Meaning
=	is equal to
≠	is not equal to
<	is less than
>	is greater than
≤	is less than or equal to
≥	is greater than or equal to

NOW LET'S LOOK AT THE INSTRUCTIONS

Both of the problem-solving sections on the GMAT have the same instructions. To avoid wasting time reading these during the test, read our version of the instructions now:

Directions: Solve the following problems, using the margins of your test booklet for space for your computations.

Numbers: This test uses only real numbers; no imaginary numbers are used or implied.

Diagrams: All diagrams in this section are drawn as accurately as possible UNLESS it is specifically noted that a diagram is "not drawn to scale." All diagrams are in a plane unless stated otherwise.

Don't Ask!

What is 6 divided by 0? The answer is "don't ask." Division by zero is undefined. There is no answer. ETS won't ever put a zero in the denominator. If you're working out a problem and you find yourself with a 0 on the bottom of a fraction, you've done something wrong. By the way, a 0 in the numerator is fine. Any fraction with a 0 on the top is 0. 0/1 = 0. 0/4 = 0.

11

Joe Bloggs, POE, and GMAT Math

In chapter 4 we introduced you to Joe Bloggs—the average test taker. Understanding how Joe thinks can be a great advantage to you on the math sections. It's important that you be able to identify the answer choices Joe Bloggs is attracted to on every math problem—easy or difficult.

Why?

On an easy problem, Joe's hunch is correct. This means that on easy problems you can trust choices that seem correct to you.

On a difficult problem, however, Joe's hunch is always wrong. By eliminating Joe's answers on the difficult problems, you can improve your odds tremendously.

Questions in each math section of the GMAT are arranged in order of difficulty—easy, medium, hard.

WHERE DOES JOE GO WRONG?

In chapter 4 we introduced Joe Bloggs by showing you how he approached a difficult math question. In that example, we pointed out one answer choice that Joe Bloggs would have been irresistibly drawn to. In fact, there were two other answer choices in that problem that might have appealed to Joe as well.

To understand how ETS comes up with traps for Joe Bloggs, let's look at that same problem again from a slightly different perspective:

15. The output of a factory was increased by 10% to keep up with rising demand. To handle the holiday rush, this new output was increased by 20%. By approximately what percent would the output now have to be decreased in order to restore the original output?

    (A)
    (B) 24%
    (C)
    (D)
    (E)

ZEN AND THE ART OF TEST WRITING

Let's put ourselves in the place of the ETS test writer who has just written this difficult math problem. He's finished with his question, and he has his correct answer (24%), but he isn't done yet. He still has four empty slots to fill in. He needs to come up with incorrect numbers for answer choices A, C, D, and E.

He *could* simply choose numbers at random, or numbers that are closely clustered around the correct answer. If the test writer did that, however, Joe Bloggs wouldn't see an obvious answer and might therefore guess at random. The test writer does *not* want Joe to guess at random. If Joe guesses at random, he might actually pick the right answer. So our test writer comes up with incorrect answer choices that whisper seductively, "Pick *me*, Joe." If Joe's going to guess, our test writer wants to make sure he guesses wrong.

Psst! Hey, Joe, Looking for a Good Time?

To come up with answers that will appeal to Joe Bloggs, the ETS test writer has to know how Joe thinks. Fortunately for the test writer, he can draw on over thirty years of statistical information ETS has compiled. From this, he knows that

1. On difficult math problems, Joe Bloggs is always attracted to easy solutions that he can find in one or two steps.

For example, Joe might just add together the numbers mentioned in the problem.

2. On difficult math problems, Joe Bloggs is attracted to numbers that he has already seen in the problem.

It's pretty silly, but frequently Joe picks a number simply because he remembers it from the problem itself.

Now let's look at the same problem complete with answer choices:

15. The output of a factory was increased by 10% to keep up with rising demand. To handle the holiday rush, this new output was increased by 20%. By approximately what percent would the output now have to be decreased in order to restore the original output?

   (A) 20%
   (B) 24%
   (C) 30%
   (D) 32%
   (E) 70%

If the test writer has done his job properly, Joe Bloggs will never even consider the correct answer (24%). He's too smitten by the other answer choices.

Here's how to crack it:

As we said in chapter 4, Joe's favorite answer to this question is undoubtedly choice (C). Joe notices that the output seems to have increased by 30% and figures that to get rid of that increase, you would have to decrease it by 30%. What Joe has just done is add the two numbers he saw in the problem. This was a one-step operation.

Another answer Joe might find enticing is choice (E). The word *percent* means "out of a hundred." If Joe adds the two numbers contained in the problem to get 30 and then subtracts the sum from 100, he gets 70. This is a two-step operation.

> On difficult math problems, Joe Bloggs is attracted to easy solutions that he can find in one or two steps.

Another answer Joe might be attracted to is choice (A). Twenty (20%) is simply one of the numbers from the problem. There is no logical reason to think this is the correct answer, but Joe isn't always logical.

Joe wants to select choice (A), (C), or (E). On a difficult question, Joe's answers are always wrong. This means that you can eliminate these three choices. At this point, if you aren't sure of how to solve the problem mathematically, guess choice (B) or (D) and move on. You'll have a fifty-fifty shot at being correct.

Even if you do think you know how to solve the problem mathematically, you might still want to guess instead of taking the time to work it out.

Why?

Suppose there's only one minute left for this math section. You're pretty sure you can solve this problem, but looking ahead to the next problem, you realize you can solve that one, too. One minute isn't enough time for two problems, though. Wouldn't it make sense to take the fifty-fifty odds on this problem in order to get to the next one?

DOES EVERY DIFFICULT MATH PROBLEM HAVE JOE BLOGGS ANSWERS?

No. Some types of problems (in particular, problems with variables in the answer choice) have no obvious solutions that can be used to trap Joe. But even when there are no obvious traps, ETS test writers are very careful in creating incorrect answer choices. They try to figure out all the mistakes a careless test taker might make, then they include those answers among the choices.

PARTIAL ANSWERS

People often go wrong on GMAT math problems by thinking that they are finished before they really are. Here's an example:

7. 22% of the cars produced in America are manufactured in Michigan. If the total number of cars produced in America is 40 million, how many cars are produced outside of Michigan?

(A) 4.4 million
(B) 8.8 million
(C) 15 million
(D) 27 million
(E) 31.2 million

Here's how to crack it

The first step in this problem is to find out how many actual cars are produced in Michigan; in other words, we need to know what 22% of 40 million equals. If you aren't sure how to do this, don't worry; we'll show you how to do percent problems in the arithmetic chapter. For the moment, take our word for it that 22% of 40 million equals 8.8 million.

If you were feeling smug about having figured this out, you might just look at the answer choices, notice that answer choice (B) says 8.8 million, and figure that you're done. Unfortunately, the problem didn't ask how many cars were produced in Michigan; it asked how many cars were *not* produced in Michigan.

ETS provided answer choice (B) just in case you got halfway through the problem and decided you'd done enough work. It was a *partial* answer. To find the correct answer you have to subtract 8.8 from 40 million. The correct answer is choice (E) 31.2 million.

You can prevent yourself from selecting partial answers by doing two things:

1. When you finish a problem, always take two seconds to reread the last line of the problem to make sure you've actually answered the question.

2. Always look at the number of the problem you're working on to decide whether you've done enough work for ETS to think you "deserve" to get the problem right. For example, that last problem was a number 7. It was a medium problem. There's no way a medium problem can be solved in just one step.

Common Sense

ETS is so caught up in trying to provide answer choices that anticipate all the mistakes a test taker might make on a problem that they often forget to make certain that all of these answer choices make sense.

Look at the following difficult problem:

14. A student took 6 courses last year and received an average grade of 100. The year before, the student took 5 courses and received an average grade of 90. To the nearest tenth of a point, what was the student's average grade for the entire two-year period?

    (A) 79
    (B) 89
    (C) 95
    (D) 95.5
    (E) 97.2

Here's how to crack it

Because this is a difficult problem, the first thing to do is see whether there are any Joe Bloggs answers. There's one big one—Joe likes answer choice (C) a lot. He figures that to find the average of the entire two-year period, all he has to do is find that the average of 90 and 100 is 95.

If this problem were that easy, it wouldn't be number 14. Eliminate choice (C).

There are no other obvious Joe Bloggs answers, but it *is* possible to eliminate a couple of other choices by using common sense. The student's average for the first year was 90. The student's average for the second year was 100. Obviously the student's second-year grades are going to bring his average *up*. We may not be sure by exactly how much, but the average for the entire two-year period has

Q: Which of the following numbers is prime?
0, 1, 15, 23, 33

to be higher than it was for the first year. Both choices (A) and (B) are less than the first year's average. We can therefore eliminate both of them.

Now we're down to a fifty-fifty shot. The answer has to be either choice (D) or (E). We can either guess and move on or start solving the problem in earnest. (By the way, the answer to this problem is choice (D), but don't worry about how to solve it just yet. We'll cover average problems in the next chapter.)

ELIMINATING CRAZY ANSWERS

A: 23. Remember, neither 0 nor 1 is prime.

Many of the problems on the GMAT are both time-consuming and difficult. You can make things easier for yourself by eliminating choices that don't make sense before you actually solve the problem. Some answer choices seem pretty crazy when you look at them in the cold light of day.

Here's an example:

15. Three typists are hired to type a 180-page report. Typist A can type 4 pages an hour, typist B can type 5 pages an hour, and typist C can type 6 pages an hour. If all three work continuously at their respective rates until the report is finished, what fraction of the report will be typed by typist A?

(A) $\frac{2}{9}$

(B) $\frac{4}{15}$

(C) $\frac{1}{3}$

(D) $\frac{4}{9}$

(E) $\frac{2}{3}$

Here's how to crack it

Is there a Joe Bloggs answer here? Joe is strongly attracted to choice (C). After all, there are three typists, so Joe (conveniently forgetting that they're working at different rates) reasons that each of them does one-third of the work. Eliminate choice (C).

Now let's try some common sense. If the three typists were working at the *same* rate, each would do one third of the work. In this case, however, the problem tells us that typist A is *slower* than the other two. Since they all plan to work continuously until the report is done, is it possible that typist A will be able to do a third of the report? No. Typist A will do *less* than a third. This means that any choice *greater* than a third is crazy. Eliminate choices (D) and (E).

(By the way, the correct answer to this problem is choice (B), but don't worry about how to solve it yet. We'll cover work problems in the algebra chapter.)

◆ You can use common sense to eliminate crazy choices even on easy and medium problems.

◆ Sometimes eliminating crazy choices will lead you directly to the correct answer.

SUMMARY

1. Joe Bloggs tends to get the easy math problems right, but he always gets the difficult math problems wrong because of the traps ETS has set for him.

2. On difficult problems, Joe Bloggs is attracted to easy solutions that he can arrive at in one or two steps. Therefore eliminate all obvious answers on difficult questions.

3. On difficult problems, Joe Bloggs is attracted to answer choices that simply repeat numbers from the problem. Therefore eliminate those choices.

4. On all problems, always take a moment to see whether the answer choices make sense. Eliminate crazy answer choices.

12

Arithmetic

Although arithmetic is only one of the three types of math tested on the GMAT, arithmetic problems comprise about half of the total number of questions. In each math section, about eight problems will involve arithmetic.

It is also interesting to note that most of these eight problems will be found in the easy and medium parts of the section. Therefore it is crucial that you know the information in this chapter cold.

Here are the specific arithmetic topics tested on the GMAT:

1. Axioms and Fundamentals (properties of integers, positive and negative numbers, even and odd). These were covered in chapter 10.

2. Arithmetic Operations

3. Fractions

4. Decimals

5. Ratios

6. Percentages

7. Averages

8. Exponents and Radicals

In this chapter we will first discuss the fundamentals of each topic and then show how ETS constructs questions based on that topic.

ARITHMETIC OPERATIONS

There are six arithmetic operations you will need for the GMAT:

1. addition $(2 + 2)$ — the result of addition is a sum or total

2. subtraction $(6 - 2)$ — the result of subtraction is a difference

3. multiplication (2×2) — the result of multiplication is a product

4. division $(8 \div 2)$ — the result of division is a quotient

5. raising to a power (x^2) — in the expression x^2 the little 2 is called an exponent

6. finding a square root — $\left(\sqrt{4}\right) = \sqrt{2 \cdot 2} = 2$

WHICH ONE DO I DO FIRST?

In a problem that involves several different operations, the operations must be performed in a particular order, and occasionally ETS likes to see whether you know what that order is. Here's an easy way to remember the order of operations:

Please Excuse My Dear Aunt Sally

This stands for Parentheses, Exponents, Multiplication, Division, Addition, Subtraction. Do operations enclosed in parentheses first; then take care of exponents; then multiply, divide, add, and subtract.

DRILL 1

Just to get you started, solve each of the following problems by performing the indicated operation in the proper order. The answers can be found on page 254.

1. $74 + (27 - 24) =$ 77

2. $(8 \times 9) + 7 =$ 79

3. $2[9 - (8 \div 2)] =$ 10

4. $2(7 - 3) + (-4)(5 - 7) =$ 8

It is not uncommon to see a problem like this on the GMAT:

5. $4[-3(3 - 5) + 10 - 17] =$

   (A) -27
   (B) -4
   (C) -1
   (D) 32
   (E) 84

There are two operations that can be done in any order, provided they are the only operations involved: **When you are adding or multiplying a series of numbers, you can group or regroup the numbers any way you like.**

$$2 + 3 + 4 \text{ is the same as } 4 + 2 + 3$$
$$\text{and}$$
$$4 \times 5 \times 6 \text{ is the same as } 6 \times 5 \times 4$$

This is called the *associative law*, but the name will not be tested on the GMAT.

The *distributive law* states that $a(b + c) = ab + ac$ and $a(b - c) = ab - ac$.

ETS likes to see whether you remember this. Sometimes the distributive law can provide you with a shortcut to the solution of a problem. If a problem gives you information in "factored form"—$a(b + c)$—you should distribute it immediately. If the information is given in distributed form—$ab + ac$—you should factor it.

> Q: According to the associative law, can you perform the following operations in any order you like?
> 2 divided by 6 divided by 3 divided by 4.
> Hint: The answer is yes *and* no.

DRILL 2

If the following problems are in distributed form, factor them; if they are in factored form, distribute them. Then do the indicated operation. Answers are on page 254.

1. $9(27 + 3)$

2. $(55 \times 12) + (55 \times 88)$

3. $a(b + c - d)$

4. $abc + xyc$

A GMAT problem might look like this:

5. If $x = 6$ what is the value of $\dfrac{2xy - xy}{y}$?

    (A) -30
    (B) 6
    (C) 8
    (D) 30
    (E) It cannot be determined.

A: There are two ways to approach the problem. You can divide from left to right. Division *must* be performed from left to right. The second way is to convert the several division operations into multiplication:
$2 \times 1/6 \times 1/3 \times 1/4$.
In this form the operations can be performed in whatever order you find most convenient.

FRACTIONS

Fractions can be thought of in two ways:

- A fraction is just another way of expressing division. The expression $\dfrac{1}{2}$ is exactly the same thing as 1 divided by 2. $\dfrac{x}{y}$ is nothing more than x divided by y. In the fraction $\dfrac{x}{y}$, x is known as the numerator, and y is known as the denominator.

- The other important way to think of a fraction is as

$$\frac{\text{part}}{\text{whole}}$$

The fraction $\dfrac{7}{10}$ can be thought of as 7 parts out of a total of 10 parts.

PEMDAS

This stands for parentheses, exponents, multiplication, division, addition, subtraction, and indicates the order in which the operations should be done. To remember, say, "Please Excuse My Dear Aunt Sally." Or, if you prefer, just say, "**PEMDAS.**"

ADDING AND SUBTRACTING FRACTIONS WITH THE SAME DENOMINATOR

To add two or more fractions that have the same denominator, simply add up the numerators and put the sum over the common denominator. For example:

$$\frac{1}{7} + \frac{5}{7} = \frac{(1+5)}{7} = \frac{6}{7}$$

Subtraction works exactly the same way:

$$\frac{6}{7} - \frac{2}{7} = \frac{(6-2)}{7} = \frac{4}{7}$$

ADDING AND SUBTRACTING FRACTIONS WITH DIFFERENT DENOMINATORS

Before you can add or subtract two or more fractions with different denominators, you must give all of them the same denominator. To do this, multiply each fraction by a number that will give it a denominator in common with the others. If you multiplied each fraction by any old number, the fractions wouldn't have their original values, so the number you multiply by has to be some value of 1.

For example, if you wanted to change $\frac{1}{2}$ into sixths, you could do the following:

$$\frac{1}{2} \times \frac{3}{3} = \frac{3}{6}$$

We haven't actually changed the value of the fraction, because we multiplied it by 1. $\frac{3}{6}$ reduces to $\frac{1}{2}$. If we wanted to add

$$\frac{1}{2} + \frac{2}{3}$$

$$\frac{1}{2} \times \frac{3}{3} + \frac{2}{3} \times \frac{2}{2}$$

$$\frac{3}{6} + \frac{4}{6} = \frac{7}{6}$$

MULTIPLYING FRACTIONS

To multiply fractions, just multiply the numerators and put the product over the product of the denominators. For example:

$$\frac{2}{3} \times \frac{6}{5} = \frac{12}{15}$$

REDUCING FRACTIONS

When you add or multiply fractions, you often end up with a big fraction that is hard to work with. You can usually reduce such a fraction. To reduce a fraction, find a factor of the numerator that is also a factor of the denominator. It saves time to find the biggest factor they have in common, but this isn't critical. You may just have to repeat the process a few times. When you find a common factor, cancel it. For example, let's take the product we just found when we multiplied the fractions above:

$$\frac{12}{15} = \frac{4 \times \cancel{3}}{5 \times \cancel{3}} = \frac{4}{5}$$

Get used to reducing all fractions (if they can be reduced) *before* you do any work with them. It saves a lot of time and prevents errors in computation.

DIVIDING FRACTIONS

To divide one fraction by another, just invert the second fraction and multiply:

$$\frac{2}{3} \div \frac{3}{4}$$

is the same thing as

$$\frac{2}{3} \times \frac{4}{3} = \frac{8}{9}$$

You may see this same operation written like this:

$$\frac{\dfrac{2}{3}}{\dfrac{3}{4}}$$

Again, just invert and multiply. This next example is handled the same way:

$$\frac{6}{\dfrac{2}{3}} = \frac{6}{1} \times \frac{3}{2} = \frac{18}{2} = 9$$

CONVERTING TO FRACTIONS

An integer can always be expressed as a fraction by making the integer the numerator and 1 the denominator. $16 = \frac{16}{1}$.

The GMAT sometimes gives you numbers that are mixtures of integers and fractions, for example, $3\frac{1}{2}$. It's easier to work with these numbers if you convert them into ordinary fractions. $3\frac{1}{2}$ would be converted like this:

Since the fractional part of this number was expressed in halves, let's convert the integer part of the number into halves as well. $3 = \frac{6}{2}$. Now just add the $\frac{1}{2}$ to the $\frac{6}{2}$. So, $3\frac{1}{2} = \frac{7}{2}$.

COMPARING FRACTIONS

In the course of a problem you may have to compare two or more fractions and determine which is larger. This is easy to do as long as you remember that you can compare fractions directly only if they have the same denominator. Suppose you had to decide which of these three fractions is largest:

$$\frac{1}{2} \quad \frac{5}{9} \quad \frac{7}{15}$$

To compare these fractions directly you need a common denominator, but finding a common denominator that works for all three fractions would be complicated and time consuming. It makes more sense to compare these fractions two at a time. We showed you the classical way to find common denominators when we talked about adding fractions earlier.

Let's start with $\frac{1}{2}$ and $\frac{5}{9}$. An easy common denominator for these two fractions is 18 (9 × 2).

$$\frac{1}{2} \qquad \frac{5}{9}$$
$$\frac{1}{2} \times \frac{9}{9} \qquad \frac{5}{9} \times \frac{2}{2}$$
$$= \frac{9}{18} \qquad = \frac{10}{18}$$

Since $\frac{5}{9}$ is bigger, let's compare it with $\frac{7}{15}$. Here the easiest common denominator is 45.

$$\frac{5}{9} \qquad \frac{7}{15}$$
$$\frac{5}{9} \times \frac{5}{5} \qquad \frac{7}{15} \times \frac{3}{3}$$
$$= \frac{25}{45} \qquad = \frac{21}{45}$$

So $\frac{5}{9}$ is bigger than $\frac{7}{15}$, which means it's also the biggest of the three.

TWO SHORTCUTS

One good shortcut is to compare fractions by cross-multiplying. The idea is that if all you need to know is which fraction is bigger, you just have to compare the new numerators.

$$9 \; \frac{1}{2} \quad \text{✕} \quad \frac{5}{9} \; 10$$

$$10 > 9, \text{ therefore, } \frac{5}{9} > \frac{1}{2}$$

You could also have saved yourself some time on the last problem by a little fast estimation. Again, which is larger?

$$\frac{1}{2} \quad \frac{5}{9} \quad \frac{7}{15}$$

Cross multiplying (with an extra step) can also be used to add fractions. Suppose we wanted to add 1/2 and 5/9. Cross multiply, then multiply along the bottom. Add the numerators and there's your answer. $\frac{1}{2} \; \text{✕} \; \frac{5}{9} = \frac{19}{18}$. Although the answer in this case is not reducible, the result of a bow tie addition can often be reduced.

Let's think about $\frac{5}{9}$ in terms of $\frac{1}{2}$. How many ninths equal a half? To put it another way, what is half of 9? 4.5. So $\frac{4.5}{9} = \frac{1}{2}$. That means $\frac{5}{9}$ is *bigger* than $\frac{1}{2}$.

Now let's think about $\frac{7}{15}$. Half of 15 is 7.5. $\frac{7.5}{15} = \frac{1}{2}$, which means that $\frac{7}{15}$ is *less* than $\frac{1}{2}$.

PROPORTIONS

A fraction can be expressed in many ways. $\frac{1}{2}$ also equals $\frac{2}{4}$ or $\frac{4}{8}$, etc. A proportion is just a different way of expressing a fraction. Here's an example:

> If 2 boxes hold a total of 14 shirts, how many shirts are contained in 3 boxes?

Here's how to crack it

The number of shirts per box can be expressed as a fraction. What you're being asked to do is express the fraction $\frac{2}{14}$ in a different way.

$$\frac{2 \text{ (boxes)}}{14 \text{ (shirts)}} = \frac{3 \text{ (boxes)}}{x \text{ (shirts)}}$$

To find the answer, all you need to do is find a value for x so that $\frac{3}{x} = \frac{2}{14}$. The easiest way to do this is to cross-multiply.

$$\frac{2}{14} = \frac{3}{x}$$

$2x = 42$, which means $x = 21$. There are 21 shirts in 3 boxes.

DRILL 3

The answers to these questions can be found on page 254.

1. $5\frac{2}{3} + \frac{3}{8} =$

2. Reduce $\frac{12}{60}$

Proportions are related to ratios (we cover ratios on page 177). Where a proportion question asks about the number of shirts *per* box, a ratio question might ask about the number of red shirts to blue shirts in a box.

3. Convert $9\frac{2}{3}$ to a fraction

4. $\dfrac{9}{2} = \dfrac{x}{4}$

A relatively easy GMAT fraction problem might look like this:

5. $\dfrac{\left(\dfrac{\dfrac{4}{5}}{\dfrac{3}{5}}\right)\left(\dfrac{\dfrac{1}{8}}{\dfrac{2}{3}}\right)}{\dfrac{3}{4}} =$

(A) $\dfrac{3}{100}$

(B) $\dfrac{3}{16}$

(C) $\dfrac{1}{3}$

(D) 1

(E) $\dfrac{7}{6}$

FRACTIONS: ADVANCED PRINCIPLES

Now that you've been reacquainted with the basics of fractions, let's go a little further. More complicated fraction problems usually involve all of the rules we've just mentioned, with the addition of two concepts: part/whole, and the rest. Here's a typical medium fraction problem:

9. A cement mixture is composed of 3 elements: by weight, $\dfrac{1}{3}$ of the mixture is sand, $\dfrac{3}{5}$ of the mixture is water and the remaining 12 pounds of the mixture is gravel. What is the weight of the entire mixture in pounds?

(A) 11.2
(B) 12.8
(C) 36
(D) 60
(E) 180

Q: There are only roses, tulips, and peonies in a certain garden. There are three roses to every four tulips and every five peonies in the garden. Expressed as a fraction, what part of the flowers in the garden are tulips?

A: To find the answer find the *whole.* We know the parts are 3 roses, 4 tulips, and 5 peonies. 3+4+5=12=the whole. What fractional part of the flowers are tulips? 4 out of a total of 12, otherwise known as $\frac{4}{12}$, or $\frac{1}{3}$.

Here's how to crack it

The difficulty in solving this problem is that the ingredients of cement are expressed in two different units of measurement. Sand and water are expressed as fractions, while gravel is expressed in pounds. At first there seems to be no way of knowing what fractional part of the mixture the 12 pounds of gravel represents; nor do we know how many pounds of sand and water there are.

The first step is to add up the fractional parts that we do have:

$$\frac{1}{3}+\frac{3}{5}=\frac{1}{3}\left(\frac{5}{5}\right)+\frac{3}{5}\left(\frac{3}{3}\right)=\frac{14}{15}$$

Sand and water make up 14 parts out of the whole of 15. This means that gravel makes up what is left over—the rest: 1 part out of the whole of 15. Now the problem is simple. Set up a proportion: gravel as part over whole equals another part over whole:

$$\frac{\text{part}}{\text{whole}}\frac{1}{15}=\frac{12}{x}\frac{\text{pounds (of gravel)}}{\text{pounds (total pounds)}}$$

Cross-multiply: $x = 180$. The answer is choice (E).

DECIMALS ARE A LOT LIKE FRACTIONS

A decimal can be expressed as a fraction, and a fraction can be expressed as a decimal.

$$.6=\frac{6}{10}\text{ which is reduced to }\frac{3}{5}$$

$$\frac{3}{5}\text{ is the same thing as }3\div5$$

$$5\overline{)3.0}^{\,.6}$$

$$= .6$$

Which would you rather figure out—the square of $\frac{1}{4}$ or the square of 0.25?

There may be a few of you out there who've had so much practice with decimals in your work that you prefer decimals to fractions, but for the rest of us, fractions are infinitely easier to deal with.

Whenever possible, convert decimals to fractions. It will save time and eliminate careless mistakes. Occasionally, however, you will have to work with decimals.

ADDING AND SUBTRACTING DECIMALS

To add or subtract decimals, just line up the decimal points and proceed as usual. Adding 6, 2.5, and 0.3 looks like this:

$$\begin{array}{r} 6.0 \\ 2.5 \\ + \ 0.3 \\ \hline 8.8 \end{array}$$

MULTIPLYING DECIMALS

To multiply decimals, simply ignore the decimal points and multiply the two numbers. When you've finished, count all the digits that were to the right of the decimal points in the original numbers you multiplied. Now place the decimal point in your answer so that there are the same number of digits to the right of it. Here are two examples:

$$\begin{array}{r} 0.3 \\ \times \ .7 \\ \hline .21 \end{array}$$

(3 times 7 = 21. There were a total of two digits to the right of the decimal point in the original numbers, so we place the decimal so that there are two digits to the right in the answer.)

$$\begin{array}{r} 2.32 \\ \times \ .03 \\ \hline .0696 \end{array}$$

(3 times 232 = 696. There were a total of four digits to the right of the decimal point in the original numbers, so we place the decimal so that there are four digits to the right in the answer.)

DIVIDING DECIMALS

The best way to divide one decimal by another is to convert the number you are dividing by (in mathematical terminology, the divisor) into a whole number. You do this simply by moving the decimal point as many places as necessary. This works as long as you remember to move the decimal point in the number that you are *dividing* (in mathematical terminology, the dividend) the same number of spaces.

For example, to divide 12 by .6, set it up the way you would an ordinary division problem:

$$.6\overline{)12}$$

To make .6 (the divisor) a whole number, you simply move the decimal point over one place to the right. You must also move the decimal one place to the right in the dividend. Now the operation looks like this:

$$6\overline{)120} \qquad 6\overline{)120}^{20}$$

To round off a decimal, look at the digit to the right of the digits place you are rounding to. If that number is 0–4, there is no change. If that number is 5–9, round up.

ROUNDING OFF DECIMALS

9.4 rounded to the nearest whole number is 9.

9.5 rounded to the nearest whole number is 10.

When ETS asks you to give an approximate answer on an easy question, it is safe to round off numbers. But you should be leery about rounding off numbers on a difficult question.

DRILL 4

The answers to these questions can be found on page 254.

1.
$$\begin{array}{r} 34.26 \\ -\ 9.6 \\ \hline \end{array}$$

2.
$$\begin{array}{r} 27.3 \\ \times\ 9.75 \\ \hline \end{array}$$

3.
$$\frac{19.6}{3.22}$$

4.
$$\frac{\frac{4}{.25}}{\frac{1}{.50}}$$

On the GMAT, there might be questions that mix decimals and fractions:

5.
$$\frac{\frac{3}{10} \times 4 \times .8}{.32}$$

(A) .96
(B) .333
(C) 3
(D) 30
(E) 96

RATIOS

Ratios are close relatives of fractions. A ratio can be expressed as a fraction and vice versa. The ratio 3 to 4 can be written as $\frac{3}{4}$ as well as in standard ratio format: 3:4.

THERE IS ONLY ONE DIFFERENCE BETWEEN A RATIO AND A FRACTION

One way of defining the *fraction* $\frac{3}{4}$ is to say that there are 3 equal *parts* out of a *whole* of 4.

Let's take the ratio of 3 women to 4 men in a room, which could also be expressed as $\frac{3}{4}$. Is 4 the whole in this ratio? Of course not. There are 3 women and 4 men, giving a total of 7 people in the room. The *whole* in a ratio is the sum of all the parts. If the ratio is expressed as a fraction, the *whole* is the sum of the numerator and the denominator.

Fraction:	Ratio:
part 3	3 women
whole 7	4 men (The *whole* is 7)

ASIDE FROM THAT, ALL THE RULES OF FRACTIONS APPLY TO RATIOS

A ratio can be converted to a percentage or a decimal. It can be cross-multiplied, reduced, or expanded—just like a fraction. The ratio of 1 to 3 can be expressed as:

$$\frac{1}{3}$$
$$1:3$$
$$0.333\ldots$$
$$33\frac{1}{3}\%$$
$$\frac{2}{6}$$
$$\frac{3}{9}$$

AN EASY RATIO PROBLEM

The ratio of men to women in a room is 3 to 4. What is the number of men in the room if there are 20 women?

Here's how to crack it

No matter how many people are actually in the room, the ratio of men to women will always stay the same: 3 to 4. What you're being asked to do is find the numerator of a fraction whose denominator is 20, and which can be reduced to $\frac{3}{4}$. Just set one fraction equal to another and cross-multiply:

$$\frac{3}{4} = \frac{x}{20} \qquad 60 = 4x, \quad x = 15$$

The answer to the question is 15 men. Note that $\frac{15}{20}$ reduces to $\frac{3}{4}$. The two fractions are equal, which is just another way of saying they are still in the same ratio.

A MORE DIFFICULT RATIO PROBLEM

The ratio of women to men in a room is 3 to 4. If there are a total of 28 people in the room, how many women are there?

This problem is more difficult because, while we are given the ratio of women to men, we do not have a specific value for either women or men. If we tried to set this problem up the way we did the previous one, it would look like this:

$$\frac{3}{4} = \frac{x}{y}$$

You can't solve an equation if it has two variables.

Here's how to crack it

The trick here is to remember how a ratio differs from a fraction. If the ratio is 3 parts to 4 parts, then there are a total of 7 parts. This means that the 28 people in that room are made up of groups of 7 people (3 women and 4 men in each group). How many groups of 7 people make up 28 people? 4 groups ($4 \times 7 = 28$).

If there are 4 groups—each made up of 3 women and 4 men—the total number of women would be 4×3, or 12. The number of men would be 4×4, or 16. To check this, make sure $\frac{12}{16}$ equals $\frac{3}{4}$ (it does) and that 12 + 16 adds up to 28 (it does).

PERCENTAGES

A percentage is just a fraction in which the denominator is always equal to 100. Fifty percent means 50 parts out of a whole of 100. Like any fraction, a percentage can be reduced, expanded, cross-multiplied, converted to a decimal, or converted to another fraction.

$$50\% = \frac{1}{2} = .5$$

Q: What is 1/4% of 40?

AN EASY PERCENT PROBLEM

The number 5 is what percent of the number 20?

Here's how to crack it

Whenever you see a percent problem, you should be thinking part/whole. In this case, the question is asking you to expand $\frac{5}{20}$ into another fraction in which the denominator is 100.

$$\frac{\text{part}}{\text{whole}} = \frac{5}{20} = \frac{x}{100} \qquad 500 = 20x \qquad x = 25\%$$

PERCENT SHORTCUTS

In the last problem, reducing $\frac{5}{20}$ to $\frac{1}{4}$ would have saved time if you knew that $\frac{1}{4} = 25\%$. Here are some fractions and decimals whose percent equivalents you should know:

$$\frac{1}{4} = .25 = 25\%$$

$$\frac{1}{2} = .50 = 50\%$$

$$\frac{1}{3} = 0.333 \text{ etc. (a repeating decimal)} = 33\frac{1}{3}\%$$

$$\frac{1}{5} = .20 = 20\%$$

◆ Some percentages simply involve moving a decimal point: To get 10 percent of any number, you simply move the decimal point of that number over one place to the left:

  10% of 6 = 0.6
  10% of 60 = 6
  10% of 600 = 60

◆ To get 1 percent of any number, you just move the decimal point of that number over two places to the left:

$$1\% \text{ of } 600 = 6$$
$$1\% \text{ of } 60 = 0.6$$
$$1\% \text{ of } 6 = .06$$

◆ To find a more complicated percentage, it's easy to break the percentage down into easy-to-find chunks:

20% of 60:   10% of 60 = 6. 20% of 60 is double 10%, so the answer is 2 × 6, or 12.

30% of 60:   10% of 60 = 6. 30% of 60 is three times 10%, so the answer is 3 × 6, or 18.

3% of 200:   1% of 200 = 2. 3% of 200 is just three times 1%, so the answer is 3 × 2, or 6.

23% of 400:   10% of 400 = 40. Therefore 20% equals 2 × 40, or 80.

1% of 400 = 4. Therefore 3% equals 3 × 4, or 12.

Putting it all together, 23% of 400 equals 80 + 12, or 92.

A: .1—There are a number of ways to calculate the answer, but the simplest is to first calculate 1% of 40 by moving the decimal point two places. This gives .4 as a result. Dividing this result by 4 gives us .1— the answer.

A MORE DIFFICULT PERCENT PROBLEM

Like advanced fraction problems, more difficult percent problems often involve remembering the principles of part/whole and the rest.

14. A motor pool has 300 vehicles of which 30% are trucks. 20% of all the vehicles in the motor pool are diesel, including 15 trucks. What percent of the motor pool is composed of vehicles that are neither truck nor diesel?

(A) 165%
(B) 90%
(C) 65%
(D) 55%
(E) 10%

Here's how to crack it

Do this problem one sentence at a time.

1. A motor pool has 300 vehicles, of which 30% are trucks. 30% of 300 = 90 trucks, which means that 210 (the rest) are *not* trucks.

2. 20% of all the vehicles are diesel, including 15 trucks. 20% of 300 = 60 diesel vehicles, 15 of which are trucks, which means there are 45 diesel vehicles that are *not* trucks.

3. What percent of the motor pool is composed of vehicles that are neither truck nor diesel? We know from sentence number 1 that there are 210 nontrucks. We know from sentence number 2 that of these 210 nontrucks, 45 are diesel. Therefore 210 − 45, or 165, are neither diesel nor truck.

The question asks what percent of the entire motor pool these 165 nondiesel nontrucks are.

$$\frac{165}{300} = \frac{x}{100} \qquad 300x = 16,500$$

$x = 55$ and the answer is choice (D).

> ### Easy Eliminations:
>
> 1. Since the problem asks us to find a portion of the entire motor pool, it's impossible for that portion to be larger than the motor pool itself. Therefore answer choice (A) 165% is crazy. Also, answer choice (A) was a trap for people who successfully got all the way to the end of the problem and then forgot that the answer was supposed to be expressed as a percent, not as a specific number.
>
> 2. If the problem simply asked what percent of the motor pool was not made up of trucks, the answer would be 70%. But since there is a further condition (the vehicles must be both nontruck and nondiesel), the answer must be even less than 70%. This makes answer choice (B) impossible, too.
>
> 3. Answer choice (C) is probably a Joe Bloggs answer. You can get it simply by adding 30 + 20 + 15.

There's a handy formula for calculating mixed groups like the one from question 14 on page 180. It isn't a priority for you to memorize (you just saw the problem calculated without it), but the formula can be helpful on some questions. Here it is: Group 1 + Group 2 - both + neither = total. Here's what that looks like using the numbers from the vehicle problem. 90 trucks + 60 diesel - 15 diesel trucks + x = 300. 135 (-135)+ x = 300 (-135). x = 165, or 55% of 300.

PERCENT INCREASE

Another type of percent problem you'll probably see on the GMAT has to do with *percentage increase* or *percentage decrease*. In these problems the trick is always to put the increase or decrease in terms of the *original* amount. Here's an example:

9. The cost of a one-family home was $120,000 in 1980. In 1988, the price had increased to $180,000. What was the percent increase in the cost of the home?

   (A) 60%
   (B) 50%
   (C) 55%
   (D) 40%
   (E) 33.3%

Here's how to crack it

The actual increase was $60,000. To find the percent increase, set up the following equation:

$$\frac{\text{amount of increase}}{\text{original amount}} = \frac{x}{100}$$

In this case, $\frac{\$60,000}{\$120,000} = \frac{x}{100}$ $x = 50$ and the answer is choice (B).

COMPOUND INTEREST

Another type of percentage problem involves *compound interest*. If you kept $1,000 in the bank for a year at 6% simple interest, you would get $60 in interest at the end of the year. Compound interest would pay you slightly more. Let's look at a compound-interest problem:

8. Ms. Lopez deposits $100 in an account that pays 20% interest, compounded semiannually. How much money will there be in the account at the end of one year?

   (A) $118.00
   (B) $120.00
   (C) $121.00
   (D) $122.00
   (E) $140.00

Easy Eliminations: Joe Bloggs doesn't know how to find compound interest, so he finds simple interest instead. In a compound-interest problem, always calculate simple interest first. $100 at 20% simple interest for one year would turn into $120, which is answer choice (B). Since compound interest is always a *little bit* more than simple interest, we can eliminate answer choices (A) and (B). Answer choice (E) is a great deal more than simple interest, so we can eliminate it, too. Only answer choices (C) and (D) are a *little bit* more than simple interest. We're down to a fifty-fifty guess.

Here's how to crack it

To find compound interest, divide the interest into as many parts as are being compounded. For example, if you're compounding interest semiannually, you divide the interest into two equal parts. If you're compounding quarterly, you divide the interest into four equal parts.

When Ms. Lopez deposited $100 into her account at a rate of 20% compounded semiannually, the bank divided the interest into two equal parts. Halfway through the year, the bank put the first half of the interest into her account. In this case, since the full rate was 20% compounded semiannually, the bank deposited 10% of $100 (10% of $100 = $10). Halfway through the year, Ms. Lopez had $110.

For the second half of the year, the bank paid 10% interest on the $110 (10% of $110 = $11). At the end of the year, Ms. Lopez had $121.00 in her account. She earned $1 more than she would have earned if the account had paid only simple interest. The answer is choice (C).

Reminder!
Averaging problems often have easy eliminations so be sure to look for them— *before* you solve.

AVERAGES

To find the *average* of a set of *n* numbers, you simply add the numbers and divide by *n*. For example:

$$\text{The average of 10, 3, and 5 is } \frac{10+3+5}{3} = 6$$

A good way to handle average problems is to set them up the same way every time. Whenever you see the word *average*, you should think:

$$\frac{\text{total sum of the items}}{\text{total number of the items}} = \text{average}$$

AN EASY AVERAGE PROBLEM

In a simple problem ETS will give you two parts of this equation, and it will be up to you to figure out the third. For example, ETS might ask:

What is the average of the numbers 3, 4, 5, and 8?

Here's how to crack it:

In this case ETS has given us the actual numbers, which means we know the total sum (3 + 4 + 5 + 8 = 20) and the total number of items (there are four numbers). What we're missing is the average.

$$\frac{\text{total sum of the items}}{\text{total number of the items}} = \text{average} \qquad \frac{20}{4} = x \qquad (x = 5)$$

Or ETS might ask:

If the average of 7 numbers is 5, what is the sum of the numbers?

Here's how to crack it

In this case we know the total number of items and the average, but not the total sum of the numbers.

$$\frac{\text{total sum of the items}}{\text{total number of the items}} = \text{average} \qquad \frac{x}{7} = 5 \qquad (x = 35)$$

A MORE DIFFICULT AVERAGE PROBLEM

This is the same problem you just did, made a little more difficult:

> The average of 7 numbers is 5. If two of the numbers are 11 and 14, what is the average of the remaining numbers?

Here's how to crack it:

Always set up an average problem the way we showed you above—and with more complicated average problems, take things one sentence at a time. Set up correctly, the first sentence says

$$\frac{\text{total sum of the averages}}{\text{total number of the items}} = \text{average} \qquad \frac{x}{7} = 5 \qquad (x = 35)$$

The sum of *all* the numbers is 35. If two of those numbers are 11 and 14, then the sum of the remaining numbers is 35 − (11 + 14), or 10. The question asks "what is the average of the remaining numbers?" Again, let's set this up properly:

$$\frac{\text{total sum of the remaining numbers}}{\text{total number of the remaining numbers}} = \text{average} \qquad \frac{10}{5} = x \qquad (x = 2)$$

Why did we divide the total sum of the remaining numbers by 5? There were only 5 remaining numbers!

MEANS

When ETS talks about an average, the words "arithmetic mean" will often follow in parentheses. This is not just to make the problem sound scarier. Arithmetic mean is the precise term for the process of finding an average that we've illustrated in the problems above.

EXPONENTS

An **exponent** is a short way of writing the value of a number multiplied several times by itself. $4 \times 4 \times 4 \times 4 \times 4$ can also be written as 4^5. This is expressed as "4 to the fifth power." The large number (4) is called the base, and the little number (5) is called the exponent.

There are several rules to remember about exponents:

♦ *Multiplying numbers with the same base:* When you multiply numbers that have the same base, you simply add the exponents.

$$6^2 \times 6^3 = 6^{(2+3)} = 6^5 \qquad (y^4)(y^6) = y^{(4+6)} = y^{10}$$

- *Dividing numbers with the same base:* When you divide numbers that have the same base, you can simply subtract the exponents.

$$\frac{3^6}{3^2} = 3^{(6-2)} = 3^4 \qquad \frac{x^7}{x^4} = x^{(7-4)} = x^3$$

- *Raising a power to a power:* When you raise a power to a power, you can simply multiply the exponents.

$$(4^3)^2 = 4^{(3 \times 2)} = 4^6 \qquad (z^2)^4 = z^{(2 \times 4)} = z^8$$

- *Distributing exponents:* When several numbers are inside parentheses, the exponent outside the parentheses must be distributed to all of the numbers within.

$$(4 \times y)^2 = 4^2 \times y^2$$

There are several operations which *seem* like they ought to work with exponents but don't.

- Does $x^2 + x^3 = x^5$?   NO!
- Does $x^6 - x^2 = x^4$?   NO!

- Does $\dfrac{\left(x^2 + y^2 + z^2\right)}{\left(x^2 + y^2\right)} = z^2$?   NO!

THE STRANGE POWERS OF POWERS

If you raise a positive integer to a power, the number gets larger. For example, $6^2 = 36$. However, raising a number to a power can sometimes have unexpected results:

- If you raise a positive fraction that is less than 1 to a power, the fraction gets *smaller*.

$$\left(\frac{1}{3}\right)^2 = \frac{1}{3} \times \frac{1}{3} = \frac{1}{9}$$

- If you raise a negative number to an odd power, the number gets *smaller*.
  $(-3)^3 = (-3)(-3)(-3) = -27$
  (Remember, –27 is smaller than –3.)

- If you raise a negative number to an even power, the number becomes positive.
  $(-3)^2 = (-3)(-3) = 9$
  (Remember, negative times negative = positive.)

- Any number to the first power = itself.

- Any number to the 0 power = 1.

Strange Powers Revealed!

Why, you might ask, is any number to the 0 power equal to 1, since any other time we multiply by 0 the result is 0? The answer is that we aren't multiplying by 0 at all. Watch closely now: 3(0) should equal 3 (–1) x 3(1), since when you add the exponents you get 3(0). Now, 3(–1) x 3(1) can be rewritten 1/3 x 3 = 3/3 =1. In other words, when a base is raised to the 0 power it means multiply the base by its reciprocal, an operation which will always equal 1.

♦ Any number to the negative power y = the reciprocal of the same number to the positive power y.

For example, $3^{-2} = \dfrac{1}{3^2} = \dfrac{1}{9}$.

Even More Strange Powers

A radical can be rewritten as a fractional exponent, and vice versa. That is, $\sqrt[3]{5} = 5^{\frac{1}{3}}$.

If this all seems a little terrifying, realize that questions which deal with strange powers show up once in a blue moon and only on the very hardest questions.

RADICALS

The square root of a positive number x is the number that, when squared, equals x. For example, the square root of 9 is 3 or –3, because 3 times 3 = 9, or –3 times –3 = 9. However, ETS is interested only in the *positive* square root. So for our purposes the square root of 9 is 3 only. The symbol for a positive square root is $\sqrt{}$. A number inside the $\sqrt{}$ is also called a *radical*.

$$\sqrt{4} = 2$$
$$\sqrt{9} = 3$$

There are several rules to remember about radicals:

1. $\sqrt{x}\sqrt{y} = \sqrt{xy}$. For example, $\sqrt{12}\sqrt{3} = \sqrt{36} = 6$

2. $\sqrt{\dfrac{x}{y}} = \dfrac{\sqrt{x}}{\sqrt{y}}$. For example, $\sqrt{\dfrac{3}{16}} = \dfrac{\sqrt{3}}{\sqrt{16}} = \dfrac{\sqrt{3}}{4}$

3. To simplify a radical, try factoring. For example, $\sqrt{32} = \sqrt{16}\sqrt{2} = 4\sqrt{2}$

4. The square root of a positive fraction less than 1 is actually larger than the original fraction. For example, $\sqrt{\dfrac{1}{4}} = \dfrac{1}{2}$.

SUMMARY

1. The six arithmetic operations are addition, subtraction, multiplication, division, raising to a power, and finding a square root.

2. These operations must be performed in the proper order (**Please Excuse My Dear Aunt Sally**).

3. If you are adding or multiplying a group of numbers, you can regroup them in any order. This is called the associative law.

4. If you are adding or subtracting numbers with common factors, you can regroup them in the following way:

   $$ab + ac = a(b + c)$$
   $$ab - ac = a(b - c)$$

   This is called the distributive law.

5. A fraction can be thought of in two ways:

   ◆ another way of expressing division

   ◆ as a part/whole

6. You must know how to add, subtract, multiply, and divide fractions. You must also know how to raise them to a power and find their roots.

7. Always reduce fractions (when you can) before doing a complicated operation. This will reduce your chances of making a careless error.

8. In tough fraction problems always think *part/whole* and *the rest*.

9. A decimal is just another way of expressing a fraction.

10. You must know how to add, subtract, multiply, and divide decimals.

11. In general it is easier to work with fractions than with decimals, so convert decimals to fractions.

12. A ratio is a fraction in all ways but one:

   $$\text{A fraction is a } \frac{\text{part}}{\text{whole}}. \text{ A ratio is a } \frac{\text{part}}{\text{part}}.$$

   In a ratio, the whole is the sum of all its parts.

13. A percentage is just a fraction whose denominator is always 100.

14. You must know the percentage shortcuts outlined in this chapter.

15. In tough percent problems, like tough fraction problems, think *part/whole* and *the rest*.

16. In a percentage increase or decrease problem, you must put the amount of the increase or decrease over the *original* amount.

17. In compound-interest problems, the answer will always be *a little bit more* than simple interest.

18. To find the average of several values, add the values and divide the total by the number of values.

19. Always set up average problems in the same way:

$$\frac{\text{total sum of the items}}{\text{total number of the items}} = \text{average}$$

20. An exponent is a shorter way of expressing the result of multiplying a number several times by itself.

21. When you multiply numbers with the same base, you simply add the exponents.

22. When you divide numbers with the same base, you simply subtract the exponents.

23. When you raise a power to a power, you multiply the exponents.

24. You *cannot* add or subtract numbers with the same or different bases by adding their exponents.

25. On the GMAT, the square root of a number x is the positive number that when multiplied by itself $= x$.

26. The two radical rules you need to know:

$$\sqrt{x}\sqrt{y} = \sqrt{xy} \qquad \sqrt{\frac{x}{y}} = \frac{\sqrt{x}}{\sqrt{y}}$$

27. There are some unusual features of exponents and radicals:

    a. The square root of a positive fraction less than one is larger than the original fraction.

    b. When you raise a positive fraction less than one to an exponent, the resulting fraction is smaller.

    c. When you raise a negative number to an even exponent, the resulting number is positive.

    d. When you raise a negative number to an odd exponent, the resulting number is still a negative number.

13

Algebra

More than a quarter of the problems in a regular problem-solving section will involve traditional algebra. These problems can often be found in the difficult third of the section, because ETS thinks algebra is difficult.

We don't. In this chapter we'll show you some powerful techniques that will enable you to solve these problems without using traditional algebra. The first half of this chapter will discuss these new techniques. The second half will show you how to do the few algebra problems that must be tackled algebraically.

NOT EXACTLY ALGEBRA: BASIC PRINCIPLES

There are certain problems in math that aren't meant to have just one specific number as an answer. Here's an example:

> What is two more than 3 times a certain number x?

To find *one* specific number that answers this question, we would need to know the value of that "certain number x." Here's the way ETS would ask the same question:

1. What is two more than 3 times a certain number x?

   (A) $3x - 2$
   (B) $3x$
   (C) $2x - 3$
   (D) $2x + 3$
   (E) $3x + 2$

Cosmic Problems

In other words, this is kind of a cosmic problem. ETS is asking you to write an equation that will answer this question no matter what the "certain number" is. x could be *any* number, and that equation would still give you the correct answer.

ETS expects you to use algebra to answer this question, but there is a better way. Since the correct answer will work for *every* value of x, why not just pick *one* value for x?

We call this **plugging in.** Plugging in is easy. There are three steps involved:

1. Pick numbers for the letters in the problem.

2. Using your numbers, find an answer to the problem.

3. Plug your numbers into the answer choices to see which choice equals the answer you found in Step 2.

Let's look at that same problem again:

1. What is two more than 3 times a certain number x?

   (A) $3x - 2$
   (B) $3x$
   (C) $2x - 3$
   (D) $2x + 3$
   (E) $3x + 2$

Here's how to crack it:

Let's pick a number for x. How about 4? In your test booklet, write in "$x = 4$" above the x in the problem. By substituting 4 for the x, we now have a specific rather than a cosmic problem. The question now reads,

"What is two more than 3 times 4?"

$3 \times 4 = 12$.

What is 2 more than 12?

14.

Using the number we chose for x, the answer to this question is 14. Write 14 in the margin next to the question and circle it. All you need to do now is figure out which of the answer choices equals 14 when you substitute 4 for x.

> When you're plugging in, always start with answer choice (A).
> If that doesn't work, try choice (E), then (B), then (D), then (C).
> In other words, start from the outside and work toward the center.

Let's start with choice (A) $3x - 2$. Plugging in 4 for x, do we get 14? No, we get 10. Eliminate.

Go to choice (E) $3x + 2$. Plugging in 4 for x, we get $12 + 2$, or 14. This is the answer we wanted. Choice (E) is the correct answer to this question.

You might be thinking, "Wait a minute. It was just as easy to solve this problem algebraically. Why should I plug in?" There are two answers:

1. This was an easy problem. Plugging in makes even difficult problems easy.

2. ETS has spent hours coming up with all the possible ways you might screw this problem up using algebra. If you make one of these mistakes, your answer will be among the answer choices, and you will pick it and get it wrong.

THERE ARE THREE KINDS OF COSMIC PROBLEMS — AND YOU CAN PLUG IN ON ALL OF THEM

A cosmic problem is any problem in which the answer choices are not specific numbers. You can plug in if you see:

1. variables in the answer choices

2. percents in the answer choices (when they are percents of some unspecified amount)

3. fractions or ratios in the answer choices (when they are fractional parts or ratios of unspecified amounts)

VARIABLES IN THE ANSWERS

ETS wants you to use algebra on problems that have variables in the answers, but plugging in is easier, faster, and less likely to produce errors. Here's an example:

10. At a photocopy center, the first 10 copies cost x cents each. Each of the next 50 copies costs 5 cents less per copy. From the 61st copy on, the cost is 2 cents per copy. In terms of x, how much does it cost in cents to have 200 copies made?

(A) $60x + 30$
(B) $50x - 10$
(C) $50(x - 5)$
(D) $60x - 110$
(E) $10x + 490$

Here's how to crack it

Pick a number for x. How about 8?

The first 10 copies = 10×8 = <u>80 cents</u>

The next 50 copies each cost 5 cents less than the first 10, so each of these copies cost $8 - 5$ or 3 cents each.

The next 50 copies = 50×3 = <u>150 cents</u>

From now on, the cost is 2 cents for any additional copies. We need a total of 200 copies. So far we've done 60 copies. We need an additional 140 copies.

The final 140 copies = 140×2 = <u>280 cents</u>

Let's add it all up.

$$
\begin{array}{r}
80 \text{ cents} \\
150 \text{ cents} \\
+ \underline{280 \text{ cents}} \\
510 \text{ cents}
\end{array}
$$

This is the answer to the question. All we have to do is find out which answer choice equals 510. Start with choice (A) $60x + 30$, and remember that we plugged in 8 for x. Does $60(8) + 30 = 510$? Yes, it does. The answer to this question is choice (A). (Try the other choices if you're not convinced.)

WHAT NUMBER SHOULD I PLUG IN?

A cosmic problem is designed to work with any number, but you'll find that certain numbers work better than others. Plugging in a number that's simple to use is obviously a good idea. In general you should stick to small numbers. But if the problem concerns hours and days, it might make sense to pick 24. If the problem concerns minutes and hours, a good number would probably be 60.

Avoid 0 and 1, and numbers that are already in the problem or the answer choices. Why? If you plug in one of these numbers, you may find that more than one answer choice appears to be correct.

Plugging numbers into a problem is much more natural to most folks' way of thinking than algebra. Has anyone ever asked a bartender, "Say, could I get $2x$ shots of whiskey, where x equals a standard shot?" The bartender might comply, but you can be sure he'd ask for your car keys first. Complicate the question with y, the ounces of alcohol in a standard shot, and z, the number of ice cubes in the glass, and you've got a real headache. Essentially, plugging in is a matter of putting numbers back into a form you are used to working with.

When deciding what number or numbers to plug in, the question to ask is: "What numbers make this problem easy for myself?"

Sometimes the best way to select a number is to use a little common sense. Here's an example:

12. If Jim can drive the distance k miles in 50 minutes, how many minutes, in terms of k, will it take him to drive 10 miles at the same speed?

(A) $\dfrac{500}{k}$

(B) $\dfrac{k}{50}$

(C) $60k$

(D) $10k$

(E) $\dfrac{50}{k}$

Here's how to crack it

ETS wants you to write a complicated equation based on the formula rate × time = distance, or perhaps set up a proportion. But this isn't necessary. Because there are variables in the answer choices, you can simply plug in.

Any number you choose to plug in for k will eventually give you the answer to this problem, but there are some numbers that will make your task even easier.

If it takes Jim 50 minutes to drive k *miles*, how long will it take him to drive *10 miles* at the same rate?

We need a number for k. What if we made k = half of 10? See how the question reads now:

If it takes Jim 50 minutes to drive 5 miles, how long will it take him to drive 10 miles at the same rate?

Suddenly the problem is simple. It will take him twice as long: 100 minutes. Now all we need to know is which of the answer choices equals 100, given that $k = 5$. Start with answer choice (A). Divide 500 by 5 and you have 100.

The answer to this question is choice (A).

PERCENTS IN THE ANSWERS

ETS wants you to use algebra on certain problems where there are percents in the answers, but plugging in is easier, and less likely to produce errors. Here's an example:

13. A merchant was selling an item at a certain price, then marked it down 20% for a spring sale. During the summer, he marked the item down another 20% from its spring price. If the item sold at the summer price, what percent of the original price did it sell for?

(A) 40%
(B) 60%
(C) 64%
(D) 67%
(E) 80%

No, *Really*, I Like Algebra

If you're comfortable with algebra, great, it'll come in very handy, but don't think that knowing algebra means you can ignore plugging in. It *will* improve your score. Make it your rule to plug in on every question you can. The technique requires some practice. Plug in on easier questions you might have solved algebraically so that when faced with medium and difficult questions plugging in comes naturally.

Q: If 80% of a certain number x is 50% of y and y is 20% of z then what is x in terms of z?

(A) $5z$

(B) $3z$

(C) $z/4$

(D) $z/5$

(E) $z/8$

Easy Eliminations: This is a difficult question. The first thing to do here is eliminate any answers that are too good to be true. The number 20 appears twice in this problem. Adding them together gives you answer choice (A). Eliminate choice (A). Joe's favorite answer is probably choice (B). Joe reasons that if an item is discounted 20% and then another 20%, there must be 60% left. Eliminate choice (B). Choice (E) seems too large. The answer is probably choice (C) or (D).

Here's how to crack it

You may have noticed that while this problem gave us lots of information, it never told us how much the item sold for originally. This is another cosmic problem. ETS wants you to write an equation that will work regardless of the original price of the item. But since this problem is supposed to work for *any* original amount, we may as well pick *one* amount.

Let's plug in 100. *When you are dealing with a percent problem, 100 is usually a convenient number.* The merchant was selling the item for $100. He discounted it by 20% for the spring sale. 20% of $100 is $20, so the spring price was $80. For the summer, he discounted it again, by 20% of the spring price. 20% of $80 is $16. Therefore he took $20 and then $16 off the original price. The summer price is $64.

The question asks what percent of the original price the item sold for. It sold for $64. What percent of 100 is 64? 64%. The answer is choice (C).

FRACTIONS OR RATIOS IN THE ANSWERS

ETS wants you to use traditional math on certain problems with fractions or ratios in the answer choices, but plugging in is easier, faster, and less likely to produce errors. Here's an example:

10. Half the graduating class of a college was accepted by a business school. One-third of the class was accepted by a law school. If one-fifth of the class was accepted to both types of school, what fraction of the class was accepted only by a law school?

(A) $\dfrac{1}{60}$

(B) $\dfrac{2}{15}$

(C) $\dfrac{1}{3}$

(D) $\dfrac{1}{2}$

(E) $\dfrac{4}{5}$

Here's how to crack it

You may have noticed that while this problem gave us lots of fractions to work with, it never told us how many people were in the graduating class. This is yet another cosmic problem. ETS wants you to find a fractional *part* without knowing what the specific *whole* is. Since this problem is supposed to work with *any* number of people in the graduating class, we may as well pick *one* number.

This problem will work with any number, but some numbers are easier to work with than others. For example, if we chose 47 for the number of people in the graduating class, that would mean that $23\frac{1}{2}$ people were accepted by a business school; while this might make a good plot for a Stephen King novel, wouldn't it be easier to pick a number that can be divided evenly by all the fractions in the problem? One number that is evenly divisible by 2, 3, and 5 is 30. So let's plug in 30 for the number of people in the graduating class.

One half of the class got into business school.

$$\left(\frac{1}{2} \text{ of } 30 = 15\right)$$

One third of the class got into law school.

$$\left(\frac{1}{3} \text{ of } 30 = 10\right)$$

One fifth of the class got into both.

$$\left(\frac{1}{5} \text{ of } 30 = 6\right)$$

ETS wants to know what fraction of the class was accepted only by a law school. Ten people were accepted by a law school, but 6 of those 10 were also accepted by a business school. Therefore 4 people out of 30 were accepted only by a law school. Reduced, $\frac{4}{30}$ is $\frac{2}{15}$, so the answer is choice (B).

WORKING BACKWARD

Any cosmic algebra problem can be solved, as we have seen, by plugging in numbers. But not all algebra problems are cosmic. What about a problem that asks for a specific numeric answer?

> A company's profits have doubled for each of the 4 years it has been in existence. If the total profits for those 4 years were $30 million, what were the profits in the first year of operation?

There is only one number in the whole world that will answer this question. If you tried plugging in amounts for the first year of operation in hopes of happening upon the correct answer, you would be busy for a very, very long time.

ETS expects you to use algebra to answer this question. They want you to assign a variable for the first year's profits, say x, in which case the second year's profits would be $2x$, the third year's profits would be $4x$, and the fourth year's profits would be $8x$. Altogether, we get $15x = 30$, and $x = 2$.

Unfortunately, it is extremely easy to make a mistake when you set up an equation. You could add up the number of x's incorrectly, or think that the profits of the third year were equal to $3x$. While this is not a difficult problem, it does represent the potential difficulties of using algebra.

ETS expects you to use algebra to answer this question, but *there is a better way*. Each time ETS asks you to find a specific numeric answer, they are forced to give you five clues. Here is how ETS would ask this question:

7. A company's profits have doubled for each of the 4 years it has been in existence. If the total profits for the last 4 years were $30 million, what were the profits in the first year of operation?

    (A) $1 million
    (B) $2 million
    (C) $4 million
    (D) $4.5 million
    (E) $6 million

Here's how to crack it

Without answer choices this problem is complicated, and the only way to solve it is to use algebra. Now, however, there are only five possible answers. One of them has to be correct. Why not **work backward** from the answer choices?

Working backward is easy. There are three steps involved:

1. Always start with answer choice (C). Plug that number into the problem and see whether it makes the problem work.

2. If choice (C) is too small, choose the next larger number.

3. If choice (C) is too big, choose the next smaller number.

Numeric answers on the GMAT are always given in order of size (with one or two rare exceptions that we'll discuss in the geometry chapter). Therefore when you're working backward, always start with answer choice (C). Plug that number into the problem and see whether it works. If it does, you've already found the answer. If it's too big, you can try a lower number. If it's too small, try a larger number.

Let's try answer choice (C).

If the first year's profits were	$4 million	
the second year's profits would be	$8 million	
the third year's profits would be	$16 million	
and the fourth year's profits would be	<u>$32 million</u>	
the total profits =	$60 million	

This is too big. The total profits were only $30 million. We don't even have to look at choice (D) or (E), which are even bigger. We can eliminate choices (C), (D), and (E).

Let's try answer choice (B).

If the first year's profits were	$2 million
the second year's profits would be	$4 million
the third year's profits would be	$8 million
and the fourth year's profits would be	<u>$16 million</u>
the total profits =	$30 million

Bingo! The correct answer is choice (B). Note that if choice (B) had been too big, the only possible answer would have been choice (A).

WHEN TO WORK BACKWARD

You can work backward as long as:

A. The answer choices are numbers.

B. The question is relatively straightforward. For example, it's easy to work backward on a question that asks, "What is x?" It's difficult and not worth the bother to work backward on a problem that asks, "What is $(x + y)$?"

> 5. If x is a positive number such that $x^2 + 5x - 14 = 0$, what is the value of x?
>
> (A) −7
> (B) −5
> (C) 0
> (D) 2
> (E) 5

Here's how to crack it

There is only one number in the world that will make this problem work, and fortunately it has to be one of the five answer choices. Let's work backward. Start with choice (C). (Zero squared) plus (zero times 5) minus 14 does *not* equal 0. Eliminate. We don't have to try choice (A) or (B) because the problem asks for a positive number. Let's try choice (D). (Two squared) plus (5 times 2)—we're up to 14 so far—minus 14 *does* equal 0. The answer is choice (D).

> **Easy Eliminations:** Obviously, if x is a positive number, choices (A), (B), and (C) are out of the question.

WORKING BACKWARD: ADVANCED PRINCIPLES

Sometimes when you're working backward you'll be able to eliminate choice (C), but you may not be sure whether you need a larger number or a smaller one.

Q: If Patrick reads twice as much as Bob but only 1/2 as much as Amy and Doug reads as much as all three others put together, how many books did Bob read last week if Doug read 7 books?

(A) 1/4 book
(B) 1/2 book
(C) 1 book
(D) 2 books
(E) 4 books

Rather than waste time trying to decide, just try all the answer choices until you hit the right one. You'll never have to try more than four of them.

10. Today Jim is twice as old as Fred, and Sam is 2 years younger than Fred. Four years ago Jim was 4 times as old as Sam. How old is Jim now?

   (A) 8
   (B) 12
   (C) 16
   (D) 20
   (E) 24

Here's how to crack it

One of these five answer choices is the right answer.

Let's work backward.

Start with choice (C). Jim is 16 years old today. He is twice as old as Fred, so Fred is 8. Sam is 2 years younger than Fred, so Sam is 6. Therefore, 4 years ago Jim was 12 and Sam was 2. If these numbers agree with the rest of the problem, then choice (C) is the answer to this question. The problem says that four years ago Jim was 4 times as old as Sam. Does 12 times 4 equal 2? No. Choice (C) is the wrong answer. Does anybody want to guess which direction to go in now? Rather than hem and haw, just try the other answers until you get the right one.

Let's try choice (D). Jim is 20 years old today. He is twice as old as Fred, so Fred is 10. Sam is 2 years younger than Fred, so Sam is 8. Therefore, four years ago Jim was 16 and Sam was 4. If these numbers agree with the rest of the problem choice (D) is the right answer. The problem says that four years ago Jim was 4 times as old as Sam. Does 4 times 4 equal 16? Yes. The answer is choice (D).

MUST BE/COULD BE

From time to time ETS will write a question that contains the words "must be," "could be," or "cannot be." This type of problem can almost always be solved by plugging in, *but you may need to plug in more than one number*. Here's an example:

5. If x and y are consecutive integers, which of the following must be an even integer?

   (A) x
   (B) y
   (C) $\dfrac{xy}{2}$
   (D) $\dfrac{x}{y}$
   (E) xy

Here's how to crack it

Plug in numbers for x and y. How about 2 for x and 3 for y? Now go through each of the answer choices. Using these numbers, choice (A) is even, but because of the words *"must be,"* we cannot assume that it will *always* be even, or that this is necessarily the right answer. Keep going. Using the numbers we plugged in, choices (B), (C), and (D) turn out to be odd. Since the question asks us for an answer that is *always* even, we can eliminate all of these. However, choice (E) is also even. We're down to either choice (A) or (E). Which is correct?

Try plugging in a different set of numbers. The problem concerns even and odd numbers, so this time let's try an odd number first. How about 3 and 4? This time choice (A) is odd. Eliminate. Choice (E) is still even; this must be our answer.

BASIC ALGEBRA

Plugging in and working backward will take care of most of your algebraic needs, but there are a few other types of problems that require some knowledge of basic algebra. After reading the rest of this chapter and working out the problems contained in it, if you still feel rusty, you might want to dig out your old high-school algebra book.

SOLVING EQUALITIES

Even the simplest equalities can be solved by working backward, but it's probably easier to solve a *simple* equation algebraically. If there is one variable in an equation, isolate the variable on one side of the equation and solve it. Here's an example:

3. If $x - 5 = 3x + 2$, then $x =$

(A) -8

(B) $-\dfrac{7}{2}$

(C) -7

(D) $\dfrac{10}{3}$

(E) $\dfrac{7}{5}$

Here's how to crack it

Get all of the xs on one side of the equation. If we subtract x from both sides we have:

$$\begin{array}{rcl} x - 5 & = & 3x + 2 \\ -x & & -x \\ \hline -5 & = & 2x + 2 \end{array}$$

Now subtract 2 from both sides:

$$\begin{array}{rcl} -5 & = & 2x + 2 \\ -2 & & -2 \\ \hline -7 & = & 2x \end{array}$$

Ancient History
The first record of algebra was found on an Egyptian papyrus dating from approximately 1700 BC.

Finally, divide both sides by 2:

$$\frac{-7}{2} = \frac{2x}{2}$$

$x = -\frac{7}{2}$. The answer is choice (B).

The Solvability Rule

You must have at least as many distinct equations as you have variables for the equations to be solvable. That is, if you are trying to figure out what x, y, and z are, you need at least three distinct equations.

SOLVING INEQUALITIES

To solve inequalities, you must be able to recognize the following symbols:

> is greater than

< is less than

≥ is greater than or equal to

≤ is less than or equal to

As with an equation, you can add or subtract a number to both sides of an inequality without changing it; you can collect similar terms and simplify them.

In fact, an inequality behaves just like a regular equation except in one way: *If you multiply or divide both sides of an equality by a negative number, the direction of the inequality symbol changes*. For example,

$$-2x > 5$$

To solve for x, you would divide both sides by –2, just as you would in an equality. But when you do, the sign flips:

$$\frac{-2x}{-2} < \frac{5}{-2} \qquad x < -\frac{5}{2}$$

SOLVING SIMULTANEOUS EQUATIONS

It's impossible to solve one equation with two variables. But if there are two equations, both of which have the same two variables, then it is possible to solve for both variables. An easy problem might look like this:

If $3x + 2y = 6$ and $5x - 2y = 10$ then $x = ?$

To solve simultaneous equations, add or subtract the equations so that one of the variables disappears.

$$\begin{aligned} 3x + 2y &= 6 \\ 5x - 2y &= 10 \\ \hline 8x &= 16 \qquad x = 2 \end{aligned}$$

In more difficult simultaneous equations, you'll find that neither of the variables will disappear when you try to add or subtract the two equations. In such cases you must multiply both sides of one of the equations by some number in order to get the coefficient in front of the variable you want to disappear to be the same in both equations. This sounds more complicated than it is. A difficult problem might look like this:

If $3x + 2y = 6$ and $5x - y = 10$, then $x = ?$

Let's set it up the same way:

$$3x + 2y = 6$$
$$5x - y = 10$$

Unfortunately, in this example neither adding nor subtracting the two equations gets rid of either variable. But look what happens when we multiply the bottom equation by 2:

$$3x + 2y = 6 \qquad \text{or} \qquad 3x + 2y = 6$$
$$(2)5x - (2)y = (2)10 \qquad\qquad \underline{+ 10x - 2y = 20}$$
$$13x \qquad = 26 \quad x = 2$$

Q: Are the following equations distinct?
(1) $3x + 21y = 12$
(2) $x + 7y = 4$

QUADRATIC EQUATIONS

On the GMAT, quadratic equations always come in one of two forms: factored or unfactored. Here's an example:

$$\underset{\text{factored}}{(x + 2)(x + 5)} = \underset{\text{unfactored}}{x^2 + 7x + 10}$$

The trick to solving a problem that involves a quadratic equation is to see which form the equation is in. If the quadratic equation is in an unfactored form, factor it immediately. If the quadratic equation is in a factored form, unfactor it. ETS likes to see whether you know how to do these things.

To unfactor a factored expression, just multiply it out:

$$(x + 2)(x + 5) = (x + 2)(x + 5)$$
$$= (x \text{ times } x) + (x \text{ times } 5) + (2 \text{ times } x) + (2 \text{ times } 5)$$
$$= x^2 + 5x + 2x + 10$$
$$= x^2 + 7x + 10$$

To factor an unfactored expression, put it into the following format and start by looking for the factors of the first and last terms.

$$x^2 + 2x - 15$$
$$= (\quad)(\quad)$$
$$= (x \quad)(x \quad)$$
$$= (x \quad 5)(x \quad 3)$$
$$= (x + 5)(x - 3)$$

Quadratic equations are usually set equal to 0. Here's an example:

4. What are all the values of x that satisfy the equation
    $x^2 + 4x + 3 = 0$?

    (A) −3
    (B) −1
    (C) −3 and −1
    (D) 3 and 4
    (E) 4

Here's how to crack it

This problem contains an unfactored equation, so let's factor it.

$$
\begin{aligned}
x^2 + 4x + 3 &= 0 \\
(x \quad)(x \quad) &= 0 \\
(x \quad 3)(x \quad 1) &= 0 \\
(x + 3)(x + 1) &= 0
\end{aligned}
$$

In order for this equation to be correct, x must be either −3 or −1. The correct answer is choice (C).

Note: This problem would also have been easy to solve by working backward. It asked a specific question, and there were five specific answer choices. One of them was correct. All you had to do was try the choices until you found the right one. Bear in mind, however, that in a quadratic equation there are usually two values that will make the equation work.

FETISHES OF GMAT TEST WRITERS

There are two types of quadratic equations the test writers at ETS find endlessly fascinating. These equations appear on the GMAT with great regularity, both in the regular math sections and the Data Sufficiency section.

$$
\begin{aligned}
(x + y)^2 &= x^2 + 2xy + y^2 \\
(x + y)(x - y) &= x^2 - y^2
\end{aligned}
$$

Memorize both of these. As with all quadratic equations, if ETS presents the equation in factored form, you should immediately unfactor it; if it's unfactored, factor it immediately.

5. If $\dfrac{x^2 - 4}{x + 2} = 5$, then $x =$

    (A) 3
    (B) 5
    (C) 6
    (D) 7
    (E) 9

A: No. Look at what equation #2 looks like multiplied by 3.
$3 (x+7y) = 3 (4)$
or $3x + 21y = 12$.
Multiply both sides by 3 and equation #1 and #2 are identical.
When one equation can be multiplied to produce the other, the equations are identical, not distinct.

Here's how to crack it

This problem contains one of ETS's fetishes. It is unfactored, so let's factor it:

$$\frac{(x+2)(x-2)}{(x+2)} = 5$$

The $(x + 2)$s cancel out, leaving us with $(x - 2) = 5$. $x = 7$ and the answer is choice (D).

RATE × TIME = DISTANCE

Any problem that mentions planes, trains, cars, bicycles, distance, miles per hour, or any other travel-related terminology is asking you to write an equation based on the formula *rate × time = distance*. This formula is easy to reconstruct if you forget it; just think of a real-life situation. If you drove at 50 miles per hour for 2 hours, how far did you go? That's right, 100 miles. We just derived the formula. The rate is 50 miles per hour. The time is 2 hours. The distance is 100 miles.

8. Pam and Sue drove to a business meeting 120 miles away in the same car. Pam drove to the meeting and Sue drove back along the same route. If Pam drove at 60 miles per hour and Sue drove at 50 miles per hour, how much longer, in minutes, did it take Sue to travel the distance than it did Pam?

   (A) 4
   (B) 10
   (C) 20
   (D) 24
   (E) 30

Here's how to crack it

As soon as you see the words "drove" and "travel," make a little chart for yourself:

$$R \times T = D$$

Pam _____

Sue _____

> $R \times T = D$ can also be written
> $T = D/R$
> $R = D/T$
> It may sometimes be easier, or faster, to start from one of the variations, but if you aren't sure, begin with the standard $R \times T = D$.

The problem says the meeting was 120 miles away from wherever they started. This tells us not only how far Pam drove but how far Sue drove as well, since she returned along the same route. We are also given the rates of both women.

Let's fill in the chart with the information we have:

$$R \times T = D$$

Pam $\quad 60 \times ? = 120$

Sue $\quad 50 \times ? = 120$

60 times what equals 120? It took Pam 2 hours to drive to the meeting. 50 times

what equals 120? It took Sue 2.4 hours to drive back from the meeting. Sue took .4 hours longer, but the problem asks for the answer in minutes. .4 equals $\frac{4}{10}$ or $\frac{2}{5}$. There are 60 minutes in an hour, so just find $\frac{2}{5}$ of 60. The answer is choice (D), 24 minutes.

WORK PROBLEMS

Another type of GMAT problem that requires an equation is the work problem. These are easy to spot because they always involve two people (or factories or machines) working at different rates. In these problems the trick is not to think about how long it takes to do an entire job, but rather how much of the job can be done in *one hour*.

7. If Sam can finish a job in 3 hours and Mark can finish a job in 12 hours, in how many hours could they finish the job if they worked on it together at their respective rates?

   (A) 1

   (B) $2\frac{2}{5}$

   (C) $2\frac{5}{8}$

   (D) $3\frac{1}{4}$

   (E) 4

Here's how to crack it

If Sam can finish a job in 3 hours, then in one hour he can finish $\frac{1}{3}$ of the job. If Mark can finish a job in 12 hours, then in one hour he can finish $\frac{1}{12}$ of the job. Working together, how much of the job can they do in one hour?

$$\frac{1}{3} + \frac{1}{12} = \frac{1}{x}$$

Now we only need to solve for x. First find a common denominator for $\frac{1}{3}$ and $\frac{1}{12}$.

$$\frac{1}{3} + \frac{1}{12} = \frac{1}{x}$$
$$\frac{4}{12} + \frac{1}{12} = \frac{1}{x}$$
$$= \frac{5}{12} = \frac{1}{x}$$

Cross-multiply and divide. $x = 2\frac{2}{5}$. The answer is choice (B).

> **Easy Eliminations:** It stands to reason that two men working together would take less time to finish a job than they would if each of them worked alone. Since Sam, working alone, could finish the job in 3 hours, it must be true that the two of them, working together, could do it in less time. The answer to this question has to be less than 3. Therefore we can eliminate answer choices (D) and (E).

FUNCTIONS

You'll know you've hit a function problem by the sensation of panic and fear you get when you see some strange symbol ($ or # or * or Δ) and say, "I studied for two months for this test and somehow managed to miss the part where they told me about $ or # or * or Δ." Relax. Any strange-looking symbol on the GMAT is just a function, and on this test functions are easy.

A function is basically a set of directions. Let's look at an example:

If $x * y = 3x - y$, then what is 4 * 2?

What the first half of this problem says is that for any two numbers with a * in between, you must multiply the number on the left by 3 and then subtract the number on the right. These are the directions. The second half of the problem asks you to use these directions with two specific numbers: 4 * 2.

To solve this problem, all we need to do is plug the specific numbers into the set of directions:

$$x * y = 3x - y$$
$$4 * 2 = 3(4) - (2)$$
$$= 12 - 2$$
$$= 10$$

Functions don't always involve two numbers. Sometimes they look like this:

13. If $\Delta x = x$ if x is positive, or $2x$ if x is negative, what is $\dfrac{\Delta 30}{\Delta -5}$?
    (A) −12
    (B) −6
    (C) −3
    (D) 6
    (E) 30

If you can follow a recipe, you can do an ETS function problem. Because function questions freak so many people out they often show up in the medium to difficult area of a section. If you can become comfortable with function problems, you'll pick up a point on a question in a portion of the test you might otherwise avoid.

Let's take this one step at a time. In this case the directions say that the function of any number x is simply that same number x, if x is positive. However, if the number x is negative, then the function of that number is $2x$. Thus:

$$\frac{\Delta 30}{\Delta -5} = \frac{30}{2(-5)} = \frac{30}{-10} \text{ or } -3 \text{ . The answer is choice (C).}$$

Don't Ignore the Function!

Joe Bloggs always tries to solve function problems as if the function just didn't exist. Eliminate answers to function problems that do this.

Easy Eliminations: Joe has no idea what to do with Δ, so he just ignores it. Because $\dfrac{30}{-5} = -6$, Joe picks answer choice (B). On the other hand, Joe might also think he can reduce functions. In other words, he might think he could do this:

$$\frac{\Delta 30}{\Delta -5} = \Delta - 6$$

The function of $-6 = -12$, so Joe might also select answer choice (A).

SUMMARY

1. Most of the algebra problems on the GMAT are simpler to solve *without* algebra, using two Princeton Review techniques: *plugging in* and *working backward*.

2. Plugging in will work on any cosmic problem; that is, any problem that does not include specific numbers in the answer choices. You can always plug in if you see

   - variables in the answer choices
   - fractional parts in the answer choices
   - ratios in the answer choices

   You can usually plug in when you see

   - percentages in the answer choices

3. Plugging in is easy. There are three steps:

   a. Pick numbers for the variables in the problem.

   b. Using your numbers, find an answer to the problem.

   c. Plug your numbers into the answer choices to see which choice equals the answer you found in Step 2.

4. When you plug in, try to choose convenient numbers—those that are simple to work with and make the problem easier to manipulate.

5. When you plug in, avoid choosing 0 or 1, or a number that already appears in the problem or in the answer choices.

6. On problems with variables in the answers that contain the words "must be" or "could be," you may have to plug in more than once to find the correct answer.

7. Working backward will solve algebra problems that are *not* cosmic—in other words, problems that are highly specific. You can always work backward on an algebra problem if the answer choices contain specific numbers, and if the question being asked is relatively straightforward.

8. Working backward is easy. There are three steps:

   a. Always start with answer choice (C). Plug that number into the problem and see whether it makes the problem work.

   b. If choice (C) is too small, choose the next larger number.

   c. If choice (C) is too big, choose the next smaller number.

9. If you see a problem with a quadratic equation in factored form, the easiest way to get the answer is to unfactor the equation immediately. If the equation is unfactored, factor it immediately.

10. Memorize the factored and unfactored forms of the two most common quadratic equations on the GMAT:

$$(x + y)^2 = x^2 + 2xy + y^2$$
$$(x + y)(x - y) = x^2 - y^2$$

11. On problems containing inequalities, remember that when you multiply or divide both sides of an inequality by a negative number, the sign flips.

12. In solving simultaneous equations, add or subtract one equation to or from another so that one of the two variables disappears.

13. Any travel-related problem is probably concerned with the formula **rate × time = distance**.

14. The key to work problems is to think about how much of the job can be done in one hour.

15. Function problems have strange symbols like $, Δ, or *, but they are really just a set of directions.

14

Geometry

Fewer than a quarter of the problems in a regular problem-solving section will involve geometry. While this tends to be the math subject most people remember least from high school, the good news is that the GMAT tests only a small portion of the geometry you used to know. It will be relatively easy to refresh your memory.

The bad news is that unlike the SAT, the GMAT does not provide you with the formulas and terms you'll need to solve the problems. You'll have to memorize them.

The first half of this chapter will show you how to eliminate answer choices on certain geometry problems without using traditional geometry. The second half will review all the geometry you need to know in order to answer the problems that must be solved using more traditional methods.

CRAZY ANSWERS

Eliminating choices that don't make sense has already proven to be a valuable technique on arithmetic and algebra questions. On geometry questions you can develop this technique into a science. The reason for this is that many geometry problems come complete with a diagram *drawn to scale*.

Most people get so caught up in solving a geometry problem geometrically that they forget to look at the diagram to see whether their answer is reasonable.

CRAZY ANSWERS ON EASY QUESTIONS

How big is angle x?

Obviously you don't know exactly how big this angle is, but it would be easy to compare it with an angle whose measure you *do* know exactly. Let's compare it with a 90-degree angle:

Angle x is less than 90 degrees. How much less? It looks as though it's about half of a 90-degree angle, or 45 degrees. Now look at the following problem, which asks about the same angle x:

When they give you a scale drawing, use it. You can almost always come up with an approximate answer.

3. In the figure above, if $BC = CD$, and angle $ADC = 90$ degrees, then what is the value of x?

(A) 45
(B) 50
(C) 70
(D) 75
(E) 100

Here's how to crack it

This is an easy problem, but before you launch into solving it, it's still a good idea to take a moment to decide whether any of the answer choices are clearly out of the question. We've already decided that angle x is less than 90 degrees, which means that answer choice (E) can be eliminated. How much less is it? Well, we estimated before that it was about half, which rules out answer choices (C) and (D) as well.

There is another way to eliminate choices (C) and (D). We can compare angle x with the other marked angle in the problem—angle DBC. If the answer to this problem is choice (C), then angle x should look exactly the same as angle DBC. Does it? No. Angle x looks a little bit smaller than angle DBC, which means that both choices (C) and (D) can be eliminated.

Eliminating crazy answers will prevent you from making careless mistakes on easy problems. (By the way, we'll show you how to solve this problem using geometry later in the chapter.)

CRAZY ANSWERS ON DIFFICULT QUESTIONS

If it's important to cross off crazy answer choices on easy questions, it's even more important to eliminate crazy answer choices when you're tackling a *difficult* geometry problem. On a difficult problem, you may not know how to find the answer geometrically, and even if you do, you could still fall victim to one of the traps ETS has placed in your path. Take a look at the following difficult geometry problem:

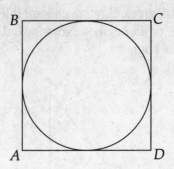

14. In the figure above, circle C is inscribed inside square ABCD as shown. What is the ratio of the area of circle C to the area of square ABCD?

(A) $\dfrac{\pi}{2}$

(B) $\dfrac{4}{\pi}$

(C) $\dfrac{\pi}{3}$

(D) $\dfrac{\pi}{4}$

(E) $\dfrac{2}{\pi}$

Here's how to crack it

This is a difficult problem, and it's worth noting that you didn't need to do this one at all. You can get a good score on the GMAT by skipping difficult questions entirely. But before you decide not to do this problem, let's see whether you can eliminate any of the answer choices just by looking at the diagram and using some common sense.

The problem asks you for the ratio of the area of the circle to the area of the square. Just by looking at the diagram, you can tell that the circle is smaller than the square. The correct answer to this question has to be the ratio of a smaller number to a bigger number. Let's look at the answer choices.

In choice (A), the ratio is π over 2. An approximate value of π is 3.14, so this really reads

$$\frac{3.14}{2}$$

Is this the ratio of a smaller number to a bigger number? Just the opposite. Therefore choice (A) is a crazy answer. Eliminate.

In choice (B), the ratio is 4 over π. This really reads

$$\frac{4}{3.14}$$

Is this the ratio of a smaller number to a bigger number? No. Choice (B) is a crazy answer. Eliminate.

In choice (C), the ratio is π over 3. This really reads

$$\frac{3.14}{3}$$

Is this the ratio of a smaller number to a bigger number? No. Choice (C) is a crazy answer. Eliminate.

Answer choices (D) and (E) both contain ratios of smaller numbers to bigger numbers, so they're both still possibilities. However, we've eliminated three of the answer choices without doing any math. If you know how to solve the problem geometrically, then proceed. If not, guess and move on. (By the way, we will show you how to solve this problem using geometry later in the chapter.)

THE BASIC TOOLS

In eliminating crazy answers, it helps to have the following approximations memorized.

$$\pi \approx 3$$
$$\sqrt{1} = 1$$
$$\sqrt{2} \approx 1.4$$
$$\sqrt{3} \approx 1.7$$
$$\sqrt{4} = 2$$

It's also useful to have a feel for the way certain common angles look:

GETTING MORE PRECISE

When a geometry problem has a diagram drawn to scale, you can get even more precise in eliminating wrong answer choices.

How?

By measuring the diagram.

The instructions at the beginning of each problem-solving section say that unless a diagram is marked "not drawn to scale," it is drawn "as accurately as possible." ETS finds it possible to draw diagrams very accurately indeed. All you need now is something with which to measure the diagram. Fortunately the folks at ETS provide you with a ruler—your answer sheet. The computer that scores your answer sheet will be very interested in the left and right edges (the markings there tell the computer what page it's scanning) and in the bulk of the page where you mark down your answer choices, but it doesn't scan the top or bottom edges of the answer sheet. You can use one of these edges to construct a ruler.

Look at the problem below:

13. In the figure above, if a line segment connecting points B and D is perpendicular to AC and the area of triangle ADC is $\dfrac{3\sqrt{3}}{2}$, then $BC = ?$

(A) $\sqrt{2}$
(B) $\sqrt{3}$
(C) 2
(D) $3\sqrt{3}$
(E) 6

Here's how to crack it

Since you probably don't have an answer sheet right now, find any straight-edged piece of paper and make a dot somewhere along the top edge. Put this dot on point A in the diagram. Now turn the edge of your piece of paper so that it lines up along AD and mark another dot along the edge of the paper next to point D. Here's how it should look:

You now have a ruler. The distance between the dots at the top of your answer sheet is exactly the same as the distance between points A and D on the diagram. Use the ruler to measure the distance between point B and C.

If you measure carefully, you'll notice that the distance between A and D is the same as the distance between B and C—exactly 2. Let's look at the answer choices. Because you memorized the values we told you to memorize earlier, you know that answer choice (A) is equal to 1.4. Eliminate. Answer choice (B) is equal to 1.7. This is close enough for us to hold on to it while we look at the other choices. Choice (C) is exactly what we're looking for—2. Choice (D) is 3 times 1.7, which equals 5.1. This is much too large. Choice (E) is even larger. Eliminate (D) and (E). We're down to choices (B) and (C). The correct answer is choice (C).

Three Important Notes

1. While all diagrams in the regular problem-solving sections of the GMAT are drawn to scale (unless otherwise indicated), they are not *all* drawn to the *same* scale. A ruler that measures 2 on one diagram won't measure 2 on another. For every new problem with a diagram, you will have to make a new ruler.

2. Diagrams marked "not drawn to scale" cannot be measured. In fact, the drawings in these problems are often purposely misleading to the eye.

3. Drawings in the Data Sufficiency section of the GMAT are *not* drawn to scale. They *cannot* be estimated with your eye or with a ruler.

WHAT SHOULD I DO IF THERE IS NO DIAGRAM?

Draw one. It's always difficult to imagine a geometry problem in your head. The first thing you should do with any geometry problem that doesn't have a diagram is sketch it out in the margin of the test booklet. And when you draw the diagram, try to draw it to scale. That way, you'll be in a position to estimate.

WHAT SHOULD I DO IF THE DIAGRAM IS NOT DRAWN TO SCALE?

The same thing you would do if there were no diagram at all—draw it yourself. Draw it as accurately as possible so you'll be able to see what a realistic answer should be.

Q: Is making a ruler cheating?

BASIC PRINCIPLES: FUNDAMENTALS OF GMAT GEOMETRY

The techniques outlined above will enable you to eliminate many incorrect choices on geometry problems. In some cases, you'll be able to eliminate every choice but one. However, there will be some geometry problems on which you will need geometry. Fortunately, ETS chooses to test only a small number of concepts.

For the sake of simplicity, we've divided GMAT geometry into five basic topics:

1. degrees and angles
2. triangles
3. circles
4. rectangles, squares, and other four-sided objects
5. solids and volume

DEGREES AND ANGLES

There are 360 degrees in a circle. It doesn't matter how large or small a circle is, it still has precisely 360 degrees. If you drew a circle on the ground and then walked a quarter of the distance around it, you would have traveled 90 degrees of that circle. If you walked halfway around the circle, you would have traveled 180 degrees of it.

An angle is formed when two line segments extend from a common point. If you think of that point as the center of a circle, the measure of the angle is the number of degrees enclosed by the lines when they pass through the edge of the circle.

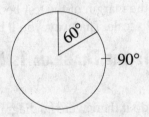

A line is just a 180-degree angle.

l is the symbol for a line. A line can be referred to as *l* or by naming two points on that line. For example, in the diagram below both points *A* and *B* are on the line *l*. This line could also be called line *AB*. The part of the line that is between points *A* and *B* is called a line segment. *A* and *B* are the end points of the line segment.

If a line is cut by another line, as in the diagram below, angle *x* and angle *y* add up to one straight line, or 180 degrees. If you knew that angle *x* equaled 120 degrees, you could find the measure of angle *y* by subtracting 120 degrees from 180 degrees. Thus angle *y* would equal 60 degrees.

Note that in the diagram above angle *x* could also be called angle *ABC*, with *B* being the point in the middle.

When two lines intersect—as in the diagram below—four angles are formed. The four angles are indicated by letters.

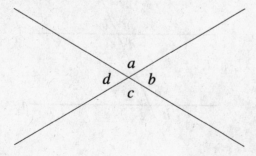

The four angles add up to 360 degrees (remember the circle).

$a + b + c + d = 360$. Angle a + angle b, since they add up to a straight line, are equal to 180 degrees. Angle b + angle c also add up to a straight line, as do $c + d$ and $d + a$. Angles that are opposite each other are called *vertical angles* and have the same number of degrees. For example, in the diagram above, angle a is equal to angle c. Angle d is also equal to angle b.

Therefore when two lines intersect, there appear to be four different angles, but there are really only two:

The 180° Rule, Part I

When you see a geometry problem that asks about angles, always look to see if two angles add up to a line, which tells you that the total of the two angles is 180 degrees. This is often the crucial little starting point that gets you solving the problem. ETS likes to construct problems in such a way that it is very easy to overlook the fact that two (or three or more) angles add up to a 180° line. So make it your habit to check.

Two lines in the same plane are said to be parallel if they could extend infinitely in both directions without touching. The symbol for parallel is $\parallel$.

Look at the diagram below:

$l_1 \parallel l_2$

When two parallel lines are cut by a third line, there appear to be eight separate angles, but there are really only two. There is a big one (greater than 90°) and a little one (less than 90°). Angle a (a big one) is also equal to angles c, e, and g. Angle b (a little one) is also equal to angles d, f, and h.

If two lines intersect in such a way that one line is perpendicular to the other, all the angles formed will be 90-degree angles. These are also known as right angles:

Angles a, b, c, and d each equal 90 degrees. The little box at the intersection of the two lines is the symbol for a right angle.

DRILL 5 (Angles and Lengths)

In the following figures, find numbers for all the variables. The answers to these problems can be found on page 254.

1.

2.

3.

4. If a driver has traveled 270 degrees around a circular race track, what fractional part of the track has he driven?

A real GMAT angle problem might look like this:

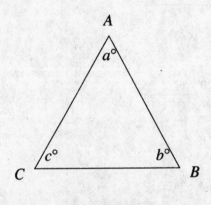

Note: Figure not drawn to scale.

5. In the figure above, if $l_1 \parallel l_2$, then which of the following angles must be equivalent?

(A) a and b
(B) g and f
(C) d and e
(D) a and d
(E) f and d

TRIANGLES

A triangle is a three-sided figure that contains three interior angles. The interior angles of a triangle always add up to 180 degrees. Several kinds of triangles appear on the GMAT:

An *equilateral* triangle has three sides that are equal in length. Because the angles opposite equal sides are also equal, all three angles in an equilateral triangle are also equal.

$$AB = BC = CA$$
$$a = b = c = 60$$

An *isosceles* triangle has two sides that are equal in length. The angles opposite those equal sides are also equal.

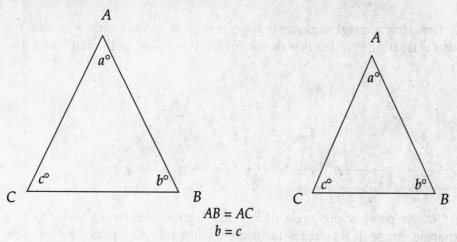

$$AB = AC$$
$$b = c$$

A *right* triangle has one interior angle that is equal to 90 degrees. The longest side of a right triangle (the one opposite the 90-degree angle) is called the *hypotenuse*.

hypotenuse

EVERYTHING ELSE YOU NEED TO KNOW ABOUT TRIANGLES

1. The sides of a triangle are in the same proportion as its angles. For example, in the triangle below, which is the longest side?

The 180° Rule, Part II

When a question involving angles has a triangle or several triangles in it remember the rule of 180 degrees in a triangle. Apply that rule every possible way you can. It is one of ETS's favorite items. They seem to have a neverending bag of tricks when it comes to questions using the simple idea of 180 degrees in a triangle.

STUDENTS' OPINIONS

According to 15,000 students surveyed, students say "classmates are smart" at:
Yale University
Stanford University
Dartmouth College
Massachusetts Institute of Technology
Georgetown University
Duke University
University of Virginia
Northwestern University
University of Maryland
University of Chicago

The longest side is opposite the longest angle. The longest side in the triangle above is *AB*. The next longest side would be *AC*.

2. *One side of a triangle can never be longer than the sum of the lengths of the other two sides of the triangle, or less than their difference.* Why? Look at the diagram below:

At the point where angle *ACB* = 180 degrees, this figure ceases to be a triangle. Angle *ACB* becomes 180 degrees when side *AB* equals the sum of the other two sides, in this case 6 + 8. Side *AB* can never quite reach 14.

By the same token, if we make angle *ACB* get smaller and smaller, at some point, when angle *ACB* = 0 degrees, the figure also ceases to be a triangle. Angle *ACB* becomes 0 degrees when side *AB* equals the difference of the other two sides, in this case 8 – 6. So *AB* can never quite reach 2.

3. The *perimeter* of a triangle is the sum of the lengths of the three sides.

perimeter = 18

4. The *area* of a triangle is equal to $\dfrac{\text{altitude} \times \text{base}}{2}$

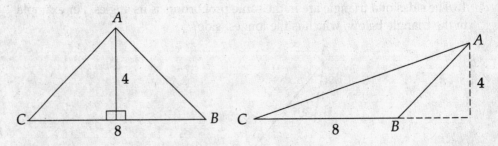

In both of the above triangles, the area = $\dfrac{4 \times 8}{2} = 16$

In a right triangle, the altitude also happens to be one of the sides of the triangle:

5. Don't expect triangles to be right side up:

This is an *isosceles* triangle.

The area of this triangle is $\dfrac{9 \times 4}{2}$, or 18.

6. In a right triangle, the square of the hypotenuse equals the sum of the squares of the other two sides. In the triangle below:

$$a^2 + b^2 = c^2$$

This is called the *Pythagorean* theorem. ETS loves to test this theorem, but usually you won't actually have to make use of it if you've memorized a few of the most common right-triangle proportions. The Pythagorean triangle that comes up most frequently on the GMAT is one that has sides of lengths 3, 4, and 5, or multiples of those numbers. Look at the following examples:

$3^2 + 4^2 = 5^2$ $6^2 + 8^2 = 10^2$
$9 + 16 = 25$ $36 + 64 = 100$

Some other Pythagorean triangles:

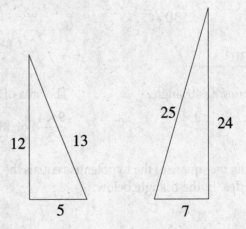

The Number of Billionaires in America	
1987	49
1988	51
1989	67
1990	66
1991	71
Source: *Forbes,*1991	

There are two other kinds of right triangles ETS loves to test. These are a little complicated to remember, but they come up so often that they're worth memorizing.

7. A *right isosceles* triangle is one that always has the following proportions:

For example:

8. A *30-60-90* triangle is one that always has the following proportions:

$\dfrac{\text{hypotenuse }\sqrt{3}}{2}$

hypotenuse

$\dfrac{\text{hypotenuse}}{2}$

30°

$\sqrt{3}$

2

60°

1

DRILL 6 (Triangles)

Find the value of the variables in the following problems. The answers can be found on page 254.

1.

45°
8
45°
x

2.

7   7
$x°$
7

3.

3
x
4

4. What value must x be less than in the triangle below? What value must x be greater than?

7
x
4

5. In the square *ABCD* below, what is the value of line segment *AC*?

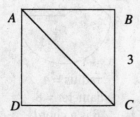

A   B

3

D   C

6. In the triangle below, what is the value of the line segment *BC*?

A real GMAT triangle problem might look like this:

7. In the diagram below, if the area of triangle *LNP* is 32, then what is the area of triangle *LMN*?

Note: Figure not drawn to scale.

(A) 24
(B) $24\sqrt{2}$
(C) $24\sqrt{3}$
(D) 32
(E) 48

CIRCLES

A line connecting any two points on a circle is called a *chord*. The distance from the center of the circle to any point on the circle is called the *radius*. The distance from one point on the circle through the center of the circle to another point on the circle is called the *diameter*. The diameter is equal to twice the radius.

radius = 4
diameter = 8
AB is a chord

The rounded portion of the circle between points *A* and *B* is called an *arc*.

The *area* of a circle is equal to πr^2.

The *circumference* (the length of the entire outer edge of the circle) is equal to $2\pi r$ or πd.

DRILL 7 (Circles)

Answer the following questions. The answers can be found on page 254.

1. In the diagram below, what is the area of the circle? What is the circumference?

2. If the area of a circle is 36π, what is the circumference?

3. In the circle below, if the arc *RT* is equal to $\frac{1}{6}$ of the circumference, what is the value of angle *x*?

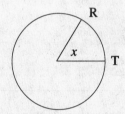

A real GMAT circle problem might look like this:

4. In the figure above, *P* is the center of the larger circle, and *N* is the center of the smaller, shaded circle. If the radius of the smaller circle is 5, what is the area of the unshaded region?

   (A) 100π
   (B) 75π
   (C) 25π
   (D) 20π
   (E) 10π

RECTANGLES, SQUARES, AND OTHER FOUR-SIDED OBJECTS

A four-sided figure is called a **quadrilateral.** The perimeter of any four-sided object is the sum of the length of its sides. A rectangle is a quadrilateral whose four interior angles are each equal to 90 degrees.

perimeter = 22   perimeter = 22

The area of a rectangle is *length* × *width*. The area of the rectangle above is therefore 3 × 8, or 24.

A *square* is a rectangle whose four sides are all equal in length. The perimeter of a square is therefore just four times the length of one side. The area of a square is just the length of one side squared.

perimeter = 4 × 5 = 20
area = 5 × 5 = 25

A *parallelogram* is a quadrilateral in which the two pairs of opposite sides are parallel to each other and equal to each other, and in which opposite angles are equal to each other. A rectangle is obviously a parallelogram, but so is a figure like this:

AB = DC
AD = BC

Angle *ADC* = angle *ABC*, and angle *DAB* = angle *DCB*.

The area of a parallelogram equals *base* × *height*.

The area of parallelogram *ABCD* = 8 × 2 = 16. (If you are having trouble picturing this, imagine cutting off triangular region *ADE* and sticking it onto the other end of the figure. What you get is a rectangle with the dimensions 8 by 2.)

SOLIDS, VOLUME, AND SURFACE AREA

The GMAT will occasionally ask you to find the volume or surface area of a three-dimensional object.

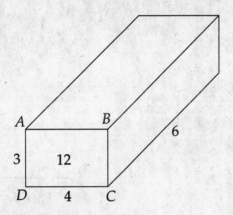

The volume of the *rectangular solid* above is equal to the area of the rectangle *ABCD* times the depth of the solid—in this case 12 × 6, or 72. Another way to think of it is *length* × *width* × *depth* = 3 × 4 × 6, or 72.

The volume of a *cube* is equal to the area of the square *WXYZ* times the depth of the cube, or again, *length* × *width* × *depth*. In the case of a square, the length, width, and depth are all the same, so the volume of a cube is always the length of any side cubed. The volume of this cube is 4 × 4 × 4, or 64.

Cut-up Cube Questions

For some unknown reason ETS likes to ask (in the medium to hard sections) about what happens when a cube gets cut up, but keep in mind that a cube has six faces. Don't forget about the bottom or the back. It might seem obvious, but weird things can happen to the mind under GMAT time pressure.

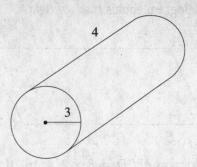

The volume of a *cylinder* is equal to the area of the circular base times the depth. The area of this circle is 9π. Thus the volume of the cylinder is 36π.

You may need to find the surface area of a solid. Surface area is just the sum of the areas of all the two-dimensional outer surfaces of the object. The surface area of a rectangular solid is just the sum of the two-dimensional areas of each of the six faces of the solid. For example, in the rectangular solid below, the surface area would be

face 1:	$3 \times 4 =$	12
face 2:	$3 \times 4 =$	12
face 3:	$3 \times 2 =$	6
face 4:	$3 \times 2 =$	6
face 5:	$4 \times 2 =$	8
face 6:	$4 \times 2 =$	$\underline{8}$
		52

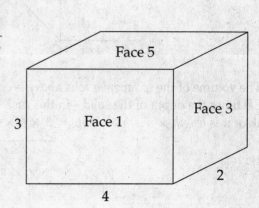

GMAT Geometry: Advanced Principles

All geometry problems (even easy ones) involve more than one step. Remember the first problem we looked at in this chapter?

3. In the figure above, if $BC = CD$, and angle $ADC = 90$ degrees, then what is the value of x?

(A) 45
(B) 50
(C) 70
(D) 75
(E) 100

Here's how to crack it:

Just by looking at the figure, we were able to eliminate answer choices (C), (D), and (E). Now let's solve the problem using geometry. The figure includes two—actually three—different triangles: *ABD, BCD,* and *ACD.* ETS wants even this easy problem to be a little challenging; there must be more than one step involved. To find angle x, which is part of triangles *ABD* and *ACD,* we must first work on triangle *BCD.*

What do we know about triangle *BCD*? The problem itself tells us that $BC = CD$. This is an isosceles triangle. Since angle *DBC* equals 70, so does angle *BDC.* Angle *BCD* must therefore equal 180 minus the other two angles. Angle *BCD* = 40. In the diagram, write in the measure of angle *BCD.*

Now look at the larger triangle, *ACD.* We know that angle *ACD* = 40, and that angle *ADC* = 90. What does angle x equal? Angle x equals 180 minus the other two angles, or 50 degrees. The answer is choice (B).

With GMAT geometry you shouldn't expect to be able to see every step a problem involves before you start solving it. Often, arriving at the right answer involves saying, "I have no idea how to get the answer, but since the problem says that $BC = CD$, let me *start* by figuring out the other angle of that triangle. Now what can I do?" At some point the answer usually becomes obvious. The main point is not to stare at a geometry problem looking for a complete solution. Just wade in there and *start*.

Walking and Chewing Gum at the Same Time

Most GMAT geometry problems involve more than one geometric concept. A problem might require you to use both the properties of a triangle and the properties of a rectangle; or you might need to know the formula for the volume of a cube in order to find the dimensions of a cube's surface area. The difficult geometry problems do not test more complicated concepts—they just pile up easier concepts.

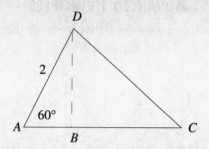

13. In the figure above, if a line segment connecting
points B and D is perpendicular to AC, and the area
of triangle ADC is $\dfrac{3\sqrt{3}}{2}$, then $BC =$

(A) $\sqrt{2}$
(B) $\sqrt{3}$
(C) 2
(D) $3\sqrt{3}$
(E) 5

Here's how to crack it

We already got the correct answer to this question by measuring; now let's solve it using geometry. If we draw in the line DB (which is perpendicular to AC), we form a 30-60-90 triangle on the left side of the diagram (triangle ADB). The hypotenuse of this triangle is 2. Using the rules we've learned, the measurements of triangle ADB are as follows:

Thus $DB = \sqrt{3}$. At first you might think we're no closer to the solution, but don't despair. Just look for somewhere else to *start*. The problem tells us that the area of triangle ADC is $\dfrac{3\sqrt{3}}{2}$. The area of a triangle is $\dfrac{\text{base} \times \text{altitude}}{2}$. DB is the altitude. Let's find out what the base is. In other words, $\dfrac{\text{base} \times \sqrt{3}}{2} = \dfrac{3\sqrt{3}}{2}$, so the base equals 3. We know from the 30-60-90 triangle that $AB = 1$. What is BC? 2. The answer is choice (C).

PLUGGING IN ON GEOMETRY?

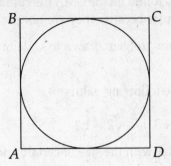

14. In the figure above, circle C is inscribed inside square *ABCD* as shown. What is the ratio of the area of circle C to the area of square *ABCD*?

(A) $\dfrac{\pi}{2}$

(B) $\dfrac{4}{\pi}$

(C) $\dfrac{\pi}{3}$

(D) $\dfrac{\pi}{4}$

(E) $\dfrac{2}{\pi}$

Advanced Principle #1: Advance!

With GMAT geometry you shouldn't expect to see every step a problem involves before you start solving it. Just get going. Wade in there and do something. With each piece you add to the puzzle the next piece to add becomes evident. In the problem on page 231 all you had to do was start with the information that *BC = CD*. That tells you that angles *CBD* and *CDB* are equal and from there everything else falls into line. Don't freeze up on geometry problems. Advance.

Here's how to crack it

We already saw this problem in the first half of the chapter when we discussed eliminating crazy answers. As you recall, we were able to eliminate answer choices (A), (B), and (C) because we determined that the correct answer had to be the ratio of a smaller number to a bigger number.

Now let's solve this problem completely. You may have noticed that the answer choices do not contain *specific numbers* for the areas of the two figures—all we have here are *ratios* in the answer choices. Sound familiar? That's right! This is just another cosmic problem, and the best way to solve it is to plug in.

To find the area of the circle, we need a radius. Let's just pick one—3. If the radius is 3, the area of the circle is 9π. Now let's tackle the square. The circle is inscribed inside the square, which means that the diameter of the circle is also the length of the side of the square. Since the radius of the circle is 3, the diameter is 6. Therefore the side of the square is 6, and the area is 36.

The problem asks for the ratio of the area of the circle to the area of the square:

$$\frac{9\pi}{36} = \frac{\pi}{4}$$ The answer is choice (D).

SUMMARY

1. While the geometry found on the GMAT is rudimentary, you will have to memorize all formulas because they are not provided on the test.

2. Always estimate any problem drawn to scale in order to eliminate crazy answer choices.

3. You must know the following values:

$$\pi \approx 3 \qquad \sqrt{2} \approx 1.4 \qquad \sqrt{3} \approx 1.7$$

4. You must be familiar with the size of certain common angles:

5. To estimate very precisely, you can use the top or bottom edge of your answer sheet as a ruler.

6. You can *never* estimate drawings on the Data Sufficiency section.

7. When no diagram is provided, make your own.

8. When the diagram is not drawn to scale, redraw it.

9. Degrees and angles:

   a. A circle contains 360 degrees.

   b. When you think about angles, remember circles.

   c. A line is a 180-degree angle.

   d. When two lines intersect, four angles are formed, but in reality there are only two.

   e. When two parallel lines are cut by a third line, eight angles are formed, but in reality there are only two: a big one and a little one.

10. Triangles:

   a. Every triangle contains 180 degrees.

   b. An equilateral triangle has three equal sides and three equal angles, all of which measure 60 degrees.

   c. An isosceles triangle has two equal sides, and the angles opposite those sides are also equal.

   d. A right triangle contains one 90-degree angle.

   e. The perimeter of a triangle is the sum of the lengths of its sides.

   f. The area of a triangle is $\dfrac{\text{altitude} \times \text{base}}{2}$.

   g. In a right triangle, the Pythagorean theorem states that the square of the hypotenuse equals the sum of the squares of the other two sides.

   h. Some common right triangles are 3-4-5 triangles and multiples of 3-4-5 triangles.

   i. Two other triangles that often appear on the GMAT are the right isosceles triangle and the 30-60-90 triangle. Memorize the formulas for these two triangles.

   j. The longest side of a triangle is opposite the largest angle; the shortest side is opposite the smallest angle.

   k. One side of a triangle can never be as large as the sum of the two remaining sides; nor can it ever be as small as the difference of the two remaining sides.

11. Circles:

   a. The circumference of a circle is $2\pi r$ or πd, where r is the radius of the circle and d is the diameter.

   b. The area of a circle is πr^2, where r is the radius of the circle.

12. Rectangles, squares, and other four-sided objects:

   a. Any four-sided object is called a quadrilateral.

   b. The perimeter of a quadrilateral is the sum of the lengths of the four sides.

   c. The area of a rectangle, or of a square, is equal to length times width.

   d. The area of a parallelogram is equal to altitude times base.

13. Solids and volume:

   a. The volume of most objects is equal to their two-dimensional area times depth.

   b. The volume of a rectangular solid is equal to length times width times depth.

   c. The volume of a cylinder is equal to the area of the circular base times depth.

14. GMAT geometry problems always involve more than one step. Difficult GMAT geometry problems layer several concepts on top of one another. Don't be intimidated if you don't see the entire process necessary to solve the problem. Start somewhere. You'll be amazed at how often you arrive at the answer.

Data Sufficiency

The Data Sufficiency section contains 20 questions to be completed in 25 minutes. Like the regular math sections, the Data Sufficiency section gets more difficult as it goes along. It helps to think of Data Sufficiency problems as being in three separate groups:

The first third	relatively easy
The second third	medium
The last third	very difficult

For each group there is a different strategy. Joe Bloggs comes in very handy on Data Sufficiency questions.

WHAT IS DATA SUFFICIENCY?

This question type requires some getting used to. When you take the exam, you'll notice that some of the people sitting around you in the examination room will spend at least the first ten minutes of the Data Sufficiency section just reading the directions. To avoid being among those unfortunate people, look at our version of the directions now:

Directions: In each of the Data Sufficiency problems below, you will find a question followed by two statements. You are not required to find the answer to the question; instead you must decide WHETHER the information given in the two statements is sufficient to answer the question, based on a knowledge of common facts (for example, the fact that an hour contains 60 minutes) and your understanding of the principles of math.

The answer to a data sufficiency question is

A   if statement (1) BY ITSELF is sufficient to answer the question but statement (2) is not sufficient by itself;

B   if statement (2) BY ITSELF is sufficient to answer the question but statement (1) is not sufficient by itself;

C   if neither statement is sufficient by itself, but if the two statements IN COMBINATION are sufficient to answer the question;

D   if EACH statement by itself is sufficient to answer the question;

E   if NEITHER statement (1) nor statement (2) is sufficient to answer the question separately or in combination.

Numbers: This test uses only real numbers; no imaginary numbers are used or implied.

Diagrams: Diagrams in Data Sufficiency are drawn to scale according to the data contained in the QUESTION, but may not be drawn to scale in light of the new information contained in the two STATEMENTS:

All diagrams lie in a plane unless stated otherwise.

Angles shown cannot have a measure of 0 degrees.

A line shown as straight cannot bend.

Relative positions of objects, points, and angles cannot change.

In triangle *QPR* above, what is the value of *y*?

(1) $x = 50$

(2) $z = 40$

Explanation: A triangle has a total of 180 degrees. Statement (1) gives us one of the three angles, but without angle *z* we cannot know the measure of angle *y*. By itself, statement (1) does not answer the question. Statement (2) gives us another of the three angles, but without angle *x*, we cannot know the measure of angle *y*. By itself, statement (2) does not answer the question. In combination, however, statement (1) and statement (2) give us two out of three of the angles of the triangle. By subtracting the sum of the two angles from the measure of the entire triangle, we can determine the value of *y*. Thus, the answer is (C).

BASIC PRINCIPLES

You can see why it is absolutely necessary to learn these directions NOW. You shouldn't even have to glance at them when you take the test. Let's start with a simple example:

Example 1

What is *x*?

(1) $2x + 4 = 14$

(2) $x + y = 7$

Here's how to crack it

Cover up statement (2). Based on statement (1) *alone*, can we answer the question "What is *x*?" Yes. Using algebraic manipulation, we can do the following:

$$2x + 4 = 14$$
$$\underline{\quad - 4 \quad -4}$$
$$2x = 10 \qquad \text{So } x = 5$$

Note that the question isn't asking us what *x* equals. The question asks only whether the information provided is sufficient to *find out* what *x* equals.

In this case it is. Statement (1) gives us enough information to answer the question "What is *x*?"

If statement (1) is sufficient, you have narrowed your answer choice down to two possibilities:

A. Statement (1) alone is sufficient, but statement (2) alone is not sufficient

or

D. EACH statement alone is sufficient

Now forget you ever saw statement (1). Cover it up with your finger and look only at statement (2). Based on statement (2) *alone*, can we find a single value for *x*?

Curiosity Killed the Clock

Data Sufficiency means just that, sufficiency: Is there enough data to solve the problem? It does not mean Problem Solving. If a question asks, "what is *x*?" it means, can a single value for *x* be found? Once you know the data is sufficient (or not) *stop* solving. It is pointless to actually find out what *x* is. Don't get curious.

No. The statement tells us that $x + y = 7$, in which case there are many possible values of x: If y equaled 2, then x could equal 5. On the other hand, if y equaled 3, then x could equal 4. Statement (2) is *not* sufficient to give us a single value for x.

Since (1) is sufficient and (2) is not, the answer to this question is choice (A).

Let's look at the same problem with the two statements reversed:

Example 2

> What is x?
>
> (1) $x + y = 7$
> (2) $2x + 4 = 14$

Here's how to crack it

Cover up statement (2) and look at statement (1). Well, we know from the previous example that $x + y = 7$ does not give us a single value for x. So this time statement (1) is *not* sufficient.

In the first example, by deciding that statement (1) was sufficient, we narrowed our answer down to choice (A) or (D).

In this example, however, because (1) is *not* sufficient, we can eliminate answer choices (A) and (D).

Now cover up statement (1) and look at statement (2). Well, we already know from the first example that $2x + 4 = 14$ gives us a single value for x.

Since we know that (2) is sufficient, but (1) is not, the answer is choice (B).

Example 3

> What is x?
>
> (1) $x + y = 7$
> (2) $y = 2$

Here's how to crack it

Cover up statement (2) and look only at statement (1). By itself, (1) is not sufficient to answer the question. Eliminate answer choices (A) and (D).

Cover up statement (1) and look at statement (2). By itself, this statement tells us what y equals, but we need a value for x. Eliminate answer choice (B).

We're down to answer choice (C) or (E).

Now let's look at the two statements at the same time. Since we know from the second statement that $y = 2$, we can substitute for y in the first statement. Now it reads $x + 2 = 7$.

Do we have a single value for x? You bet!

Since neither statement by itself is sufficient, but both statements together are sufficient, the answer is choice (C).

Example 4

> What is x?
>
> (1) $2x + 4 = 14$
> (2) $3x = 15$

The Equation Rule I

You must have as many equations as you have variables for the data to be sufficient. For example: $x = y + 1$ cannot be solved without another *distinct* equation. For more on this see page 200 in the section on solving simultaneous equations.

Here's how to crack it

Cover up statement (2). Based on statement (1) *alone*, can we get a single value for *x*? Yes. Using algebraic manipulation, we know that $x = 5$.

Since statement (1) is sufficient, we are already down to two possible answer choices: (A) or (D).

Now cover up statement (1). Based on statement (2) *alone*, can we get a single value for *x*? Yes. Using algebraic manipulation, we find that, again, $x = 5$.

Since each statement alone is sufficient, the answer is choice (D).

Example 5

What is *x*?

(1) $x + y = 7$
(2) $y + z = 3$

Here's how to crack it

Cover up statement (2). Based on statement (1) alone, can we get a single value for *x*? No. Eliminate answer choices (A) and (D).

Cover up statement (1). Based on statement (2) alone, we still can't arrive at a single value for *x*. Eliminate answer choice (B).

We're down to answer choice (C) or (E).

Looking at both statements together, can we find a single value for *x*?

No. Because there are three different variables in the two equations, *x* could have many different values.

Since statements (1) and (2) are not sufficient by themselves OR together, the answer is choice (E).

DANISH DATA SUFFICIENCY

In the examples above you may have noticed that we were already using the Process of Elimination. In Data Sufficiency a little knowledge goes a long way. Suppose you saw the following Data Sufficiency problem:

12. How tall is Frank?

(1) Frank is 6'2".
(2) Frank er en stor mand.

When we don't know something about a problem, our impulse is to skip the entire problem. Since you probably don't speak Danish, you have no idea whether the second statement is sufficient to answer the question.

However, it would be a mistake to skip this question.

HEADS YOU WIN A DOLLAR; TAILS YOU LOSE A QUARTER

Let's focus on what you DO know. Cover up statement (2). Based on statement (1) *alone*, do you know how tall Frank is? Of course. He is 6'2". Since statement (1) is sufficient, the answer to this question is either

A. Statement (1) alone is sufficient

or

D. EACH statement ALONE is sufficient

The Equation Rule II (part i)

Just because there is only one variable doesn't mean an equation has just one solution. When an equation has one variable and that variable is to an *odd* power the equation can definitely be solved. For example: $3\pi x^3 = 10^{-2}$. This equation has one variable, *x*. (π is a constant, not a variable.) The number 10 is raised to the negative 2, an even power, but that doesn't matter because ten is not a variable. How do you solve this equation? Who cares? All we need to say is that the equation *can* be solved.

By using POE, you've narrowed your choice down to two possibilities. You now have a fifty-fifty chance of getting this question correct, even though you know absolutely nothing about statement (2).

TAILS YOU LOSE A QUARTER; HEADS YOU WIN A DOLLAR

As long as you know *something* about a Data Sufficiency problem, you can do some shrewd guessing. Look at the following problem:

> 12. How tall is Frank?
>   (1) Frank er en stor mand.
>   (2) Frank is pretty tall.

Since we have no idea what statement (1) says, let's cover it up and look at statement (2). Based on statement (2) *alone*, can you tell exactly how tall Frank is? Of course not. Since (2) is not sufficient, you can rule out choices (B) and (D).

By using POE in this case, you've narrowed your choice down to three possibilities—a one-in-three shot—even though the only thing you knew for certain about this problem was that one of the statements *did not* work.

CAN'T MAKE HEADS OR TAILS OF THE FIRST STATEMENT?

If you're having trouble understanding the first statement, skip it for a minute and look at the second statement. If it is sufficient, you can eliminate answer choices (A), (C), and (E) and be down to a fifty-fifty guess—choice (B) or (D). If it is not sufficient, you can eliminate answer choices (B) and (D), and have a one-in-three shot at getting the problem right.

HOW DOES JOE DO ON DATA SUFFICIENCY?

Joe Bloggs does well on the easy Data Sufficiency problems. He gets a few of the medium problems, and then he gets *all* of the difficult problems wrong.

This is bad news for Joe, but good news for you. On the early problems, if you pay close attention to the method we've outlined in the preceding five examples, you'll get the correct answer most of the time. There are no tricks in those first eight problems. ETS has designed them so that Joe will get most of them right.

On the medium problems, however, it isn't enough to merely understand the directions; you must begin using POE to eliminate answers. Some of these medium problems will contain traps that ETS hopes will trip you up. We'll show you some of ETS's favorite traps in just a minute.

On the difficult problems, virtually every question contains a trap. Joe Bloggs invariably picks the wrong answer on the last seven problems of Data Sufficiency. By learning to recognize the traps ETS has set for Joe, you can eliminate even more wrong answers. Sometimes all that remains is the correct answer.

DATA SUFFICIENCY MATH VERSUS PROBLEM-SOLVING MATH

In terms of mathematical content, the Data Sufficiency section tests the same kinds of topics tested by the regular math sections. You'll find problems

The Equation Rule II (part ii)

When an equation has one variable but that variable is raised to a even power, the equation might or might not have a single solution; you just have to solve. For example: $x^2 = 4$. This equation has two solutions, 2 and −2. (It's one of ETS's favorite traps because it looks so easy. Joe Bloggs never thinks of negative numbers.)
$x^2 + 4x + 4 = 0$.
This equation has one solution. Factored, it equals $(x + 2)(x + 2) = 0$. Therefore x must equal −2.

involving integers, percents, averages, ratios, algebra, and geometry. Only the format is different.

Let's do an easy "regular" math problem and then turn it into a Data Sufficiency problem.

3. A certain factory has filled 92 orders. If the total number of orders on file is 230, what percent of the orders have been filled?

(A) 20%
(B) 30%
(C) 40%
(D) 50%
(E) 60%

If you've already done the math review in the preceding chapters, this problem should be very easy. It's a percent problem, and as soon as you see the word "percent," you should immediately be thinking

$$\frac{\text{part}}{\text{whole}} = \frac{92}{230} = \frac{x}{100}$$

(the answer, by the way, is (C) 40%)

Now let's turn this same problem into a Data Sufficiency problem.

3. If a certain factory has filled 92 orders, what percent of the total number of orders has been filled?

(1) The total number of orders on file is 230.
(2) The number of orders the factory has already filled represents two-fifths of the total number of orders.

Here's how to crack it

Although the problem is now in a different format, the math involved is exactly the same. Again, as soon as you see the word "percent," you should be thinking

$$\frac{\text{part}}{\text{whole}}$$

Without looking at the two statements, let's look at the information contained in the question itself and set that up as a part-over-whole equation:

$$\frac{\text{part}}{\text{whole}} \frac{92}{?} = \frac{x}{100}$$

As this equation stands, there is no way to find a value for x. We have the **part** (the number of orders that have already been filled), but we do not have the **whole** (total number of orders).

Cover up statement (2). Does statement (1) alone give us the missing whole? Yes, it does. Therefore, the answer to this question is either choice (A) or (D).

Now cover up statement (1). Statement (2) expresses the number of orders already filled as a fraction of the total number of orders. Remember, a fraction is *also* a part over whole. Let's see what we have:

In the right margin:

Equations Rule Tricks and Traps

You've already seen ETS's favorite trap: $x^2 = 4$. Remember, x could be 2 or –2. A single variable to any even power (except 0) can have both a positive and a negative value.

$$\frac{\text{part}}{\text{whole}} \quad \frac{2}{5} = \frac{x}{100}$$

Can we find a value for x in this equation? Of course. Therefore statement (2) is also sufficient, and the answer to this question is choice (D).

MATH IS MATH IS MATH

All Data Sufficiency problems are just standard math problems in a new format. Look for the clue that tells you what to do, then see whether the two statements provide you with enough information to answer the question.

EXCEPT ON YES OR NO QUESTIONS

Leave it to ETS to come up with a way to give you five different answer choices on a "yes or no" question. Let's look at an example:

7. Did candidate x receive more than 40% of the 30,000 votes cast in the general election?

   (1) Candidate y received 45% of the votes.
   (2) Candidate x received exactly 11,000 votes.

Here's how to crack it

When all is said and done, the answer to this question is either yes or no.

Cover up statement (2). Does statement (1) alone answer the question? If you were in a hurry, you might think so. Many people just assume that statement (1) is talking about candidate x—in which case they get the problem wrong. Other people notice that statement (1) is talking about candidate y but assume that these are the only two candidates running in the election (in which case, since candidate y received 45%, candidate x must have received 55%). Since the problem doesn't *say* that there were only two candidates, statement (1) doesn't answer the question.

Now cover up statement (1) and let's look at statement (2). This seems more promising. Like the problem we saw earlier involving factory orders, this problem is also about percents, so again we think:

$$\frac{\text{part}}{\text{whole}} \quad \frac{11,000}{30,000} = \frac{x}{100}$$

Using algebraic manipulation, we learn that $x = 36.6\%$. At which point many people say, "The guy got less than 40%—this statement doesn't answer the question, either."

But they're wrong.

JUST SAY NO

Broken down to its basics, the question we were asked was, "Did he get more than 40% of the vote—yes or no?"

Statement (2) *does* answer the question. The answer is, "No, he didn't."

On a yes or no Data Sufficiency problem, if a statement answers the question in the affirmative *or* in the negative, it is sufficient. The answer to question number 7 above is choice (B).

Equations Tricks and Traps

$x + 3y - 7 = x^2 (x^{-1}) + y$
This looks like two variables in one equation, which would mean we need at least one more equation to solve, but look again. If you combine the xs on the right, you'll see that each side of the equation has one x. The xs can be subtracted, leaving you with just one variable, y. The equation can be solved.

How to Keep It All Straight

Since there can be as many as nine yes or no problems in a Data Sufficiency section, it's a good idea to have a strategy. When yes or no questions involve variables, there's a good way to keep everything straight. Here's an example:

> 10. Is *x* an integer?
>   (1) 5*x* is a positive integer
>   (2) 5*x* = 1

Here's how to crack it

As always, cover up statement (2). Look only at statement (1). Let's plug in a value for *x*, a number that anyone, even Joe Bloggs, might pick. How about 2? We know that $5 \times 2 = 10$, which is a positive integer. Is 2 an integer? Yes.

What we've just found is *one case* in which the answer to question 10 is yes. If *x* is *always* an integer, then the answer is always yes, and statement (1) is sufficient. If *x* is *never* an integer, the answer would always be no, and statement (1) would *still* be sufficient (remember, the answer to a yes or no question can be no).

But if statement (1) gives us an answer that is sometimes yes and sometimes no, then the statement is no good.

By plugging in, we found *one case* in which the answer to the question is yes. Now all we need to do is see whether we can find *one case* in which the answer to the question is no. The statement says,

> (1) 5*x* is a positive integer

Most numbers we could plug in for *x* to make the statement true are integers. Is there ANY value of *x* that makes the statement true, but isn't itself an integer?

What if *x* were $\frac{1}{5}$?

We know that $5 \times \frac{1}{5} = 1$, which *is* a positive integer; but now *x* is *not* an integer. By plugging in $\frac{1}{5}$, we have found one case in which the answer is no. Since statement (1) gives us an answer that is sometimes yes and sometimes no, the statement is not sufficient. Now we're down to (B), (C), or (E).

Cover up statement (1) and look at statement (2):

> (2) 5*x* = 1

To make this statement true, *x must* equal $\frac{1}{5}$. Is *x* an integer? No. We have now found *one case* in which the answer is no. Is there any other number we could plug in for *x* that would make the statement true? No.

Since statement (2) gives us an answer that is *always* no, the statement is sufficient, and the answer to this question is choice (B).

Equations Tricks and Traps

Some equations are not distinct. When one equation can be multiplied to equal the other equation, the equations are not distinct.
For example:
x + *y* = 4
4*x* + 4*y* = 16
These are not distinct equations. There is not enough data yet to solve for *x* or *y*.

Dr. Livingstone, I Presume?

Stanley would not have done well on the GMAT with that kind of careless presumption. The test makers at ETS like to see whether they can get you to make careless assumptions. Here's an example:

8. Two people went into an executive trainee program at the same time. How much more money per week does trainee A now earn than trainee B?

   (1) Trainee A earns $300 per week more than she did when she began the program.
   (2) Trainee B earns $100 more per week than she did when she began the program.

Here's how to crack it

In this problem everyone's first impression is that the answer is choice (C) (both statements together are sufficient). Most people make the perfectly natural assumption that both trainees started at the same salary. But do we *know* this?

Never Assume

On medium or difficult questions, you can never assume *anything*. The answer to this question is choice (E) because the two trainees may have had different starting salaries.

12. At a business dinner, people were offered coffee or tea. If all the diners had either coffee or tea, how many of the diners had tea?

    (1) Of 60 people at the dinner, 10% had tea.
    (2) Fifty-four people had coffee.

Here's how to crack it

Statement (1) is sufficient because 10% of 60 = 6. Now look at statement (2). At first glance this seems sufficient as well. We just found out from statement (1) that there were a total of 60 people at the dinner. If 54 of them had coffee, then the other 6 had tea, which agrees with the number we got in statement (1). There is only one hitch: Statement (2) by itself does not tell us the total number of people at the dinner. We are subconsciously relying on information in statement (1).

Just Because One Statement Seems to Agree with the Other Doesn't Mean They Are Necessarily Saying the Same Thing

If statement (2) had said "two people had coffee," you would have eliminated it right away. But because it seemed to agree with statement (1), it became much more tempting. Just remember: When you look at statement (2), *always cover up statement* (1) *and forget you ever saw it.* The answer to this question is choice (A).

CRACKING DATA SUFFICIENCY: ADVANCED PRINCIPLES

When our students take their first practice GMAT with us, they generally get less than 10 percent of the difficult Data Sufficiency problems correct. When you consider that random guessing would have gotten them 20 percent correct, you begin to see that the axiom we gave you for the regular math sections is true here as well:

On difficult problems, answers that seem correct at first glance are never correct. By eliminating the answers Joe Bloggs wants to pick, you can improve the odds tremendously.

JOE'S FAVORITE ANSWERS

Joe Bloggs's initial reaction to a difficult Data Sufficiency question is, "I don't know how to do this." This statement doesn't seem to help Joe in answering the question. Therefore on questions he perceives to be difficult, Joe's favorite answer is usually choice (E) (statements (1) and (2) TOGETHER are not sufficient).

His second favorite answer is choice (C) (BOTH statements TOGETHER are sufficient, but neither statement alone is sufficient). Joe likes choice (C) because he assumes that a difficult question like this one will need a lot of information.

Joe's favorite answers on tough Data Sufficiency questions are choices (E) and (C), but that doesn't mean these will never be the answer to difficult questions. We should eliminate choice (E) and/or (C) *only* when they are Joe Bloggs's first or second impulse.

16. If $xy \neq 0$, what is the value of $\dfrac{x^4 y^3 z^2}{y^2 x^2 y^1 z^2}$?

(1) $x = 3$
(2) $y = 5$

Here's how to crack it

Joe's *first* impulse here might be to pick answer choice (E). He sees an expression with xs, ys, and zs, but the two statements underneath give values only for x and y.

If Joe thinks for a minute, he might realize that there is a z^2 in the numerator and a z^2 in the denominator. These cancel out, eliminating all the zs in the expression. Joe's *second* impulse might be to pick answer choice (C). He now sees an equation with xs and ys, and assumes he will need values for both in order to answer the question.

Having eliminated Joe's answers, we're down to choices (A), (B), or (D). If that's as far as you have time to get on this problem, guess and move on. You have a one-in-three shot of getting it right—good odds.

The correct answer is answer choice (A). The y^2 and the y^1 in the denominator can be consolidated to form y^3. The ys cancel out.

When Joe Thinks a Tough Question Is Easy

The only time the correct answer to a tough Data Sufficiency question will actually turn out to be (E) or (C) is when Joe is convinced that the question is easy.

19. What was the combined average attendance at Memorial Stadium for the months of June and July?

    (1) The average attendance for the month of June was 23,100, and the average attendance for the month of July was 25,200.
    (2) There were 20 games played in June at the stadium and 22 games played in July.

Here's how to crack it

Joe thinks this is an easy one. Statement (1) gives us the average attendance for June and the average attendance for July. Joe probably decides this is sufficient by itself. He thinks you can get the total average of the two months by averaging the two averages. (You—having completed our chapter on arithmetic—know better.) Joe looks at statement (2) and doesn't see any attendance figures at all. He picks answer choice (A).

Because he is convinced that this is an easy question and that the answer is choice (A), Joe Bloggs never even considers his two favorite answers—choices (E) and (C). *This* time he *knows* he's right!

But, of course, he is wrong. The answer to this question is choice (C). An average is the *total* sum of values divided by the total number of values. We need to know the number of games in each month in order to find out the *total* number of people attending.

Putting It All Together

Eliminating Joe Bloggs answers gives you an enormous advantage on Data Sufficiency problems. But by coupling this technique with POE, you can do even better. Remember our Danish question?

12. How tall is Frank?

    (1) Frank is 6'2".
    (2) Frank er en stor mand.

Using POE, and completely ignoring statement (2), we were able to get down to a fifty-fifty choice. Since statement (1) unequivocally answers the question, we knew the answer had to be choice (A) or (D). Now suppose this had been question 20 instead of question 12. We were already down to a fifty-fifty choice. The answer is choice (A) or (D).

Consider for a moment: Which of the two remaining choices does Joe like?

Since Joe doesn't know anything about statement (2), he'll probably choose (A). This is question 20. There's no way Joe's answer could be correct. In that case we'd better pick answer choice (D).

Here's one last example:

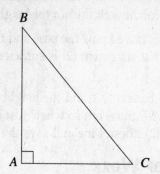

Q: What is the value of y?
(1) x − y = 3
(2) y (x⁰) = 0

19. If the perimeter of right triangle *ABC* above is $3+3\sqrt{3}$, what is the area of the triangle?

    (1) Side *AC* ≠ side *AB*.
    (2) Angle *ABC* = 30 degrees.

Here's how to crack it

The area of a triangle is $\frac{1}{2}$ *base* × *height*. Joe looks at statements (1) and (2) and sees neither the length of the base nor the length of the height. Joe likes choice (E) a lot on this problem. He doesn't see how he can get the area of the triangle from this information. Joe might also be tempted by choice (C) just because it seems like he is being given an awful lot of information; maybe, he reasons, there's some formula he doesn't know about.

Let's look at the problem seriously now. Cover up statement (2). Statement (1) tells us only that two of the sides of the triangle are not equal. Is there any conceivable way this information could help us find the base and the height of the triangle? No, statement (1) doesn't answer the question. Since statement (1) is not sufficient by itself, we can eliminate answer choices (A) and (D).

We are left with three choices: (B), (C), or (E).

Are any of these choices Joe Bloggs answers? Well, yes. We decided a moment ago that choice (E) was definitely Joe Bloggs and that, in fact, choice (C) might be as well. It therefore seems quite likely that the answer is choice (B).

Here's how ETS wants you to crack it

Statement (2) tells us that the right triangle is a 30-60-90 triangle. If you have already read our chapter on geometry, you know that the dimensions of a 30-60-90 triangle are always in the same proportion: The short side (the side opposite the 30-degree angle) is always equal to half the hypotenuse, and the middle side is always equal to the short side times $\sqrt{3}$. If we call the short side x, then the hypotenuse is $2x$ and the middle side is $x\sqrt{3}$. Thus the formula for the perimeter of a 30-60-90 triangle is $3x + x\sqrt{3}$, where x is the side opposite the 30-degree angle. If we set this equal to the actual perimeter of the triangle, we can solve for x.

$$3x + x\sqrt{3} = 3 + 3\sqrt{3}$$

After a lot of work solving for x, it turns out that $x = \sqrt{3}$. This is equal to the base of our triangle. We can now figure out the height, which would be the short side ($\sqrt{3}$) times $\sqrt{3}$, or 3. If we know the base and the height, we can figure out the area, which means that statement (2) is sufficient, and the answer is choice (B).

Wait a minute! If the base is $\sqrt{3}$ and the height is 3, doesn't this agree with statement (1) that $AC \neq AB$? Sure, but so what? Just because statement (1) seems to *agree* with statement (2) doesn't mean it says the same thing.

THAT WAS A LOT OF WORK

This problem was very difficult and took a long time if you actually tried to solve it mathematically, the way ETS wanted you to. You will notice that we got the same answer within only a few seconds by using a combination of POE and the Joe Bloggs technique.

Using our method isn't infallible, but unless you're extremely good at Data Sufficiency, you'll probably do better on the last seven problems by using POE and Joe Bloggs than you will by trying to figure out the answer mathematically.

There just isn't time.

A: B. The question is difficult and Joe answers his favorites, E or C. You should see that Statement (1) is clearly not sufficient alone. Statement (2), alone is sufficient. *Any number* to the zero power equals 1. Statement (2) says in effect, *y* times 1 equals zero. Clearly then, *y* equals zero. To solve for *x* you would need to use the information in both statements, but that wasn't the question.

SUMMARY

1. The Data Sufficiency questions are presented in order of difficulty. The first third are relatively easy, the second third are medium, and the last third are very difficult.

2. The instructions for this section are very complicated. Memorize them now. Here is a pared-down checklist:

   ◆ If only the first statement answers the question, the answer is choice (A).

   ◆ If only the second statement answers the question, the answer is choice (B).

   ◆ If you need both statements together to answer the question, the answer is choice (C).

   ◆ If both statements individually answer the question, the answer is choice (D).

   ◆ If neither statement, together or separately, answers the question, the answer is choice (E).

3. Use the Process of Elimination to narrow down the field. If you *know* that one statement is sufficient, you are already down to a fifty-fifty guess. If you *know* that one statement is *not* sufficient, you are already down to a one-in-three guess.

4. If you are stuck on statement (1), skip it and look at statement (2). POE will be just as helpful.

5. The math content of the Data Sufficiency section is exactly the same as it is on the regular math sections.

6. As you would in the regular math sections, look for the clues that tell you how to solve a particular problem.

7. When a problem asks a "yes or no" question, remember that the answer can be no.

8. In "yes or no" questions, a statement is sufficient if it always gives us the *same* answer: always yes or always no. If the answer is sometimes yes and sometimes no, the statement is insufficient.

9. In the medium and difficult portions of the Data Sufficiency section, you must be on guard against careless assumptions.

10. In the *difficult* portions of the Data Sufficiency section:

    ◆ If Joe Bloggs *thinks* the problem is difficult, his favorite answers are choices (E) ("there isn't enough information") or (C) ("this problem needs all the information it can get").

    ◆ If Joe Bloggs thinks the problem is easy, he will be drawn to choices (A), (B), or (D).

11. On difficult Data Sufficiency questions, Joe's answer is always wrong.

12. By combining the techniques of POE and Joe Bloggs, you can do some very shrewd guessing on the most difficult problems. If you *know* that one statement is sufficient, you're already down to a fifty-fifty choice. Is Joe Bloggs attracted to either of the two answers that remain? If he is, pick the other one. If you *know* that one statement is not sufficient, you have a one-in-three shot at guessing the right answer. Is Joe attracted to any of these three? If he is, choose among the remaining answers.

PART V

Answer Key to Drills

DRILL 1
(page 167)

1. 77
2. 79
3. 10
4. 16
5. choice (B)

DRILL 2
(page 168)

1. $9 \times 30 = 270$
2. $55 \times 100 = 5500$
3. $ab + ac - ad$
4. $c(ab + xy)$
5. $\dfrac{12y - 6y}{y} = \dfrac{y(6)}{y} = 6$, choice (B)

DRILL 3
(pages 172–173)

1. $\dfrac{145}{24}$ or $6\dfrac{1}{24}$
2. $\dfrac{1}{5}$
3. $\dfrac{29}{3}$
4. 18
5. choice (C)

DRILL 4
(page 176)

1. 24.66
2. 266.175
3. 6.09
4. 8
5. choice (C)

DRILL 5 (Angles and Lengths)
(pages 219–220)

1. $x = 110°$
2. $x = 50°$ $y = 130°$ $z = 130°$
3. $x = 60°$ $y = 120°$ $z = 120°$
4. $\dfrac{3}{4}$
5. choice (D)

DRILL 6 (Triangles)
(pages 225–226)

1. $x = 8$
2. $x = 60$
3. $x = 5$
4. x must be less than 11 and greater than 3
5. $3\sqrt{2}$
6. $2\sqrt{3}$
7. choice (B)

DRILL 7 (Circles)
(page 227)

1. area = 25π, circumference = 10π
2. circumference = 12π
3. $60°$
4. choice (B)

PART

VI

The Princeton Review
GMAT Diagnostic Test

Graduate Management Admission Test

GMAT ANALYTICAL WRITING ASSESSMENT

GENERAL DIRECTIONS

The Analytical Writing Assessment consists of two tasks:

ANALYSIS OF AN ISSUE   (30 minutes)

ANALYSIS OF AN ARGUMENT   (30 minutes)

For the <u>Analysis of an Issue</u> task, you will need to explore the complexities of an issue and explain your own point of view on that issue.

For the <u>Analysis of an Argument</u> task, you will need to analyze the reasoning behind an argument and write a critique of that argument.

WRITING YOUR RESPONSES

For each task, take a few minutes to think about the question and plan a response before you begin writing. Take care to organize your ideas and develop them fully, but leave time to reread your response and make any revisions that you think are necessary.
Feel free to cross out or insert words, but please write legibly.

EVALUATION OF YOUR RESPONSES

College and university faculty members from various subject matter areas, including management education, will evaluate the overall quality of your thinking and writing. They will consider how well you organize, develop, and express your ideas about the issue or argument presented; provide relevant supporting reasons and examples; and control the elements of standard written English.

The directions contained in this booklet appear in "Analytical Writing Assessment," a paper presented at GMAC's 1994 Annual Meeting. GMAC does not endorse this booklet. The Princeton Review is not affiliated with Princeton University or GMAC.

ANALYSIS OF AN ISSUE

Time — 30 minutes

Directions: In this section, you will need to analyze the issue presented below and explain your views on it. The question has no "correct" answer. Instead, you should consider various perspectives as you develop your own position on the issue.

Read the statement and directions, and then make any notes in your test booklet that will help you plan your response. Begin writing your response on the separate answer document. Make sure that you use the answer document that goes with this writing task.

QUESTION

"Some municipalities have recently enacted wide-ranging bans on public tobacco smoking due to alarming reports on the dangers of secondhand smoke. Some have even gone as far as to prohibit smoking in all public areas, including those that are privately owned, such as restaurants and movie theaters. While smoking bans in publicly-owned areas may be justified, bans are certainly not justified for private property. Private ownership should mean just that: property owners should be free to set their own rules concerning behavior on their premises."

Which do you find more compelling, the argument that smoking should be banned in all public areas, including privately owned public areas, or the response to it? Explain your position using relevant examples, drawn from your personal experience, observations, or readings.

NOTES

Use the space below to plan your response. Any writing on this page will not be evaluated.

ANALYSIS OF AN ARGUMENT

Time — 30 minutes

<u>Directions:</u> In this section, you will need to write a critique of the argument presented below. You may, for example, consider what questionable assumptions underlie the thinking, what alternative explanations or counterexamples might weaken the conclusion, or what sort of evidence could help strengthen or refute the argument.

Read the argument and directions, and then make any notes in your test booklet that will help you plan your response. Begin writing your response on the separate answer document. Make sure that you use the answer document that goes with this writing task.

QUESTION

"There is no need for government to police the problem of sexual harassment in the workplace, because the market will take care of the problem itself. Now that everyone is aware of this problem, businesses will have to 'clean up their acts' in order to attract the most qualified female employees, since it is obvious that a woman will choose to work in an atmosphere where there is no harassment over one in which such harassment occurs."

Discuss how logically convincing you find this argument. In explaining your point of view, be sure to analyze the line of reasoning and the use of evidence in the argument. Also discuss what, if anything, would make the argument more sound and persuasive, or would help you to better evaluate its conclusion.

NOTES

Use the space below to plan your response. Any writing on this page will not be evaluated.

SECTION 2
Time—25 minutes
16 Questions

<u>Directions</u>: In this section solve each problem, using any available space on the page for scratchwork. Then indicate the best of the answer choices given.

<u>Numbers</u>: All numbers used are real numbers.

<u>Figures</u>: Figures that accompany problems in the text are intended to provide information useful in solving the problems. They are drawn as accurately as possible EXCEPT when it is stated in a specific problem that its figure is not drawn to scale. All figures lie in a plane unless otherwise indicated.

1. If $(16)(3)^2 = x(2^3)$, then $x =$

   (A) 81
   (B) 72
   (C) 18
   (D) 16
   (E) 8

2. Starting at 9 a.m. on a certain day, snow began to fall at a rate of $1\frac{1}{4}$ inches every two hours until 3 p.m. If there were already $2\frac{1}{4}$ inches of snow on the ground at 9 a.m., how many inches of snow were on the ground at 3 p.m. that day?

   (A) $3\frac{3}{4}$
   (B) 6
   (C) 7
   (D) $7\frac{1}{2}$
   (E) $9\frac{3}{4}$

3. At a Wall Street company, 70 percent of this year's new employees are graduates of business schools and the remainder are graduates of liberal arts colleges. If 550 new employees were hired this year, what is the difference between the number of new business school employees and the number of new liberal arts employees?

   (A) 55
   (B) 220
   (C) 240
   (D) 385
   (E) 440

GO ON TO THE NEXT PAGE.

Important Note:
Section 1 of this test was the experimental section and has been left out since it did not count toward your score.

---

4. $(165)^2 - (164)^2 =$

(A)   1
(B)   2
(C)   4
(D) 325
(E) 329

5. The formula $E = \sqrt{\dfrac{a}{6}}$ describes the relationship between the length of the edge E of a cube and the surface area a of the cube. How much longer is the edge of a cube with a surface area of 1350 than the edge of one with a surface area of 600?

(A)   5
(B) 15
(C) 150
(D) 250
(E) 750

6. If y is an odd integer, which of the following must be an even integer?

(A) $y + 2$
(B) $y + 6$
(C) $2y - 1$
(D) $3y$
(E) $3y + 1$

7. If $x = \dfrac{5}{6} + \dfrac{15}{18} - \dfrac{10}{12}$, then $(x - 1)^3 =$

(A) $-\dfrac{1}{216}$

(B) $-\dfrac{1}{6}$

(C) $\dfrac{1}{6}$

(D) $\dfrac{27}{216}$

(E) $\dfrac{125}{216}$

8. There are 240 doctors and nurses at a hospital. If the ratio of doctors to nurses is 5 to 7, how many nurses are at the hospital?

(A) 20
(B) 60
(C) 100
(D) 140
(E) 180

GO ON TO THE NEXT PAGE.

9. If the temperature rises 25 percent from *d* degrees to 60 degrees, then 60 − *d* =

(A) 12
(B) 30
(C) 35
(D) 48
(E) 85

10. A computer is programmed to generate a list of multiples of prime numbers 2, 3, and 5, as shown below:

Program 1- *List multiples of 2*
Program 2- *List multiples of 3*
Program 3- *List multiples of 5*

How many integers between 1 and 100 will appear on all three of the lists of programs produced above?

(A) None
(B) 1
(C) 3
(D) 5
(E) An infinite number of integers

11. A grocer is storing small cereal boxes in large cartons that measure 25 inches by 42 inches by 60 inches. If the measurement of each small cereal box is 7 inches by 6 inches by 5 inches, then what is the maximum number of small cereal boxes that can be placed in each large carton?

(A)   25
(B) 210
(C) 252
(D) 300
(E) 420

12. Sue is now 10 years younger than Jane. If in 5 years, Jane will be twice as old as Sue, how old will Sue be in 3 years?

(A)   6
(B)   8
(C) 11
(D) 14
(E) 18

13. The price for a pair of cuff links is $1. The price for a 5-pair package of cuff links is $3.40. The 5-pair package is what percent cheaper per pair than 5 pairs purchased separately?

(A) 63%
(B) 62%
(C) 47%
(D) 32%
(E) 20%

GO ON TO THE NEXT PAGE.

14. If x, y, and z are non-zero numbers such that $1 \geq y > x$ and $xy = z$, which of the following cannot be true?

(A) $y > z$
(B) $y = z$
(C) $z = x$
(D) $x > z$
(E) $z > 0$

15. A company bought a total of 60 computers and 20 printers to modernize billing operations. If the price of each computer was three times the price of each printer, what percent of the total cost of the purchase was the total cost of the printers?

(A) 10%
(B) 11%
(C) 15%
(D) 20%
(E) 25%

16. A machine costs m dollars per day to maintain and n cents for each unit it produces. If the machine is operated 7 days a week and produces r units in a week, which of the following is the total cost, in dollars, of operating the machine for a week?

(A) $7m + 100nr$

(B) $\dfrac{700\,m + nr}{100}$

(C) $m + nr$

(D) $\dfrac{7m + 100nr}{100}$

(E) $700mnr$

STOP

IF YOU FINISH BEFORE TIME IS CALLED, YOU MAY CHECK YOUR WORK ON THIS SECTION ONLY.
DO NOT TURN TO ANY OTHER SECTION IN THE TEST.

SECTION 3
Time—25 minutes
18 Questions

Directions: Each passage in this group is followed by questions based on its content. After reading a passage, choose the best answer to each question and fill in the corresponding oval on the answer sheet. Answer all questions following a passage on the basis of what is <u>stated</u> or <u>implied</u> in that passage.

The two main theories of arbitration may be described as judicial and political. One might even go so far as to characterize them by saying
Line that the first is based on how arbitration is
(5) supposed to work, while the second is based on how it does in fact work.

The judicial theory implies that a "just" solution of the dispute does in fact exist, and that it is the duty of the arbitrator to decide on the
(10) principles and the facts involved. The arbitrator sits as a private judge, called upon to determine the legal rights and the economic interests of the parties involved as these rights and interests are demonstrated by the information provided by the
(15) parties themselves. The political theory, on the other hand, regards arbitration as an extension of both collective bargaining and, of course, collective coercion. The arbitrator functions as a sensitive instrument of sorts, accurately recording
(20) the relative strengths of the parties and making sure that the lion gets his share.

To some extent, however, these opposing theories represent a confusion between arbitration and conciliation, the act of appeasing both parties
(25) to a dispute without necessarily rendering a just or pragmatic decision. The notion of compromise that dominates conciliation may also guide arbitration, although, in the process of arbitration, the result necessarily requires the
(30) decision of an outsider rather than an accommodation between the parties themselves. Nevertheless, since to some the idea of arbitration necessarily involves absolute "rights," compromise is likely to be regarded as the
(35) solution of the timid or the unprincipled. Arbitration grounded in political theory, while more likely to permit conciliation, is therefore less preferable to both parties in a dispute, despite the obvious practicality of compromise.

1. The primary purpose of the passage is to
   (A) provide examples of the social failures that make arbitration necessary
   (B) describe the origin of two theories of arbitration
   (C) compare two conflicting theories of dispute arbitration
   (D) discuss the relative merits of arbitration and conciliation
   (E) outline the successive stages of collective bargaining

2. It can be inferred from the passage that all of the following are elements of the political theory of arbitration EXCEPT
   (A) an evaluation of the balance of power between disputing parties
   (B) a willingness on the part of both parties to accept compromise
   (C) a relative disregard of the importance of moral right in the dispute
   (D) an understanding that any compromise must appear to be just
   (E) an extension of collective bargaining

GO ON TO THE NEXT PAGE.

3. Which of the following, if true, would most effectively weaken the author's assessment of the drawbacks of the political theory of arbitration?

(A) Litigation is becoming a more popular alternative to arbitration.

(B) A system of checks and balances was put in place to reduce the likelihood of finding biased arbitrators.

(C) Contending parties in most disputes establish compromise as one of their most important goals.

(D) The process of arbitration uncovered new strategies for avoiding conflicts between contending parties.

(E) Resolution of the problem of the opposing rights of the parties involved in labor settlements can be achieved.

4. It can be inferred from the passage that the political theory of arbitration

(A) will eventually be replaced by a more efficient system of judicial compromise

(B) is not solely concerned with principles of justice

(C) suffers from most disputants' unwillingness to accept compromise

(D) may replace conciliation as the most practical means of resolving disputes

(E) is unlikely to be chosen by disputants unless they are coerced

5. According to the judicial theory of arbitration, an arbitrator would base his or her decision on

(A) information supplied by the parties involved in arbitration

(B) the notion of compromise that dominates conciliation

(C) decisions rendered by judges in similar cases

(D) the relative strengths of the parties involved

(E) whatever appears to both parties to be a fair settlement of the dispute

6. It can be inferred from the passage that efforts at conciliation are

(A) unlikely to be highly regarded by proponents of the judicial theory of arbitration

(B) absent from most well-regarded theories of arbitration

(C) most effective when neither party is responsible for a final decision

(D) inextricably linked with the concept of "rights"

(E) necessary to any dispute resolution under current theories of arbitration

7. According to the passage, the political theory of arbitration

(A) leaves no room for dissension

(B) implies that there is a just solution to all disputes

(C) directly contradicts the notion of compromise

(D) is grounded in political theory

(E) is based on how arbitration actually works

GO ON TO THE NEXT PAGE.

Anthropologists who study orangutans, distant cousins of the human race, find in the animals' behavior hints of how our earliest ancestors may
Line have lived. It has long been accepted that
(5) primates originally dwelt in the treetops and only migrated to the ground as forests began to dwindle. While to a certain extent all primates except humans spend at least some time dwelling in trees, the orangutan hardly ever ventures to the
(10) forest floor. Adult orangutans can grow as heavy as 330 pounds and live for decades, requiring copious amounts of fruit simply to stay alive. Thus, they become very jealous of the territory where they find their food. Compounding this
(15) territoriality are the breeding habits of orangutans, since females can only breed every few years and, like humans, give birth not to litters but single offspring.

Consequently, orangutans are solitary,
(20) territorial animals who have difficulty foraging in any part of the forest where they were not raised. Orangutans taken from poachers by customs agents undergo incredible hardship on their return to the wild. Incorrectly relocating a male
(25) orangutan is especially problematic, often ending in the animal's death at the hands of a rival who sees not only his territory but also the females of his loosely knit community under threat from an outsider. While humans, like chimpanzees, are
(30) more gregarious and resourceful than orangutans, the latter provide anthropologists with useful information about the behavior of prehominid primates and how apelike behavior influenced our ancestors' search for food and family beneath the
(35) forest's canopy.

8. The primary purpose of this passage is to

(A) describe some behavioral and evolutionary characteristics of orangutans
(B) analyze the reasons why early primates left their forest dwellings
(C) illustrate the dangers posed to orangutans by poachers
(D) show how orangutan behavior differs from that of other primates
(E) criticize anthropologists who misinterpret orangutan behavior

9. The author of the passage discusses "orangutans taken from poachers" (line 22) in order to

(A) stress the importance of preserving orangutans as a species
(B) indicate the widespread practice of animal poaching
(C) refute the theory that orangutans can live in a variety of environments
(D) contrast the behavior of orangutans with that of other apes
(E) emphasize the consequences of orangutan territoriality

10. The passage indicates that it is difficult to return orangutans to the wild for which of the following reasons?

   I. The threat posed by newcomers to other orangutans' territory
   II. The conflict between males over available females
   III. The scarcity of available food in the orangutan's environment

(A) I only
(B) I and II only
(C) I and III only
(D) II and III only
(E) I, II, and III

GO ON TO THE NEXT PAGE.

11. Which of the following can be inferred about differences between the behavior of orangutans and that of other ape species?

  (A) While orangutans spend much of their time in the treetops, other apes live exclusively on the ground.
  (B) Orangutans and other types of apes are all sociable species, but orangutans are more likely to bond for life.
  (C) Apes such as chimpanzees rely less upon their size than the average orangutan does.
  (D) Orangutans spend less time in the company of other members of their species than do some other apes.
  (E) Because of their stringent territoriality, orangutans are less likely to elude capture by poachers than are other apes.

12. According to the author, anthropologists study the behavior of orangutans in order to

  (A) prevent orangutans from becoming the target of poaching
  (B) assist customs agents in the relocation of orangutans
  (C) analyze the causes and consequences of contemporary human behavior
  (D) prevent larger orangutans from eliminating their weaker rivals
  (E) better understand the factors that influenced human evolution

13. Which of the following are factors that the author indicates contribute to the orangutan's territoriality?

  (A) The lack of available food and the antisocial nature of orangutans
  (B) The orangutan's need for large quantities of food and the infrequency with which they mate
  (C) The threat posed by poachers and the orangutan's inability to protect itself from them
  (D) The difficulties that orangutans have when compelled to socialize with other ape species such as chimpanzees
  (E) The constant dangers that present themselves whenever one orangutan encounters another

14. It can be inferred from the passage that one development responsible for the evolution of distinct ape species was

  (A) early primates' inability to survive in the forest
  (B) the shrinking of the available primitive forest
  (C) the growth of human and chimpanzee communities
  (D) the orangutan's eventual dominance of the treetops
  (E) the encroachment of other species into the primitive forest

GO ON TO THE NEXT PAGE.

The Romans—for centuries the masters of war and politics across Europe, Northern Africa, and Asia Minor—have often been criticized for
Line producing few original thinkers outside the realm
(5) of politics. This criticism, while in many ways true, is not without its problems. It was, after all, the conquest of Greece that provided Rome with its greatest influx of educated subjects. Two of the great disasters in intellectual history—the
(10) murder of Archimedes and the burning of Alexandria's library—both occurred under Rome's watch. Nevertheless, a city that was able to conquer so much of the known world could not have been devoid of the creativity that
(15) characterizes so many other ancient empires.

Engineering is one endeavor in which the Romans showed themselves capable. Their aqueducts carried water hundreds of miles along the tops of vast arcades. Roman roads, built for
(20) the rapid deployment of troops, crisscross Europe and still form the basis of numerous modern highways that provide quick access between many major European and African cities. Indeed, a large number of these cities owe their
(25) prominence to Rome's economic and political influence.

Many of those major cities lie far beyond Rome's original province, and Latin-derived languages are spoken in most Southern European
(30) nations. Again a result of military influence, the popularity of Latin and its offspring is difficult to underestimate. During the centuries of ignorance and violence that followed Rome's decline, the Latin language was the glue that held
(35) together the identity of an entire continent. While seldom spoken today, it is still studied widely, if only so that such masters of rhetoric as Cicero can be read in the original.

It is Cicero and his like who are perhaps the
(40) most overlooked legacy of Rome. While far from being a democracy, Rome did leave behind useful political tools that serve the American republic today. "Republic" itself is Latin for "the people's business," a notion cherished in democracies
(45) worldwide. Senators owe their name to Rome's class of elders; Representatives owe theirs to the Tribunes who seized popular prerogatives from the Senatorial class. The veto was a Roman notion adopted by the historically aware framers
(50) of the Constitution, who often assumed pen names from the lexicon of Latin life. These accomplishments, as monumental as any highway or coliseum, remain prominent features of the Western landscape.

15. The author describes "two of the great disasters in intellectual history" (lines 8-12) in order to

(A) establish a point directly related to the main argument
(B) show that certain historical claims are inaccurate
(C) demonstrate the importance of certain historical data
(D) disprove the claims made by others with a different view
(E) concede the partial accuracy of an opposing view

GO ON TO THE NEXT PAGE.

16. According to the passage, ancient Roman roads

    (A) connected many major cities in ancient
        Europe
    (B) are engineering marvels unequaled in modern
        times
    (C) are similar in some respects to modern
        highways
    (D) were products of democratic political
        institutions
    (E) caused the development of modern European
        cities

17. According to the passage, which of the following
    accurately describes the Latin language?

    I.   It spread in part due to Rome's military
         power.
    II. It is reflected in modern political concepts.
    III. It is spoken today in some parts of Europe.

    (A) I only
    (B) II only
    (C) I and II only
    (D) I and III only
    (E) II and III only

18. It can be inferred from the passage that the
    framers of the Constitution

    (A) were familiar with certain aspects of
        Roman government
    (B) were similar to the Roman elders
    (C) embraced the veto as the hallmark of
        Roman democracy
    (D) overlooked Cicero's contributions to the
        theory of democracy
    (E) formed a government based on worldwide
        democracy

STOP

IF YOU FINISH BEFORE TIME IS CALLED, YOU MAY CHECK YOUR WORK ON THIS SECTION ONLY.
DO NOT TURN TO ANY OTHER SECTION IN THE TEST.

SECTION 4

Time—25 minutes

16 Questions

<u>Directions</u>: In this section solve each problem, using any available space on the page for scratchwork. Then indicate the best of the answer choices given.

<u>Numbers</u>: All numbers used are real numbers.

<u>Figures</u>: Figures that accompany problems in the text are intended to provide information useful in solving the problems. They are drawn as accurately as possible EXCEPT when it is stated in a specific problem that its figure is not drawn to scale. All figures lie in a plane unless otherwise indicated.

94.08

A

94.07

1. A portion of a thermometer above is calibrated to show degrees in equal increments. If the temperature indicates a reading at level A, what is the temperature?

(A) 94.069
(B) 94.070
(C) 94.079
(D) 94.080
(E) 94.790

2. The owner of a boutique decides to calculate the percentage of customers who purchase hats. If 40 percent of the store's customers decide to purchase items, and of those customers 15 percent purchase hats, what percent of the store's customers purchase hats?

(A) 4%
(B) 6%
(C) 15%
(D) 24%
(E) 55%

3. The result obtained when x is multiplied by y is equal to ten times the result obtained when y is subtracted from x. If y equals 5, what does x equal?

(A) 50
(B) 25
(C) 15
(D) 10
(E) 5

GO ON TO THE NEXT PAGE.

4. $\left[1-\left(\dfrac{2}{3}\right)^2\right]^2 =$

(A) $-\dfrac{1}{3}$

(B) $\dfrac{1}{27}$

(C) $\dfrac{125}{729}$

(D) $\dfrac{25}{81}$

(E) $\dfrac{5}{9}$

5. After reading $\dfrac{3}{5}$ of his biology homework on Monday night, Bernie read $\dfrac{1}{3}$ of his remaining homework on Tuesday night. What fraction of his original homework would Bernie have to read on Wednesday night to complete his biology assignment?

(A) $\dfrac{1}{15}$

(B) $\dfrac{2}{15}$

(C) $\dfrac{4}{15}$

(D) $\dfrac{2}{5}$

(E) $\dfrac{4}{5}$

6. If $x \neq 1$, then $\dfrac{3x^2 + 6x - 9}{3x - 3} =$

(A) $x + 1$
(B) $x - 1$
(C) $3x + 1$
(D) $x + 3$
(E) $3x + 3$

$$a = \left(\dfrac{1}{10}\right)^2$$

$$b = \dfrac{1}{5}$$

$$c = \sqrt{\dfrac{1}{100}}$$

7. The values of a, b, and c are shown above. Which of the following is correct?

(A) $a < b < c$
(B) $a < c < b$
(C) $b < c < a$
(D) $c < a < b$
(E) $c < b < a$

GO ON TO THE NEXT PAGE.

8. If $\frac{1}{y} = 3\frac{1}{2}$, then $\frac{1}{y+2} =$

(A) $\frac{7}{16}$

(B) $\frac{4}{7}$

(C) $\frac{7}{9}$

(D) $\frac{7}{8}$

(E) $\frac{16}{7}$

9. Laura borrowed $240, interest free, from her parents to pay for her college education. If she pays back $2\frac{1}{2}$ percent of this amount quarterly, and has already paid $42.00, for how many months has she been paying back her loan?

(A) 6
(B) 7
(C) 19
(D) 21
(E) 24

10. The function * is defined by the equation $a * b = \frac{ab}{b-a}$, where $a \neq b$. Which of the following has a value of 3?

(A) 1 * 3
(B) 3 * 0
(C) 2 * 6
(D) 6 * 2
(E) 4 * −1

11. A store raised the price of an item by exactly 10 percent. Which of the following could NOT be the resulting price of the item?

(A) $5.50
(B) $7.60
(C) $11.00
(D) $12.10
(E) $75.90

12. If when a certain integer x is divided by 5 the remainder is 2, then each of the following could also be an integer EXCEPT

(A) $\frac{x}{17}$

(B) $\frac{x}{11}$

(C) $\frac{x}{10}$

(D) $\frac{x}{6}$

(E) $\frac{x}{3}$

GO ON TO THE NEXT PAGE.

13. In a certain flower shop, which stocks four types of flowers, there are $\frac{1}{3}$ as many violets as carnations, and $\frac{1}{2}$ as many tulips as violets. If there are equal numbers of roses and tulips, what percent of the flowers in the shop are carnations?

(A) 10%
(B) 33%
(C) 40%
(D) 50%
(E) 60%

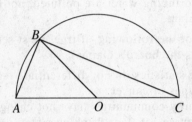

Note: Figure not drawn to scale

14. If triangle AOB is equilateral, O is the center of the semicircle ABC, and the radius of semicircle ABC is 6, what is the length of BC?

(A) 12
(B) $6\sqrt{3}$
(C) 10
(D) $6\sqrt{2}$
(E) $\sqrt{42}$

15. A car averages 40 miles per hour for the first 6 hours of a trip and averages 60 miles per hour for each additional hour of travel time. If the average speed for the entire trip is 55 miles per hour, how many hours long is the trip?

(A) 8
(B) 12
(C) 16
(D) 18
(E) 24

16. How many integers between 100 and 150, inclusive, can be evenly divided by neither 3 nor 5?

(A) 33
(B) 28
(C) 27
(D) 26
(E) 24

STOP

IF YOU FINISH BEFORE TIME IS CALLED, YOU MAY CHECK YOUR WORK ON THIS SECTION ONLY.
DO NOT TURN TO ANY OTHER SECTION IN THE TEST.

SECTION 5

Time—25 minutes

16 Questions

Directions: For each question in this section, select the best of the answer choices given.

1. A mail order company recently had a big jump in clothing sales after hiring a copywriter and a graphic artist to give its clothing catalog a magazine-like format designed to appeal to a more upscale clientele. The company is now planning to launch a housewares catalog using the same concept.

The company's plan assumes that

(A) other housewares catalogs with magazine-like formats do not already exist
(B) an upscale clientele would be interested in a housewares catalog
(C) the same copywriter and graphic artist could be employed for both the clothing and housewares catalogs
(D) a magazine-like format requires a copywriter and a graphic artist
(E) customers to whom the old clothing catalog appealed would continue to make purchases from catalogs with the new format

2. Civic Leaders: The high cancer rate among our citizens is the result of hazardous materials produced at your plant.

Board of Directors: Our statistics show that rates of cancer are high throughout the valley in which the plant is situated because local wells that supply drinking water are polluted, not because of the plant.

Which of the following, if true, most seriously weakens the board's claims?

(A) The statistics do not differentiate between types of cancer.
(B) Nearby communities have not changed the sources of their drinking water.
(C) Cancer-causing chemicals used at the plant are discharged into a nearby river and find their way into local wells.
(D) The plant both uses and produces chemicals that have been shown to cause cancer.
(E) Some of the pollutants cited by the board as contaminating the local wells have been present in the wells for decades.

GO ON TO THE NEXT PAGE.

3. Television programming experts maintain that with each 1% increase in the prime-time ratings of a television station there is a 3.5% increase in the number of people who watch its evening news program. However, in the last ten years at Channel NTR, there was only one year of extremely high prime-time ratings—and during that year, fewer people than ever watched Channel NTR's evening news program.

Which of the following conclusions can properly be drawn from the statements above?

(A) When a news program has good ratings, the channel as a whole will have good ratings.

(B) The programming experts neglected to consider daytime news programs.

(C) The year of high ratings at NTR was a result of two hit shows which were subsequently canceled because of contractual problems.

(D) The ten-year period in question is not representative of normal viewing patterns.

(E) Prime-time ratings are not the only factor affecting how many people watch an evening news program.

4. The people least likely to be audited by the Internal Revenue Service this year are those who have been audited at least once since 1985 and who were found to have made no mistakes in filing their returns during that audit.

Of the following people, who is MOST likely to be audited by the IRS?

(A) A person who was audited in 1986 but was not found to have made any mistakes in filing his return.

(B) A person who was audited in 1986 and whose lawyer corrected several mistakes in the tax return prior to the filing deadline.

(C) A person whose spouse was convicted of tax fraud in 1987, who was then audited and found to have made no mistakes.

(D) A person who was last audited in 1984, and had no mistakes uncovered by the IRS during that audit.

(E) A person who was audited in each of the past five years, but was found to have made no mistakes in any of the filings.

5. James's grade point average puts him in the top third of the graduating class of college A. Nestor is in the top tenth of the same class. Elizabeth has the same grade point average as Nestor. Nancy has a lower grade point average than Elizabeth.

If the information above is true, which of the following must also be true?

(A) James has a higher grade point average than Elizabeth

(B) James has a higher grade point average than Nancy

(C) Nestor has a higher grade point average than Nancy

(D) Elizabeth and Nancy both have a higher grade point average than James

(E) Nestor and James both have a higher grade point average than Nancy

GO ON TO THE NEXT PAGE.

6. Whenever a major airplane accident occurs, there is a dramatic increase in the number of airplane mishaps reported in the media, a phenomenon that may last for as long as a few months after the accident. Airline officials assert that the publicity given the gruesomeness of major airplane accidents focuses media attention on the airline industry, and the increase in the number of reported accidents is caused by an increase in the number of news sources covering airline accidents, not by an increase in the number of accidents.

Which of the following, if true, would seriously weaken the assertions of the airline officials?

(A) The publicity surrounding airline accidents is largely limited to the country in which the crash occurred.
(B) Airline accidents tend to occur far more often during certain peak travel months.
(C) News organizations do not have any guidelines to help them decide how severe an accident must be for it to receive coverage.
(D) Airplane accidents receive coverage by news sources only when the news sources find it advantageous to do so.
(E) Studies by government regulators show that the number of airplane flight miles remains relatively constant from month to month.

Questions 7-8 are based on the following:

Investing in real estate would be a profitable venture at this time. A survey in *House* magazine revealed that 85% of the magazine's readers are planning to buy a second home over the next few years. A study of the real estate industry, however, revealed that the current supply of homes could only provide for 65% of that demand each year.

7. Which of the following, if true, reveals a weakness in the evidence cited above?

(A) Real estate is a highly labor-intensive business.
(B) Home builders are not evenly distributed across the country.
(C) The number of people who want second homes has been increasing each year for the past ten years.
(D) Readers of *House* magazine are more likely than most people to want second homes.
(E) *House* magazine includes articles about owning a second home as well as articles about building a second home.

8. Which of the following, if true, would undermine the validity of the investment advice in the paragraph above?

(A) Some home owners are satisfied with only one home.
(B) About half of the people who buy homes are investing in their first home.
(C) About half of the people who buy homes have to take out a mortgage to do so.
(D) Only a quarter of the homes that are built are sold within the first two weeks.
(E) Only a quarter of those who claim that they want a second home actually end up purchasing one.

GO ON TO THE NEXT PAGE.

9. Traffic safety experts predict that the installation of newly designed air bags in all cars in the United States would reduce the average number of fatalities per traffic accident by 30 percent. In order to save lives, the Department of Transportation (DOT) is considering requiring automobile manufacturers to install air bags of this design in all cars produced after 1998.

Which of the following, if true, represents the strongest challenge to the DOT's proposal?

(A) Air bags of the new design are more given to being inadvertently triggered, an occurrence that can sometimes result in fatal traffic accidents.

(B) The DOT is planning to require automobile manufacturers to produce these air bags according to very strict specifications.

(C) After installing air bags in new cars, automobile manufacturers will experience an increase in sales.

(D) The proposed air bag installation program will adversely affect the resale of cars manufactured prior to 1998.

(E) As production costs increase, the profits of many domestic automobile dealers show a marked decrease.

10. A newly discovered disease is thought to be caused by a certain bacterium. However, recently released data notes that the bacterium thrives in the presence of a certain virus, implying that it is actually the virus that causes the new disease.

Which of the following pieces of evidence would most support the data's implication?

(A) In the absence of the virus, the disease has been observed to follow infection by the bacterium.

(B) The virus has been shown to aid the growth of bacterium, a process which often leads to the onset of the disease.

(C) The virus alone has been observed in many cases of the disease.

(D) In cases where the disease does not develop, infection by the bacterium is usually preceded by infection by the virus.

(E) Onset of the disease usually follows infection by both the virus and the bacterium.

11. Because of a recent drought in Florida during the orange-growing season, the price of oranges this season will be three times the usual price. This will drive up the cost of producing orange juice and thus push up the price of orange juice for the consumer.

Which of the following, if true, most seriously weakens the argument above?

(A) The recent drought was not as severe as scientists predicted.

(B) States other than Florida also supply oranges to orange juice manufacturers.

(C) Other ingredients are used in the production of orange juice.

(D) Last year the price of oranges was actually lower than the average price over the past ten years.

(E) The price of oranges will eventually be $0.48 per crate.

GO ON TO THE NEXT PAGE.

Questions 12-13 are based on the following:

Local phone companies have monopolies on phone service within their areas. Cable television can be transmitted via the wires that are already in place and owned by the phone companies. Cable television companies argue that if the telephone companies were to offer cable service, these telephone companies would have an unfair advantage, because their cable transmissions could be subsidized by the profits of their monopolies on phone service.

12. Which of the following, if true, would ease the cable companies' fear of unfair competition?

(A) In order to use existing telephone wire, telephone companies would need to modernize their operations, a process so expensive it would virtually wipe out all profit from their monopoly for the foreseeable future.
(B) If a phone company were to offer cable service within a particular area, it would have a monopoly within that area.
(C) The cost of television service, whether provided by cable or telephone companies, scales; that is, the total cost of transmission rises only marginally as more homes are added to the network.
(D) Cable programming that offers more channels is already available through satellite dish, but the initial cost of the dish is extremely high.
(E) Cable television will never be able to compete with the burgeoning video rental industry, especially as more homes now have video cassette recorders than ever did before.

13. On the basis of the information provided in the passage above, which of the following questions can be answered?

(A) Are phone companies as efficient as cable companies in providing reliable and inexpensive service?
(B) If phone companies were allowed to provide cable service, would they want to do so?
(C) Do the cable companies believe that the local phone companies make a profit on phone service?
(D) Are local phone companies forbidden to offer cable service?
(E) Is it expected that phone companies will have a monopoly on cable service?

14. In the past year, there has been a large drop in the number of new cars sold, due to harsh economic conditions in the marketplace and high taxes. At the same time, the average price paid for a new car has risen dramatically.

Which of the following, if true, best explains the increase in the average price of a new car?

(A) The price of used cars has climbed steadily over the past ten years.
(B) There will be a tax reduction later in the year which is expected to aid moderate and low income families.
(C) The market for expensive cars has been unaffected by the current economic conditions.
(D) Economic conditions are expected to get significantly worse before the end of the year.
(E) Low demand for trucks and vans has led to lower production in the factories.

GO ON TO THE NEXT PAGE.

15. Informed people generally assimilate information from several divergent sources before coming to an opinion. However, most popular news organizations view foreign affairs solely through the eyes of our State Department. In reporting the political crisis in foreign country B, news organizations must endeavor to find alternative sources of information.

Which of the following inferences can be drawn from the argument above?

(A) To the degree that a news source gives an account of another country that mirrors that of our State Department, that reporting is suspect.

(B) To protect their integrity, news media should avoid the influence of State Department releases in their coverage of foreign affairs.

(C) Reporting that is not influenced by the State Department is usually more accurate than are other accounts.

(D) The alternative sources of information mentioned in the passage might not share the same views as the State Department.

(E) A report cannot be seen as influenced by the State Department if it accurately depicts the events in a foreign country.

16. A light bulb company produces 2,000 light bulbs per week. The manager wants to ensure that standards of quality remain constant from week to week. The manager, therefore, claims that out of 2,000 light bulbs produced per week, 500 light bulbs are rejected.

Of the following, the best criticism of the manager's plan is that the plan assumes that

(A) light bulb manufacturers cannot accept all light bulbs that are produced

(B) the overall quality of the light bulbs would not be improved if the total number of light bulbs produced were reduced

(C) each light bulb that is reviewed is worthy of being reviewed

(D) it is difficult to judge the quality of a light bulb

(E) the 1,500 light bulbs that are accepted will be of the same quality from week to week

STOP

IF YOU FINISH BEFORE TIME IS CALLED, YOU MAY CHECK YOUR WORK ON THIS SECTION ONLY.
DO NOT TURN TO ANY OTHER SECTION IN THE TEST.

SECTION 6

Time—25 minutes

20 Questions

<u>Directions</u>: Each of the data sufficiency problems below consists of a question and two statements, labeled (1) and (2), in which certain data are given. You have to decide whether the data given in the statements are <u>sufficient</u> for answering the question. Using the data given in the statements <u>plus</u> your knowledge of mathematics and everyday facts (such as the number of days in July or the meaning of *counterclockwise*), you are to fill in oval

    A   if statement (1) ALONE is sufficient, but statement (2) alone is not sufficient to answer the question asked;

    B   if statement (2) ALONE is sufficient, but statement (1) alone is not sufficient to answer the question asked;

    C   if BOTH statements (1) and (2) TOGETHER are sufficient to answer the question asked, but NEITHER statement ALONE is sufficient;

    D   if EACH statement ALONE is sufficient to answer the question asked;

    E   if statements (1) and (2) TOGETHER are NOT sufficient to answer the question asked, and additional data specific to the problem are needed.

<u>Numbers:</u>   All numbers used are real numbers.

<u>Figures:</u>   A figure in a data sufficiency problem will conform to the information given in the question, but will not necessarily conform to the additional information given in statements (1) and (2).

          You may assume that lines shown as straight are straight and that angle measures are greater than zero.

          You may assume that the positions of points, angles, regions, etc., exist in the order shown.

          All figures lie in a plane unless otherwise indicated.

<u>Note:</u>   In questions that ask for the value of a quantity, the data given in the statements are sufficient only when it is possible to determine exactly one numerical value for the quantity.

<u>Example:</u>

In △ *PQR*, what is the value of *x* ?

(1) *PQ = PR*
(2) *y* = 40

<u>Explanation:</u> According to statement (1), *PQ = PR*; therefore, △ *PQR* is isosceles and *y* = *z*. Since *x* + *y* + *z* = 180, it follows that *x* + 2*y* = 180. Since statement (1) does not give a value for *y*, you cannot answer the question using statement (1) alone. According to statement (2), *y* = 40; therefore, *x* + *z* = 140. Since statement (2) does not give a value for *z*, you cannot answer the question using statement (2) alone. Using both statements together, since *x* + 2*y* = 180 and the value of *y* is given, you can find the value of *x*. Therefore, the answer is C.

GO ON TO THE NEXT PAGE.

A   Statement (1) ALONE is sufficient, but statement (2) alone is not sufficient.
B   Statement (2) ALONE is sufficient, but statement (1) alone is not sufficient.
C   BOTH statements TOGETHER are sufficient, but NEITHER statement ALONE is sufficient.
D   EACH statement ALONE is sufficient.
E   Statements (1) and (2) TOGETHER are NOT sufficient.

1. What is the area of triangular region T?

   (1) The base of triangle T is 12.

   (2) The ratio of the height of T to the base of T is 3:1.

2. Bob purchased 18 cans of soda, some of which contained diet soda. How many of the cans did not contain diet soda?

   (1) Of the cans Bob purchased, the number containing diet soda is equal to the number not containing diet soda.

   (2) Of the cans Bob purchased, the number containing diet soda is odd.

3. In 1988, was the number of people in City X greater than three times the number of people in City Y?

   (1) In 1988, there were approximately 1.1 million more people in City X than in City Y.

   (2) In 1988, the 300,000 Mormons in City X made up 20 percent of its population, and the 141,000 Buddhists in City Y made up 30 percent of its population.

4. If point X is directly north of point Y and directly west of point Z, what is the distance from point X to point Z?

   (1) The distance from Y to Z is 20.

   (2) The distance from X to Y is equal to half the distance from Y to Z.

GO ON TO THE NEXT PAGE.

A   Statement (1) ALONE is sufficient, but statement (2) alone is not sufficient.
B   Statement (2) ALONE is sufficient, but statement (1) alone is not sufficient.
C   BOTH statements TOGETHER are sufficient, but NEITHER statement ALONE is sufficient.
D   EACH statement ALONE is sufficient.
E   Statements (1) and (2) TOGETHER are NOT sufficient.

5. Is v equal to the average (arithmetic mean) of s, t, and u?

   (1) $s + t + u = 3v$

   (2) $\dfrac{s+t+u}{6} = \dfrac{v}{2}$

6. What is the maximum capacity in cups of a pail that contains only sand and is filled to three-fourths of its capacity?

   (1) If one cup of sand were added to the pail, it would be filled to seven-eighths of its capacity.

   (2) If two cups were removed from the pail, it would be filled to one-half of its capacity.

7. What is the value of x?

   (1) $x^2 = 4x$

   (2) x is an even integer.

8. Marc must visit either the library or the University Center. Which of these two buildings is a greater distance from his home?

   (1) It takes Marc an average of 20 minutes to ride his bike from his home to the library.

   (2) It takes Marc an average of 20 minutes to ride his bike from the library to the University Center.

9. Is x^3 equal to 125?

   (1) $x > 4$

   (2) $x < 6$

GO ON TO THE NEXT PAGE.

A Statement (1) ALONE is sufficient, but statement (2) alone is not sufficient.
B Statement (2) ALONE is sufficient, but statement (1) alone is not sufficient.
C BOTH statements TOGETHER are sufficient, but NEITHER statement ALONE is sufficient.
D EACH statement ALONE is sufficient.
E Statements (1) and (2) TOGETHER are NOT sufficient.

10. Over a seven-week period a company monitored the output of two of its branches, C and D. Each week the company calculated how many units were produced in each branch. The branch that produced the greatest number of units for four or more of the seven weeks was considered the more efficient branch. Which office was deemed the more efficient?

(1) Over the seven-week period Branch C produced twice as many units as Branch D.

(2) The branch that was more efficient was known by the fifth week.

11. All of the tickets for two real estate seminars, F and G, were either purchased or given away, and the ratio of F tickets to G tickets was 2 to 1. Of the total number of F tickets and G tickets, what percentage was purchased?

(1) The total number of F tickets and G tickets is 240.

(2) Of the F tickets, exactly 60 percent were purchased, and of the G tickets, exactly 80 percent were purchased.

12. What is the greatest common factor of positive integers x and y?

(1) The greatest common factor of $\frac{x}{2}$ and $\frac{y}{2}$ is 5.

(2) x and y are even.

13. If x and y are positive integers, is $x + 4y$ odd?

(1) y is odd.

(2) x is odd.

GO ON TO THE NEXT PAGE.

A   Statement (1) ALONE is sufficient, but statement (2) alone is not sufficient.
B   Statement (2) ALONE is sufficient, but statement (1) alone is not sufficient.
C   BOTH statements TOGETHER are sufficient, but NEITHER statement ALONE is sufficient.
D   EACH statement ALONE is sufficient.
E   Statements (1) and (2) TOGETHER are NOT sufficient.

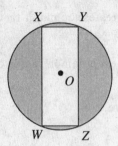

14. Rectangle *WXYZ* is inscribed in a circle with center *O* as shown above. If the diameter of the circle is equal to 16, then what is the area of the shaded region?

(1) *WZ* = *OW*

(2) *XW* < *XY*

15. Is rectangular block *B* a cube?

(1) At least two faces of rectangular block *B* are square.

(2) The volume of rectangular block *B* is 64.

16. Is the statement $0 < y < 1$ true?

(1) $0 < \sqrt{y} < 1$

(2) $y^2 = \dfrac{1}{4}$

17. In the figure above, what is the length of *PQ* times the length of *RS*?

(1) The length of *PQ* is 5.

(2) The length of *QR* times the length of *PR* is equal to 12.

GO ON TO THE NEXT PAGE.

A   Statement (1) ALONE is sufficient, but statement (2) alone is not sufficient.
B   Statement (2) ALONE is sufficient, but statement (1) alone is not sufficient.
C   BOTH statements TOGETHER are sufficient, but NEITHER statement ALONE is sufficient.
D   EACH statement ALONE is sufficient.
E   Statements (1) and (2) TOGETHER are NOT sufficient.

18. If P is a set of integers and 3 is in P, is every positive multiple of 3 in P?

   (1) For any integer in P, the sum of 3 and that integer is also in P.

   (2) For any integer in P, that integer minus 3 is also in P.

	s	
u	t	8
	4	

19. If t is a multiple of prime number s, is t a multiple of s^2?

   (1) $s < 4$

   (2) $t = 18$

20. A computer generates non-zero numbers for the figure above so that the product of the numbers along any vertical column is equal to the product of the numbers in any horizontal row. What number does s represent?

   (1) u equals 6.

   (2) t equals 2.

STOP

IF YOU FINISH BEFORE TIME IS CALLED, YOU MAY CHECK YOUR WORK ON THIS SECTION ONLY.
DO NOT TURN TO ANY OTHER SECTION IN THE TEST.

SECTION 7

Time—25 Minutes

22 Questions

<u>Directions</u>: In each of the following sentences, some part of the sentence or the entire sentence is underlined. Beneath each sentence you will find five ways of phrasing the underlined part. The first of these repeats the original; the other four are different. If you think the original is better than any of the alternatives, choose answer A; otherwise choose one of the others. Select the best version and blacken the corresponding space on your answer sheet.

This is a test of correctness and effectiveness of expression. In choosing answers, follow the requirements of standard written English; that is, pay attention to grammar, choice of words, and sentence construction. Choose the answer that expresses most effectively what is presented in the original sentence; this answer should be clear and exact, without awkwardness, ambiguity, or redundancy.

1. Violence in the stands at soccer matches has gotten so pronounced in several European countries that some stadiums have adopted new rules that aim <u>to identify fans of visiting teams and that seat them</u> in a separate area.

   (A) to identify fans of visiting teams and that seat them
   (B) to identify fans of visiting teams and seat them
   (C) to identify fans of visiting teams for seating
   (D) at identifying fans of visiting teams so as to seat them
   (E) at identifying fans of visiting teams and that seat them

2. Despite the recent election of a woman to the office of prime minister, the status of women in Pakistan <u>is little changed from how it was</u> in the last century.

   (A) is little changed from how it was
   (B) is a little changed from how it was
   (C) has changed little
   (D) has changed little from how it has been
   (E) is little changed from the way it was

GO ON TO THE NEXT PAGE.

3. In the last twenty years, despite the chauvinism of European connoisseurs, California wines <u>are respected</u> throughout the world.

   (A) are respected
   (B) are becoming better respected
   (C) which have gained respect
   (D) have gained respect
   (E) have since become respected

4. Recently there has been increased debate <u>over if a budget surplus should go towards lower taxes or increased spending</u> on social programs.

   (A) over if a budget surplus should go towards lower taxes or increased spending
   (B) over whether a budget surplus should go towards lowering taxes or increasing spending
   (C) about a budget surplus going towards lower taxes or increasing spending
   (D) about if lower taxes should come from a budget surplus or spending increases
   (E) concerning a budget surplus and its going towards lower taxes or increased spending

5. Chicago, <u>where industrial growth in the nineteenth century was more rapid than any other American city</u>, was plagued by labor troubles like the Pullman Strikes of 1894.

   (A) where industrial growth in the nineteenth century was more rapid than any other American city
   (B) which had industrial growth in the nineteenth century more rapid than that of other American cities
   (C) which had growth industrially more rapid than any other American city in the nineteenth century
   (D) whose industrial growth in the nineteenth century was more rapid than any other American city
   (E) whose industrial growth in the nineteenth century was more rapid than that of any other American city

GO ON TO THE NEXT PAGE.

6. With total sales <u>of less than three hundred thousand dollars and fewer</u> new subscribers than last year, the New England Theatre Company is in danger of losing its building.

(A) of less than three hundred thousand dollars and fewer
(B) lower than three hundred thousand dollars and less
(C) lesser than three hundred thousand dollars and fewer
(D) fewer than three hundred thousand dollars and less
(E) of fewer than three hundred thousand dollars and of fewer

7. A recent *New York Times* editorial criticized the city's election board for, first of all, failing to replace outmoded voting machines prone to breakdowns, and <u>secondarily, for their failure to</u> investigate allegations of corruption involving board members.

(A) secondarily, for their failure to
(B) secondly, for their failure to
(C) secondly, that they failed and did not
(D) second, that they failed to
(E) second, for failing to

8. <u>Two week notice being given to employers before leaving</u> a job is the generally accepted protocol.

(A) Two week notice being given to employers before leaving
(B) Giving notice to employers of two weeks before having to leave
(C) Two weeks' notice to give to employers before leaving
(D) Giving notice to employers two weeks before leaving
(E) To give two weeks' worth of notice before having to leave

9. Upset by the recent downturn in production numbers during the first half of the year, <u>the possibility of adding worker incentives was raised by the board of directors at its quarterly meeting</u>.

(A) the possibility of adding worker incentives was raised by the board of directors at its quarterly meeting
(B) the addition of worker incentives was raised as a possibility by the board of directors at its quarterly meeting
(C) added worker incentives was raised by the board of directors at its quarterly meeting as a possibility
(D) the board of directors raised at its quarterly meeting the possibility of worker incentives being added
(E) the board of directors, at its quarterly meeting, raised the possibility of adding worker incentives

10. IRS provision 354-B requires <u>that an S corporation with assets of greater than $200,000 send W-2 forms to their full- and part-time employees on or before Jan. 31</u>.

(A) that an S corporation with assets of greater than $200,000 send W-2 forms to their full- and part-time employees on or before Jan. 31
(B) an S corporation with assets of greater than $200,000 send W-2 forms to their full- and part-time employees on or before Jan. 31
(C) that an S corporation with assets of greater than $200,000 send W-2 forms to its full- and part-time employees on or before Jan. 31
(D) an S corporation with assets of greater than $200,000 to send W-2 forms to their full- and part-time employees on Jan. 31 or before
(E) an S corporation with assets of greater than $200,000 send W-2 forms to its full- and part-time employees on or before Jan. 31

GO ON TO THE NEXT PAGE.

11. <u>Just as the European countries of the early eighteenth century sought to exploit the resources of our continent, so too</u> are we now attempting to extract energy and minerals from the ocean bed.

(A) Just as the European countries of the early eighteenth century sought to exploit the resources of our continent, so too

(B) The European countries of the early eighteenth century sought to exploit the resources of our continent, and in a similar way

(C) Like the case of the European countries of the early eighteenth century who sought to exploit the resources of our continent, so too

(D) As in the exploitation of the resources of our continent by European countries of the early eighteenth century,

(E) Similar to the European countries which sought in the early eighteenth century to exploit the resources of our continent

12. In 1978 a national study found that not only had many contractors licensed by a self-policing private guild failed to pass qualifying exams, <u>they in addition falsified their references</u>.

(A) they in addition falsified their references

(B) they had their references falsified in addition

(C) but they had also falsified their references

(D) they had also falsified their references

(E) but their references were falsified as well

13. An attempt <u>to ratify the Equal Rights Amendment, begun almost two decades ago,</u> has been unsuccessful despite efforts by many important groups, including the National Organization for Women.

(A) to ratify the Equal Rights Amendment, begun almost two decades ago,

(B) begun almost two decades ago, for ratifying the Equal Rights Amendment

(C) begun for ratifying the Equal Rights Amendment almost two decades ago

(D) at ratifying the Equal Rights Amendment, begun almost two decades ago,

(E) that has begun almost two decades ago to ratify the Equal Rights Amendment

14. When evidence of financial wrongdoing by an elected official surfaces, it is the electorate who must decide <u>whether the evidence warrants censuring him or ousting him</u> from office.

(A) whether the evidence warrants censuring him or ousting him

(B) if there is evidence that warrants a censure or an ousting of him

(C) whether or not the evidence warrants the censuring or ousting of him

(D) if there is evidence that warrants censuring him or his ousting

(E) if the evidence would warrant that he be censured or that he be ousted

15. Because the enemy's new ship is the quietest <u>and it is therefore the most elusive submarine, it is being increasingly viewed</u> by the military as a threat to security.

(A) and it is therefore the most elusive submarine, it is being increasingly viewed

(B) it is therefore the most elusive of submarines, and it has increased the view

(C) and therefore the most elusive submarine, it is being increasingly viewed

(D) and therefore it is the most elusive of submarines, there is an increasing view

(E) therefore being the most elusive of submarines, it is increasingly viewed

GO ON TO THE NEXT PAGE.

16. The economic forces which may affect the new public offering of stock include sudden downturns in the market, hedging and other investor strategies for preventing losses, <u>loosening the interest rates in Washington, and fearing that the company may still be undercapitalized</u>.

(A) loosening the interest rates in Washington, and fearing that the company may still be undercapitalized

(B) loosening the interest rates in Washington, and a fear of the company still being undercapitalized

(C) a loosening of the interest rates in Washington, and fearing that the company may still be undercapitalized

(D) a loosening of the interest rates in Washington, and a fear of the still undercapitalized company

(E) a loosening of the interest rates in Washington, and a fear that the company may still be undercapitalized

17. Like the government that came before it, which set new records for growth, <u>laissez-faire capitalism is the cornerstone of the new government</u>.

(A) laissez-faire capitalism is the cornerstone of the new government

(B) the cornerstone of the new government is laissez-faire capitalism

(C) laissez-faire capitalism is the new government's cornerstone

(D) the new government has made laissez-faire capitalism its cornerstone

(E) the new government has a laissez-faire cornerstone of capitalism

18. During the 1980s it became clear <u>that soliciting private funds was far more efficient for environmentalists who sought financial aid</u> than to go to state or federal agencies.

(A) that soliciting private funds was far more efficient for environmentalists who sought financial aid

(B) that for environmentalists who sought financial aid, it was far more efficient to solicit private funds

(C) that for environmentalists seeking financial aid, private organizations were far more efficient to go to

(D) for environmentalists seeking financial aid, going to private organizations was far more efficient

(E) for environmentalists who sought financial aid, private organizations were far more efficient

19. The major areas of medicine in which lasers are effective <u>is in the cutting and closing of blood vessels, and in the destruction</u> of tumors.

(A) is in the cutting and closing of blood vessels, and in the destruction

(B) are the cutting and closing of blood vessels, and also the case of destroying

(C) are the cutting, closing of blood vessels, and in the destroying

(D) are the cutting and closing of blood vessels, and the destruction

(E) is in the cutting and closing of blood vessels, and the destroying

GO ON TO THE NEXT PAGE.

20. Since the movie was released seventeen UFOs have been sighted in the state, <u>which is more than had been sighted</u> in the past ten years together.

    (A) which is more than had been sighted
    (B) more than had been sighted
    (C) more than they had sighted
    (D) more than had reported sightings
    (E) which is more than had reported sightings

21. Ignoring the admonitions of his staff, the chief financial officer accepted the advice of the consulting company because <u>he believed that the standardized accounting procedures would prove not only inexpensive but</u> reliable indicators of economic performance.

    (A) he believed that the standardized accounting procedures would prove not only inexpensive but
    (B) the standardized accounting procedures will prove both inexpensive and also
    (C) he believed the standardized accounting procedures would prove themselves to be both inexpensive and
    (D) he believed that the standardized accounting procedures would prove to be both inexpensive and
    (E) standardized accounting procedures will prove his belief that they are both inexpensive and

22. A large rise in the number of housing starts in the coming year should boost new construction dollars by several billion dollars, <u>making the construction industry's economic health much more robust than five years ago</u>.

    (A) making the construction industry's economic health much more robust than five years ago
    (B) and make the construction industry's economic health much more robust than five years ago
    (C) making the construction industry's economic health much more robust than it was five years ago
    (D) to make the construction industry's economic health much more robust than five years ago
    (E) in making the construction industry's economic health much more robust than it was five years ago

STOP

IF YOU FINISH BEFORE TIME IS CALLED, YOU MAY CHECK YOUR WORK ON THIS SECTION ONLY.
DO NOT TURN TO ANY OTHER SECTION IN THE TEST.

ANSWER KEY

Section 2	Section 3	Section 4	Section 5	Section 6	Section 7
1. C	1. C	1. C	1. B	1. C	1. B
2. B	2. D	2. B	2. C	2. A	2. C
3. B	3. C	3. D	3. E	3. B	3. D
4. E	4. B	4. D	4. D	4. C	4. B
5. A	5. A	5. C	5. C	5. D	5. E
6. E	6. A	6. D	6. B	6. D	6. A
7. A	7. E	7. B	7. D	7. E	7. E
8. D	8. A	8. A	8. E	8. E	8. D
9. A	9. E	9. D	9. A	9. E	9. E
10. C	10. B	10. C	10. C	10. E	10. C
11. D	11. D	11. B	11. B	11. B	11. A
12. B	12. E	12. C	12. A	12. A	12. C
13. D	13. B	13. E	13. C	13. B	13. A
14. B	14. B	14. B	14. C	14. A	14. A
15. A	15. E	15. E	15. D	15. E	15. C
16. B	16. A	16. D	16. E	16. A	16. E
	17. C			17. B	17. D
	18. A			18. A	18. B
				19. E	19. D
				20. A	20. B
					21. D
					22. C

HOW TO SCORE THE PRINCETON REVIEW GMAT DIAGNOSTIC TEST

When you take the real exam, the proctors will collect your text booklet and bubble sheet and send your answer sheet to New Jersey where a computer (yes, a big old-fashioned one that has been around since the 1960s) looks at the pattern of filled-in ovals on your answer sheet and gives you a score. We couldn't include even a small computer with this book, so we are providing this more primitive way of scoring your exam.

DETERMINING YOUR SCORE

STEP 1   Add up the total number of questions you got right from all six sections:

(A) _____

STEP 2   Add up the number of questions you got wrong:

(B) _____

STEP 3   Now, divide the incorrect number by 4:

(C) (B) ÷ 4 = _____

STEP 4   Subtract this last figure from the number correct. This will give you your corrected raw score:

(A) – (C) = _____

STEP 5   To find your scaled point score, look up your corrected raw score on the conversion table on next page.

CONVERSION TABLE FOR TOTAL SCORES GMAT

Corrected Raw Score	Total Scaled Score	Corrected Raw Score	Total Scaled Score	Corrected Raw Score	Total Scaled Score	Corrected Raw Score	Total Scaled Score
108	800	78	640	48	490	18	330
107	800	77	640	47	480	17	330
106	800	76	630	46	480	16	320
105	790	75	630	45	470	15	320
104	790	74	620	44	470	14	310
103	780	73	620	43	460	13	300
102	780	72	610	42	460	12	300
101	770	71	610	41	450	11	290
100	760	70	600	40	440	10	290
99	750	69	600	39	440	9	280
98	750	68	590	38	430	8	280
97	740	67	580	37	430	7	270
96	730	66	580	36	420	6	260
95	730	65	570	35	420	5	250
94	720	64	570	34	410	4	240
93	720	63	560	33	410	3	230
92	710	62	560	32	400	2	220
91	710	61	550	31	400	1	210
90	700	60	550	30	390	0	200
89	700	59	540	29	390		
88	690	58	540	28	380		
87	690	57	530	27	380		
86	680	56	530	26	370		
85	680	55	520	25	370		
84	670	54	520	24	360		
83	670	53	510	23	360		
82	660	52	510	22	350		
81	660	51	500	21	350		
80	650	50	500	20	340		
79	650	49	490	19	340		

**Answers and
Explanations to the
Diagnostic Test**

ANSWERS AND EXPLANATIONS
to the Princeton Review GMAT Diagnostic

SECTION ONE

This was the experimental section and has been left out since it did not count toward your score.

SECTION 2—PROBLEM SOLVING

1. **(C)** Rather than multiply out each side of the equation, let's simplify. We can rewrite 16 as 2^4. If we cancel 2^3 from each side of the equation, we are left with $2(3)^2 = x$. The correct answer is (C) 18.

2. **(B)** It snowed from 9 a.m. until 3 p.m., for a total of six hours. The rate of snowfall was $1\frac{1}{4}$ inches every <u>two</u> hours. So to find the snowfall during those three 2-hour periods, multiply $1\frac{1}{4}$ times 3, for a total of $3\frac{3}{4}$ inches. You'll notice that this is the number in answer choice (A), but we aren't quite done yet. There were already $2\frac{1}{4}$ inches on the ground. To get the total number of inches, we need to add $3\frac{3}{4}$ to $2\frac{1}{4}$. The answer is (B) 6.

   By the way, if you picked choice (E), you probably thought the rate of snowfall was $1\frac{1}{4}$ inches per hour. As usual, ETS made sure your answer was there waiting for you. Could we have ballparked this problem a bit? Sure. There were already $2\frac{1}{4}$ inches on the ground, and the snow was falling at a rate of $1\frac{1}{4}$ every two hours. Clearly choice (A) was going to be too small.

3. **(B)** What kind of problem was this? A percent problem. 70% of the 550 new employees were B-school graduates. 70% of 550 = 385. If you were rushing you might have chosen choice (D) 385, but we weren't done yet. The other 30% were B.A.s. 30% of 550 = 165. The problem wants to know the difference between 385 and 165. To find the difference, simply subtract. The correct answer is (B) 220.

   Could we have ballparked? Sure. The difference between 70% and 30% is 40%, or slightly less than half of the 550 new employees. Choices (D) and (E) were both greater than half. Choice (A) was much too small. For a quick way to compute these percents, turn back to page 180.

4. **(E)** Rather than multiply out completely, let's focus on the units digit of both numbers. We may not need to know exactly what 165^2 equals, if we know what its units digit equals. 5^2 gives us a units digit of 5, so whatever the entire number will be, its units digit will be 5. We may not need to know exactly what 164^2 equals, if we know what its units digit equals. 4^2 gives us a units digit of 6, so whatever the entire number is going to be, its units digit will be 6. The problem asks you to subtract the second number from the first. Again, we don't know what either number is exactly, but we do know that the first number ends in a 5 and the second ends in a 6. When you subtract one from the other, what will the units digit be?

$$
\begin{array}{r}
\_\,,\_\_\ 5 \\
-\ \_\,,\_\_\ 6 \\
\hline
9
\end{array}
$$

The correct answer is (E) 329.

5. (A) While this looks like a geometry problem, it is actually simply a matter of plugging the numbers provided into the formula. Let's start with the surface area of 600. To find $\sqrt{\dfrac{600}{6}}$, first divide 600 by 6 to get 100. The square root of $100 = 10$. To find $\sqrt{\dfrac{1350}{6}}$, first divide 1350 by 6 to get 225. The square root of $225 = 15$. The problem asks how much longer 15 is than 10. The correct answer is choice (A) 5.

6. (E) Variables in the answer choices means this is a plug-in problem—a total gift as long as you use our techniques—but the word "must" means you may have to plug in *twice* to be sure you have the right answer. Whenever you plug in, be sure to write the number you are using above the variable so you won't forget it as you work. Since y must be an odd integer, let's use 3. Now, all we have to do is plug 3 into each of the answer choices. Any choice that does *not* yield an even integer can be crossed off immediately. If more than one of the choices yields an even integer, we will have to plug in a second number for y to see which choice *always* yields an even number. Using 3 as our value for y, we find that choices (A), (B), (C), and (D) all yield odd numbers. Therefore the correct answer is choice (E).

7. (A) In this fraction problem, many students would be tempted to use a common denominator of 18. However, if you take a second to look at the fractions involved, you will notice that the second two fractions can be reduced. $\dfrac{15}{18} = \dfrac{5}{6}$ and $\dfrac{12}{10} = \dfrac{5}{6}$ as well. This saves a lot of time. x turns out to equal $\dfrac{5}{6} + \dfrac{5}{6} - \dfrac{5}{6}$ —in other words, $\dfrac{5}{6}$.

Now let's plug in $\dfrac{5}{6}$ for x in the second part of the equation. $\left(\dfrac{5}{6} - 1\right)^3 = \left(-\dfrac{1}{6}\right)^3$. The correct answer is choice (A) $-\dfrac{1}{216}$.

Could we have ballparked? Sure. As soon as you know that the number in the parentheses is going to be negative, you could have eliminated choices (C), (D), and (E). A negative number to an odd power always stays negative.

8. (D) The key word in this problem is "ratio." To find the number of nurses, we must convert the ratio to a fraction. If the ratio of doctors to nurses is 5 to 7, then the "whole" is $5 + 7$, or 12. The fraction of nurses at the hospital is $\dfrac{7}{12}$. Let's set up an equation: $\dfrac{7}{12} = \dfrac{x}{240}$ The correct answer is choice (D) 140.

If you picked choice (C), you found the number of *doctors* at the hospital.

Could we have ballparked? Sure. Once we knew that the fraction of nurses at the hospital was $\dfrac{7}{12}$, we could see that the actual number of nurses had to be slightly more than half of the total $\left(\dfrac{6}{12} \text{ would be exactly half}\right)$. This allows us to eliminate choices (A), (B), and (C) because they are all less than half, and choice (E) because it is much greater than half.

9. (A) ETS wants you to write an equation here. The correct equation would be $d + .25d = 60$. Then you would have to subtract your result from 60 to get the final answer.

However, there is a much faster way. Let's backsolve. Ordinarily, when you backsolve you want to start with choice (C), but in this case choice (B) is much easier: If $60 - d = 30$, then $d = 30$, which is a nice round number to work with. Let's see if plugging in 30 for d makes the problem work. According to the problem, the temperature rises 25% from d degrees to 60 degrees. If $d = 30$, could this be true? No way! 25% of 30 is only a bit more than 7. D must be much larger. And if d is much larger, then $60 - d$, which is what we are looking for, must be much smaller than choice (B). There is only one choice smaller than (B). The correct answer is choice (A) 12.

10. (C) To appear on all three lists, a number would have to be a multiple of 2, 3, and 5, all at the same time. What kind of number is a multiple of all three of these numbers? A number that has 2, 3, and 5 as factors. If we multiply $2 \times 3 \times 5$, we get 30. 30 is therefore a multiple of 2, 3, and 5. How many numbers like this are there between 1 and 100? 30 is the first one, 60 is the second, and 90 is the third. The correct answer is choice (C) 3.

11. (D) This volume problem is potentially difficult because there may be more than one way to stack the boxes inside the carton. We need to find the *maximum* number that will fit. Let's start by worrying about one layer of cereal boxes inside the carton—in other words, let's start in two dimensions instead of three. Later we'll worry about the height of the box, but for now consider a rectangle that is 25 by 42.

As with any geometry problem without a diagram, it is essential that you make your own drawing. How many smaller rectangles measuring 5 by 7 will fit in this larger 25 by 42 rectangle? You can actually draw in the smaller boxes if you want. You will notice that you can fit 5 sides of 5 inches along the 25 inch side. You

can fit 6 sides of 7 inches along the 42 inch side. This means that you can fit 5×6, or 30 boxes in one layer of the carton. Now, how many layers of boxes fit in the carton? The carton is 60 inches tall. Each of the boxes is 6 inches tall. How many layers of 6 inches fit into 60? That's right, 10. The correct answer to this problem is 10 times 30, which is choice (D) 300. We know this is the maximum number because we used up all the space in the carton.

12. (B) This is a great backsolve problem. Instead of writing an equation, just try plugging the answer choices back into the problem until you find the correct answer. As usual, you want to start with choice (C).

Let's suppose for a moment that Sue will be (C) 11 years old in 3 years. That means that right now she is 8. The problem says Sue is now 10 years younger than Jane. If Sue is now 8, then Jane is now 18.

According to the problem, in five years Jane will be twice as old as Sue. Let's see if these numbers make that true: in five years, Sue will be 13 and Jane will be 23. Obviously, choice (C) is wrong, so we eliminate it. At this point in most backsolve problems you can tell whether you need a larger or a smaller number, which enables you to eliminate several other answer choices as well. However, sometimes you may not be able to see in which direction to go. Can you tell in this case if we want a larger or a smaller number? You may have noticed that in choice (C), Sue's age ended up being slightly *more* than half Jane's age. Sue's age will have to start out a bit smaller to make the problem work. However, if you didn't notice that, don't get worried. Rather than wasting time trying to figure out which direction to go in, just pick a direction, and see what happens. At worst, you'll just try each of the answers until you get the right one.

Let's try choice (B). If Sue will be 8 in three years, then she is 5 right now. Sue is now 10 years younger than Jane, so Jane is 15 right now. In five years, Sue will be 10 and Jane will be 20. Bingo! Jane's age in five years is twice Sue's. The correct answer is choice (B). Note that choice (E), the Joe Bloggs answer in this question, was simply the sum of all the numbers in the problem. If that's all this problem took it wouldn't have been number 12.

13. **(D)** The five-pair package costs $3.40, which works out to 68 cents per pair, as opposed to the $1.00 per pair if purchased individually. Thus, the savings per pair if you buy the package is 32 cents. What percent cheaper is this? $\frac{32}{100}$, or choice (D).

14. **(B)** As soon as you see variables in the answer, you should be thinking "plugging in." In order for (B) to be true, x would have to equal 1. This is impossible, since x must be smaller than y and only y can equal 1. The correct answer is choice (B).

15. **(A)** This is a cosmic plugging in problem. Notice that no specific price is ever mentioned. You could use an equation to solve this problem, but it would be infinitely easier to plug in prices. The problem says that the price of each computer was three times the price of a printer. Let's make the price of a printer $100, which would make the price of a computer $300. 20 printers at $100 each works out to $2,000, and 60 computers at $300 each works out to $18,000. The question wants to know what percent of the total cost was the cost of all the printers. The total cost (using the numbers we plugged in) was $20,000. The cost of the printers was $2,000.

$$\frac{\$2,000}{\$20,000} = \frac{x}{100}$$

The correct answer is choice (A) 10%. Notice that choice (D) was a Joe Bloggs answer, merely repeating a number from the problem itself.

16. **(B)** Based on the variables in the answer choices, this is yet another plug-in problem. Let's pick 5 for m, 200 for n and 8 for r. Of course, any numbers will work, but the problem was much easier to figure out if we picked a number for n that easily converted into dollars, since the answer to the question is supposed to be in dollars. Based on these numbers, one week would cost $35 in maintenance, and $16 for production, for a total cost of $51. Now, all we have to do is figure out which answer choice equals 51 when we plug in our numbers for m, n, and r. The correct answer is choice (B).

Section 3—Reading Comprehension

Passage 1

Paragraph one compares two theories of arbitration—judicial and political.

Paragraph two briefly describes each theory.

Paragraph three relates arbitration to the idea of conciliation, and ultimately decides that the judicial theory of arbitration is preferable.

1. **(C)** The passage did not mention the larger social failures that might make arbitration necessary (A), nor the origin of the theories (B) or the stages of bargaining (E). The confusion between arbitration vs. conciliation *was* discussed, but was this the main idea of the passage? Nope. The correct answer was choice (C), a good paraphrase of the main idea of the passage.

2. **(D)** This specific question has a good lead phrase: "political theory." Running your finger down the passage, you would find it on line 15. Remember, this is an except question—the choice that was *not* discussed in relation to political theory is correct: choice (D). This was said about judicial theory a bit earlier in the passage.

3. **(C)** Litigation, biased arbitrators, new strategies for avoiding conflicts, and resolution of the rights of different parties—all of these are outside the scope of this passage.

   Choice (C) is correct because if the two parties' goal is compromise, then compromise would actually *be* the "just or pragmatic" decision.

4. **(B)** This specific question has the same lead phrase we found in question 2: "political theory." The answer to the question can be found in lines 15–21. We know from the beginning of the paragraph that the judicial theory is "just." But the sentence that describes the political theory begins with the trigger word, "on the other hand." We also see it described as "collective coercion." The correct answer is choice (B).

5. **(A)** This specific question has a good lead phrase: "judicial theory." We'll find it at the beginning of the second paragraph. Choices (B), (D) and (E) would all be true of the political theory, not the judicial theory. Choice (C) is not mentioned in the passage. The correct answer is choice (A).

6. **(A)** This specific question also has a good lead phrase: "conciliation." We'll find it in the third paragraph. (B) and (C) are not discussed in the passage. Choice (D) gets it wrong: compromise is not compatible with absolute "rights." Choice (E) is too extreme. Which of the two theories is conciliation linked to? If you said political, you are doing just fine—so the answer is choice (A).

7. **(E)** The answer to this question is in line 5. Choices (A), (B), and (C) are all based on the judicial theory. Choice (D) might have seemed tempting but it was pretty broad for a specific question. The correct answer was choice (E).

Passage 2

It's a science passage, and like many real ETS passages, not particularly well written.

Paragraph one says the orangutan, studied by scientists for its resemblance to early humans, lives in trees and is very territorial.

Paragraph two describes the orangutan's solitary territorial behavior which resembled that of early humans.

8. **(A)** The answer to this general question came from understanding the main idea. The passage did not analyze the *reasons* primates left trees (B), or devote itself to a discussion of poachers (C), or do a point-by-point comparison of orangutans with other primates (D), or criticize anthropologists (E). The correct answer is choice (A).

9. **(E)** This specific question has a line number. Remember to read a bit above and below the cited lines. The answer to this question actually came just *below* the quote. The poacher example is simply a further illustration of orangutans' territorial nature. The correct answer is choice (E).

10. (B) It's a good idea to save I, II, III questions for last since they often require you to answer three questions for the price of one.

Fortunately, in this case, the question is discussing the same topic you were just reading about for question number 9. Both statements I and II were mentioned in lines 24–26. Statement III was not. The correct answer is choice (B).

11. (D) This is a specific question with no line number, and, really, no lead word. We're looking for differences between orangutans and other types of apes. The only other type of monkey mentioned is a chimpanzee who is said to be more gregarious in lines 29-30. The correct answer is choice (D).

12. (E) This specific question also has a good lead word: "anthropologists." We found it in two places, at the very beginning and the very end of the passage. You were probably down to choices (C) and (E). Why was (C) wrong? Because anthropologists only see parallels with *early* man.

13. (B) This specific question also has a good lead word: "territoriality." You'll find it in the second half of the first paragraph, which discusses two causes: the need for large amounts of food, and breeding habits. You were probably down to (A) or (B). Why was (A) wrong? It didn't discuss both food and breeding habits. Choice (B) was correct.

14. (B) The second sentence of the first paragraph ends, ". . . and only migrated to the ground as forests began to dwindle." That gives us choice (B).

Passage 3
This was the longest passage, so it made sense to leave it for last.
Paragraph one says that ancient Rome has been criticized for lack of originality, but the criticism is wrong.
Paragraph two gives the example of Rome's engineering innovations.

Paragraph three gives the example of the influence of their language (Latin) on other languages. Paragraph four gives the example of Rome's political innovations.

15. (E) This specific question has a line number. Remember to read a bit above and below the cited lines. The two disasters cited are mentioned to give an example of Rome's failings, before countering with a number of Rome's successes. The best answer was choice (E).

16. (A) This specific question also has a good lead phrase: "Roman roads." You'll find it in the beginning of the second paragraph. Choice (C) is wrong because these roads are not just similar to modern highways—they form the *basis* of these highways. Choice (E) is a bit too extreme. The cities may owe their prominence to these roads, but they were not "caused" by the roads. The correct answer (choice (A)) is a paraphrase of lines 19–23.

17. (C) It's a good idea to save I, II, III questions for last since they often require you to answer three questions for the price of one.

However, this is also a specific question with a good lead phrase: "Latin language." You'll find it in the third paragraph. The correct answer is choice (C). If you were tempted by statement III, remember, while Latin derivatives are widely spoken today, the passage says Latin itself is "seldom spoken today." If you said, "Well, what about the Vatican?" you forgot that as far as ETS is concerned, only what's said in the passage is relevant.

18. (A) This specific question also has a good lead phrase: "framers of the Constitution." You'll find it in the last paragraph. You may have been down to choices (A) and (C). Choice (C) used extreme language, and went a bit too far. Great as the veto is, did the founding fathers consider it the "hallmark" of democracy? The passage doesn't say so. The correct answer was choice (A).

Section 4—Problem Solving

1. **(C)** In this decimal question, choices (A) and (E) are off the scale. Choices (B) and (D) are the smallest and greatest numbers on the scale, but the mercury in the thermometer is a little less than 94.08. The correct answer is choice (C).

2. **(B)** This is a cosmic plug-in problem. Let's say there were 100 customers. 40 of them purchase something. The problem says that 15% of the 40 purchase hats. 15% of 40 is 6. The correct answer is choice (B). We could have used ballparking to eliminate choice (E) which was greater than the percentage of customers who bought *anything*, let alone hats.

3. **(D)** Let's translate the first sentence: $xy = 10(x - y)$. If $y = 5$, then x must equal 10. The correct answer is choice (D).

4. **(D)** Use PEMDAS to perform the operations in the correct order. Start with the innermost set of parentheses: first, square $\frac{2}{3}$, then subtract that from 1, finally square the result. The correct answer is choice (D). You could have used ballparking to eliminate choice (A) because the square of any number is always positive.

5. **(C)** To get this fraction problem correct, you needed to remember the concept of "the rest." If Bernie reads $\frac{3}{5}$ of his homework on Monday, that means $\frac{2}{5}$ remains to be read. He reads $\frac{1}{3}$ of the $\frac{2}{5}$ (remember, in math the word "of " always means multiply) or $\frac{2}{15}$ on Tuesday.

How much of his assignment has he done so far? $\frac{3}{5} + \frac{2}{15}$. Using the bowtie, this works out to $\frac{11}{15}$. How much remains? The correct answer is choice (C) $\frac{4}{15}$.

6. **(D)** You could use the quadratic formula, but it would be just as easy to plug in since there are variables in the answer choices. Pick a value for x, solve the equation and then find out which answer choice yields the same number. If we let $x = 2$, we get $\frac{15}{3}$, or 5. Which answer choice equals 5? That's right, choice (D) $x + 3$.

7. **(B)** The first step in this medium problem is to simply the values of a, b, and c. $a = \frac{1}{100}$, $b = \frac{1}{5}$, and $c = \frac{1}{10}$. The correct answer is choice (B).

8. **(A)** $3\frac{1}{2}$ is equal to $\frac{7}{2}$. If $\frac{1}{y} = \frac{7}{2}$, then $y = \frac{2}{7}$. We can now plug this value into the equation:

$$\frac{1}{\frac{2}{7} + \frac{14}{7}} \text{ or } \frac{7}{16}$$

The correct answer is choice (A).

9. **(D)** Laura is paying back 2.5 percent of the loan each quarter of the year. 2.5% of $240 is $6.00. If she has already paid $42.00, that means she has paid that $6.00 for seven quarters. How many months is that? Each quarter of the year is 3 months. The correct answer is choice (D).

10. (C) Answering a function problem is simply a matter of following directions. In this case, the directions say that whenever you see two numbers a and b with a $*$ between them, you should multiply them and then divide by $b - a$. Now you have to try out each of the answer choices until you find the one that equals 3. The correct answer is choice (C).

11. (B) In this backsolving question, four of the five choices could be the result of raising a price by 10%. One of them could not. You might have noticed that it was relatively easy to figure out two of the choices. Choice (A) $5.50 was clearly the result of adding 10% of $5.00 (50 cents) to $5.00. Choice (C) was clearly the result of adding 10% of $10.00 (or $1) to $10.00. Thus, we could eliminate (A) and (C). If this was as far as you could get, it made sense to guess among the remaining answer choices. Remember, if you can eliminate even one choice, you should guess. To eliminate the other two answer choices was tougher, and it helped to try to extrapolate from one of the choices that was easier to see. For example, we knew that choice (C) was the result of adding 10% of $10 (or $1) to $10. Mathematically, what did we do? We took an amount x, added 10% of x to that and set it equal to $11.00:

$$x + .1(x) = \$11.$$

and x turned out to equal $10, a round number.

Let's try this with choice (D) $12.10:

$$x + .1(x) = \$12.10$$

If you do the math, x turns out to equal $11.00, a round number. We can eliminate choice (D).

Let's try it with choice (B) $7.60. This time, x is *not* a round number at all; it works out to about $6.9090..., a repeating decimal. The correct answer is choice (B).

12. (C) As always, when there are variables in the answer choices, the easiest thing to do is plug in. If you always get a remainder of 2 when you divide x by 5, then x has to be some multiple of 5 plus 2 more. In other words, x could be 7 or 12 or 17 or 22, etc. Now, we have to go through the answer choices plugging in numbers for x that allow them to be integers as well. For example, in choice (A), if we plugged in 17 for x, that would give us $\frac{17}{17}$ which is an integer. Cross off choice (A). In choice (B) if we plugged in 22, we would get $\frac{22}{11}$ which is an integer. Cross off choice (B). In choices (D) and (E) plugging in the number 12 would make both choices integers. Only choice (C) can never be an integer as long as x can be divided by 5 with a remainder of 2. The correct answer is choice (C).

13. (E) As an algebra question, this is pretty tough. However, if you plug in, it is pretty easy. There are $\frac{1}{3}$ as many violets as carnations. Let's say there are 30 carnations. That would mean there are 10 violets. There are $\frac{1}{2}$ as many tulips as violets, which means there are 5 tulips. And there are equal numbers of roses and tulips, which means there are 5 roses. Let's add this up

> 30 carnations
> 10 violets
> 5 tulips
> 5 roses
> _____
> 50 flowers

What percent are carnations? $\frac{30}{50} = \frac{x}{100}$. The correct answer is choice (E) 60%. Choice (B) was the Joe Bloggs answer.

14. (B) First redraw the diagram to scale, so you can see what's going on. If you redraw carefully, making sure that $AB = AO = BO$, you will be able to guesstimate, and eliminate several answer choices even if you don't know much geometry. Use the side of your answer sheet to measure your redrawn BC. Is it equal to 12? Of course not. 12 is the diameter of the circle. BC must be smaller. Cross off choice (A). Choice (E) does not come out to a whole number, but it is close to the square root of 49, or 7. Could BC be this small? No way. If you drew your diagram accurately, BC should be a little bigger than 10. The correct answer is choice (B).

Geometrically speaking, any triangle inscribed inside a semicircle forms a 90-degree angle. If triangle ABO is equilateral, that means that angle OAB is 60 degrees. Thus triangle ABC is a 30-60-90 triangle, with sides $6 - 6\sqrt{3} - 12$.

15. (E) As soon as you see the words "car" and "trip," you should be thinking $R \times T = D$. Did you also notice that this problem could be solved by working backward? Let's start with choice (C) 16 hours.

The first 6 hours were driven at 40 MPH for a total of 240 miles. That leaves 10 hours at 60 mph for a total of 600 miles. To find the average speed, divide the total distance (840) by the total number of hours (16). If the result is 55 mph, we have our answer. Unfortunately, $\frac{840}{16} = 52.5$ so we can cross off choice (C), but we can do even better than that: we can also cross off choices (A) and (B). To get from 52.5 up to 55, we need a *greater* number of hours. The answer is either (D) or (E). Let's try (E) 24.

The first 6 hours were driven at 40 MPH for a total of 240 miles. That leaves 18 hours at 60 mph for a total of 1080 miles. To find the average speed, divide the total distance (1320) by the total number of hours (24). The result is 55 mph, and the correct answer is choice (E). You could probably have used ballparking to eliminate choice (B). If the first six hours were at 40 mph and the second six hours were at 60 mph, what would the average speed have been? That's right: 50 mph. We needed a larger number. This would have allowed you to eliminate choice (A) as well as choice (B).

16. (D) Let's first figure out how many integers between 100 and 150 can be divided by 5. You could count it out on your fingers ("100, 105, 110, 115..." etc.), which gives you 11, or you could subtract 100 from 150 and then divide by 5, which gives you 10 and then you have to remember that the problem says "inclusive" meaning you have to add one more to make 11.

Now, let's figure out how many integers between 100 and 150 can be divided by 3. Again, you could count on your fingers or you could subtract 100 from 150 and then divide by 3, which gives you 16 and since 100 is not divisible by 3, you don't have to add one more. 11 + 16 = 27, which is answer choice (C), but we aren't done yet. There were three numbers in the 3 pile that were also in the 5 pile, and we can't count count them twice—105, 120, and 135. So, that's 14 in the 3 pile. 14 and 11 is 25, but the question asks how many of the integers between 100 and 150 inclusive are NOT divisible by 3 or 5. There are 51 integers between 100 and 150 inclusive. Of these, 25 are divisible by either 3 or 5. So 51 – 25 gives us the correct answer of 26. Choice (D) is correct.

Section 5—Critical Reasoning

1. **(B)** This is an analogy argument. The magazine-like houseware catalog is being launched because the company expects it to appeal to the same upscale clientele that its clothing catalog appealed to. The key word in the passage that might have alerted you to the analogy was the word "same." The assumption on which this argument depends is that the two catalogues are analogous—that it actually will attract the same clientele. (A), (C), (D), and (E) are all outside the scope of the argument. The correct answer is choice (B).

2. **(C)** This is a causal argument. The civil leaders are saying that the plant's hazardous waste is the cause of high cancer rates in the area. The company directors propose an alternate cause: polluted drinking water. How do we weaken the directors' argument? The correct answer is choice (C), which says that it is the hazardous wastes from the company that are contaminating the drinking water. In other words, there is no alternate cause; the primary cause is creating the secondary cause that the company is trying to blame. (A), (B), and (E) are outside the scope of the argument. Choice (D) is attractive, but does not directly attack the board's claims, nor does it say that the cancerous materials are contaminating the environment.

3. **(E)** This is a causal argument. According to the experts, high prime-time ratings cause the ratings of the evening news show to increase as well. However, at Channel NTR, this was not found to be true. What conclusion can we draw from this? The correct answer is choice (E) which asks us to consider that there might be alternate causes. (A), (B), and (C) are outside the scope of the argument, while choice (D) would have been more likely to be correct had this been a statistical argument.

4. **(D)** According to the passage, you are least likely to be audited if you have recently been audited and found not to have made mistakes. Thus it would seem evident that you would be most likely to be audited if you had not been audited for a while, but when you were last audited you were found to have made lots of mistakes. Unfortunately, there is no answer choice like that. We need the best choice we can find. Choice (B) seems attractive at first, but as long as the lawyer corrected the mistakes before the IRS caught them, choice (B) is effectively identical to choice (A). Choice (C) seems attractive because the spouse was convicted of tax fraud, but if you picked it, you were thinking beyond the scope of the argument. This taxpayer was audited recently and no mistakes were found. Choice (E) describes a person who is extremely unlikely to be audited given the criteria outlined in the argument. Thus, choice (D) is the best answer: The taxpayer has not been audited since 1984, and although he or she was not then found to have made any mistakes, this is the furthest away we can get from the criteria.

5. **(C)** This is an all-some-most question. The clue that gives this away is the word "must" in the question. It is often helpful to sketch out all-some-most questions for yourself. A sketch might look like this:

Nestor = Elizabeth

James - ? - Nancy

Nestor and Elizabeth are equivalent. Nancy has a lower average than Elizabeth, but we don't know where she ranks in terms of James. Now, just read through the choices for something that MUST be true. The correct answer is choice (C)

6. (B) This is a statistical argument. The officials are asserting that there is in fact no increase in actual mishaps during the months after an accident, but an increase in the number of news sources *reporting* the mishaps—in other words, they are arguing that the statistics are not representative. To weaken this assertion, we would have to show that the statistics are in fact representative. Choice (B) does this by implying that certain months are more likely to have more frequent accidents due to high volume of flights. Choice (A) is outside the scope of the argument. Choices (C), (D), and (E) would all *strengthen* the assertions of the officials.

7. (D) This is a statistical argument. The conclusion, that it would be a good idea to invest in real estate, is based on a survey that implies that there will be more demand than supply. To weaken a statistical argument, we need to show that the survey was not representative. Which choice does this? Answer choice (D) shows that the readers of *House* magazine are more likely to want to buy a house than the general public—making the survey less than representative. The rest of the answer choices were out of the scope of the argument.

8. (E) Question 7 was asking us to weaken the evidence. Question 8 is asking us to weaken the conclusion that was based on the evidence. In both cases, the correct answer will show that the statistics are not representative. In question 8, the correct answer is choice (E) which does exactly this. If only a quarter of the people who claimed in the survey to want a second home actually buy one, this undermines the validity of the survey, and thus the validity of the investment advice as well.

9. (A) Choices (D) and (E) are negative aspects of the DOT's proposal, but negative only in an economic sense. Choice (A) represents a stronger challenge to the proposal, since it raises the possibility that the new design that is supposed to save lives may inadvertently cost additional lives.

10. (C) The last line of this argument gives away its type: "... the virus that *causes* ..." The cause of a certain disease was thought to be one thing, but now is believed to be something else. Recent evidence suggests that the cause is a virus (which also nourishes the bacterium once thought to be the cause of the disease). To support a causal argument, you take away possible alternate causes. Choice (C) does this by showing that while both virus and bacterium are often present at the same time, the virus has been found *without* the bacterium in many cases of the disease. Choice (A) directly contradicts this, suggesting that the bacterium is the sole cause. Choices (B) and (E) suggest that the virus plays a supporting role to the bacterium. Choice (D) is outside the scope of the argument. The correct answer is choice (C).

11. (B) According to the passage, a drought in Florida will drive up the overall price of orange juice. Let's use this question as a scope workshop.

Choice (A): According to the argument, there was a drought in Florida. This is not changed by saying the drought was less severe than scientists had predicted before the drought.

Choice (B): This seriously weakens the argument. If the drought in Florida only affects part of this year's orange crop—the part produced in Florida—then the price of orange juice might not be so severely affected.

Choice (C): While other materials may be used in the making of orange juice, we have to feel that oranges are at least an important ingredient. If the drought decreases the Florida orange crop, this is likely to affect prices unless there is another supply.

Choice (D): Who cares that the price was lower than usual last year? The argument says only that it will go up *this* year.

Choice (E): Since we have nothing to compare it to, the price per crate is meaningless.

12. (A) Choices (C), (D), and (E) are outside the scope of the argument. Choice (B) would not ease the fears of the cable companies—rather the reverse. The correct answer is choice (A).

13. (C) To conclusively answer a question, neither the question nor the answer can be hypothetical. Choices (A), (B), and (E) discuss events that might or might not happen in the future. Choice (D) is not discussed in the passage. The correct answer is choice (C), because the cable companies' position is based on their assumption or knowledge that the telephone companies are turning a profit.

14. (C) *Used* cars, a tax reduction sometime in the *future*, a change of economic conditions in the *future*, and the demand for *trucks* are all irrelevant in explaining the recent increase in the price of new cars. Thus, choice (C) seems to be the best answer, even if we aren't immediately sure why. This is a tough question, and you may not have seen during the minute and some-odd seconds that you had to spend on it during the test, why (C) would explain the increase in the "average price paid for a new car." However, if harsh economic situations are preventing ordinary people from buying cars, but not preventing rich people from buying expensive cars, then the "average price paid for a car" would rise.

15. (D) To get an inference question correct, you almost never actually want to infer. Look for an answer that seems ludicrously obvious. Choice (A) implies that the State Department's views are always likely to diverge from other news sources, which is not only silly, but something ETS would be unlikely to say. (B) implies that the State Department should never be used as a news source, which goes way too far. (C) also goes much further than the passage itself. (E) is a bit bizarre, since sometimes the State Department is bound to be right. (D) is the correct answer because the argument makes it clear that the "alternative" sources of information would provide the "divergent" opinions mentioned in the first sentence.

16. (E) The manager's aim is constant quality, yet his solution—to reject 500 bulbs every week—presupposes that there will be exactly 500 defective bulbs every week. Choice (E) points this out. If you chose choice (C), you were in too much of a hurry. If (C) had said, "each light bulb that is *rejected* is worthy of being *rejected*," that would have been a better answer.

SECTION 6—DATA SUFFICIENCY

1. (C) The area of a triangle is

$$\frac{\text{base} \times \text{height}}{2}$$

Statement (1) alone gives us the base, but not the height, so we are down to (B), (C), or (E). Statement (2) alone gives us the ratio of the height to the base, but doesn't give us a specific number for either, so eliminate (B). Let's see if the *combination* of the two statements will help. If the base is 12 and the ratio of the height to the base is 3:1, then we can figure out exactly what the height is as well:

$$\frac{3}{1} = \frac{x}{12}$$

The correct answer is choice (C). Remember, in data sufficiency you don't have to solve a problem; you merely want to know that you *can* solve a problem based on either or both of the statements.

2. (A) The original question tells us the total number of cans. Statement (1) tells us there is an equal number of diet and non-diet cans. This answers the question (there are 9 of each, not that we really needed to know to get this data sufficiency question correct.) We are down to (A) or (D).

Statement (2) may seem to *agree* with statement (1) because we may have noticed that the number of diet cans supplied by the information in statement (1) happens to be odd. However there are lots of odd numbers. The correct answer is choice (A).

3. (B) Statement (1) tells us how many *more* people were in City X than in City Y, but since we don't know the total population of either, we can't definitively answer this "yes or no" question. We're down to (B), (C), or (E).

At first glance, statement (2) may not seem helpful since it talks about Mormons and Buddhists, but in fact, this statement is sufficient. The 300,000 Mormons make up 20% of the population of City X, meaning that we can compute the entire population (five times 300,000, not that we needed to know the exact figure.) The 141,000 Buddhists make up 30% of City Y, meaning that we can compute the entire population of City Y as well. Is this information enough to answer this question with a definitive yes or no? Of course. The correct answer is choice (B).

4. (C) Remember, in geometry problems where there is no diagram, your first step should be to draw your own. In this case, your diagram should look like this:

Statement (1) tells us the distance from Y to Z. This is one side (the hypotenuse, as it happens) of the right triangle, but since we don't know any of the angles except for angle YXZ (which must be 90 degrees), we will need one other side in order to figure out the third. We're down to (B), (C), or (E).

Statement (2) tells us that the distance from X to Y is half the distance from Y to Z. By itself, this gives us no actual numbers. We're down to (C) or (E).

Putting the two statements together, we know that YZ is 20 and that XY is half of that, or 10. Using the Pythagorean theorem ($a^2 + b^2 = c^2$) we could figure out the distance from X to Z. Thus the correct answer is choice (C).

5. (D) The average of any three numbers is the sum of those numbers divided by 3. In this "yes or no" question, you are being asked if the average of three numbers equals v. By dividing both sides by 3, statement (1) can be rewritten as

$$\frac{s+t+u}{3}$$

Obviously, this answers the question. We're down to (A) or (D).

By dividing both sides by 2, statement (2) can be rewritten as

$$\frac{s+t+u}{3} = \frac{2v}{2}$$

As soon as we cancel the 2's on the right, we see that statement (2) also answers the question. The correct answer is choice (D).

6. (D) In this fraction problem, we must convert fractions to actual numbers. Statement (1) says that 1 cup of sand would fill the pail from $\frac{3}{4}$ to $\frac{7}{8}$.

Using the bowtie, this translates to a change of $\frac{1}{8}$. Thus, one cup = $\frac{1}{8}$ of the pail. The pail holds a total of 8 cups. This answers the question, so we are down to (A) or (D).

Statement (2) says that removing two cups would reduce the pail from $\frac{3}{4}$ to $\frac{1}{2}$. In other words, the difference $\left(\frac{1}{4}\right)$ is equal to 2 cups, and the entire pail holds 8 cups. This, too, answers the question, so the correct answer is choice (D).

7. (E) The last of the so-called "easy" questions, problem 7 is already fairly tricky. You might think that if $x^2 = 4x$, then x must equal 4, but this is not necessarily so. What if x were 0? In data sufficiency, when ETS asks for the value of x, they mean the one and only value of x. Statement (1) gives us two possible values. It is not sufficient, and we are down to (B), (C), or (E).

Statement (2) by itself narrows down the answer to every single even integer in the world, which is not very helpful.

Combining the two statements might at first appear to help. If statement (1) gives us two alternatives (4 and 0), wouldn't statement (2) (which limits the answer to only even integers) eliminate one of them? Well, no. 4 and 0 are *both* even numbers. The correct answer is choice (E).

8. (E) Let's leave aside for a moment the question of whether Marc was traveling at the same speed on his trips to the library and the University Center (although you can bet that ETS would not leave this aside). Statement (1) only tells us the time it takes to bicycle to the library. Since it says nothing about the University center, this is insufficient, and we are down to (B), (C), or (E).

Statement (2) only tells us the time it takes to ride from the library to the center. By itself, this is also insufficient. We're down to (C) and (E).

When we put the two statements together, we might be tempted to assume that the three sites (home, the library, and the University Center) are all in a straight line, but of course, we can't assume anything of the kind. What if Marc travels 20 minutes due north of his house to get to the library, then travels 20 minutes due south to get to the University Center, which just happens to be across the street from his home? The correct answer to this question is choice (E).

9. (E) The question "Is $x^3 = 125$?" can be rewritten as "Is $x = 5$?" This is a "yes or no" question, and the best way to tackle it is to plug in twice. In statement (1), we can plug in 5, in which case the answer to the question "is $x^3 = $ to 125" is "yes" or 6, in which case the answer is "no." Thus, since we are getting two different answers depending on the numbers we plug in, statement (1) is not sufficient. We're down to (B), (C), or (E).

In statement (2), we can plug in 5, in which case the answer is "yes" or 4, in which case the answer is "no." Eliminate choice (B).

To see if the answer is (C), we must choose a number that satisfies the conditions of both statements (1) and (2) at the same time. We can plug in 5, in which case the answer is "yes." You may have been tempted to choose (C) at this point since no other integer will satisfy the two equations at the same time, but does this problem limit us to picking integers? Nope. What about 4.5? Or 5.2? In either of these cases, the answer would be "no." Thus, since we are getting two different answers depending on the numbers we plug in, the combination of statements (1) and (2) is not sufficient either, and the correct answer is choice (E).

10. (E) While statement (1) makes Branch C seem pretty darn capable, we must answer the question based on the criteria given in the question: the more efficient is considered the branch that produced the greatest number of units for four or more of the seven weeks. Statement (1) doesn't tell us *when* Branch C produced its units. Perhaps all Branch C's units were produced in the last week. In spite of the fact that, according to the statement, Branch C produced many more units than Branch D, it doesn't necessarily fit the criteria. We're down to (B), (C), or (E).

Statement (2) by itself isn't sufficient either. We're down to answer choices (C) or (E). The combination of the two statements might seem to be sufficient, but we still don't know if it was Branch C that was the more efficient. The correct answer is choice (E).

11. (B) Using information from statement (1) which gives us the total number of tickets, and from the question itself, which gives us the ratio of one type of ticket to another, we can figure out exactly how many F tickets and G tickets there were. But this doesn't help us to figure out what percentage of these tickets were purchased as opposed to given away. We're down to (B), (C), or (E).

Statement (2) does not give us the total number of actual tickets, but in this case, that doesn't matter. All we need to know to answer the question is the percentage of each type that were purchased, and the ratio of one type to the other. The correct answer is choice (B).

Still confused about why statement (2) is sufficient? Let's plug in. The ratio of F to G was 2 to 1, so let's say there were 20 F tickets and 10 G tickets, for a total of 30 tickets. Statement (2) says 60% of the F tickets (60% of 20 = 12) and 80% of the G tickets (80% of 10 = 8) were purchased. That's a total of 20 tickets purchased out of a total of 30. Can we figure out what percentage that is? Of course.

12. (A) As usual, whenever you see variables you should try to plug in. Statement (1) tells us that the greatest common factor of $\frac{x}{2}$ and $\frac{y}{2}$ is 5. Let's plug in some numbers for x and y that make this true. How about 10 for x and 20 for y. How did we pick these numbers? Well, first of all, $\frac{x}{2}$ and $\frac{y}{2}$ have to be non-fraction numbers in order to be divisible by *any* integer, which means that x and y must both be divisible by 2. Second of all, to have 5 as a factor, both x and y have to be divisible by 5. If x and y have to be divisible by both 2 and by 5, they both have to be divisible by 2 times 5 or 10. You could also just mess around until you find two numbers that work. If $x = 10$ and $y = 20$, then what is the greatest common factor of x and y? You got it: 10. Because this is a data sufficiency question, the exact answer doesn't matter, but it is important to be sure that you will always get the same answer. You could try plugging in a few more values for x and y, but in this case, you won't find a greater common factor than 10. We're down to (A) or (D).

While it appears to agree with statement (1), statement (2) gives us much less specific information. By plugging in, you'll see that there could be many different answers to the question using statement (2). The correct answer is choice (A).

13. **(B)** "Is $x + 4y$ odd?" is a "yes or no" question. Before we look at the statements, notice that 4 times *any* integer is always going to be even. Thus, in this case, it doesn't matter whether y is even or odd. We don't need to know anything about y. Since $4y$ will always be even, what number plus an even number makes an odd number? That's right: an odd number. To answer this question affirmatively, x would have to be odd. To answer this question in the negative, x would have to be even. Since this is a "yes or no" question, in which either a yes *or* a no is sufficient to answer the question, all we need to know is *something* about x. Statement (1) tells us nothing about x. So is $x + 4y$ odd? It might be and it might not. This statement is not sufficient to answer the question definitively. We're down to (B), (C), or (E).

Statement (2) tells us that x is odd. If this is the case, then $x + 4y$ will *always* be odd. The correct answer is choice (B). Note that on this question, the too-obvious answer is choice (C). If you were in a hurry, you might think you needed to know about both x and y to answer the question.

14. **(A)** Remember, in data sufficiency, the diagrams are *never* drawn to scale. Always make it a point to redraw the diagram as the two statements add information. To get the area of the shaded region, we need to subtract the area of the rectangle from the area of the circle. The question itself gives us the diameter of the circle (16), which enables us to find its area. Now all we need is the area of the rectangle. Statement (1) tells us that the base of the rectangle is equal to the radius of the circle (1/2 of the diameter) which we know to be 8. We don't have the height of the rectangle, but we can figure it out. $WZ = 8$. WY is equal to the diameter of the circle, or 16. These two segments form two sides of a right triangle WZY. We can use the Pythagorean theorem to find the third side ZY. We're down to (A) or (D).

Statement (2) merely tells us that one side of the rectangle is less than another. This does not help to answer the question. The correct answer is choice (A).

15. **(E)** This is a yes or no question. Statement (1) tells us that 2 faces of the rectangle are square. A rectangle has 6 faces. If all 6 are square, then the block is a cube. But if only some of them are square, then the block is not a cube. If you try drawing this yourself, you will see that it is possible to sometimes get a cube and sometimes get a rectangular solid, so we are down to (B), (C), or (E).

Statement (2) tells us that the volume of the block is 64. You may have realized that 64 is the cube root of 4, and decided that this means the solid must be a cube with dimensions $4 \times 4 \times 4$. Unfortunately, there are other dimensions that would also yield a block with a volume of 64. We're down to (C) or (E).

Combining the two statements does not help either. It is still possible to draw this as a cube ($4 \times 4 \times 4$) or as a rectangular solid ($2 \times 2 \times 16$). The correct answer is choice (E). Joe Bloggs might have picked (A) under the mistaken impression that if any side of the solid was a square, then the entire solid must be a cube. Joe might also have picked choice (C), feeling that the best way to answer this question was to throw the kitchen sink at it.

16. **(A)** To solve this "yes or no" question, plug values into the two statements. Joe Bloggs liked statement (2) because he forgot that y could equal $-\frac{1}{2}$. However only statement (1) answered the question: On the GMAT, square roots are always positive. The correct answer is choice (A).

17. **(B)** Statement (1) only gives the length of PQ, so we're down to (B), (C), or (E). At first glance, statement (2) doesn't seem to help, but in fact it is sufficient to answer the question. The key to this problem is area. The area of any triangle is $B \times \frac{H}{2}$, but you can consider any side of the triangle to be the base. For example, the area of this figure could be written as $PQ \times \frac{RS}{2}$, or as $QR \times \frac{PR}{2}$. In other words, these are equivalent equations, and the correct answer is choice (B). Joe Bloggs might have taken the kitchen sink approach to this one and chosen (C).

18. **(A)** To find the answer to this "yes or no" question, try plugging in to the two statements, starting with the one number that you know is in the set: 3. Statement (1) gives us all the positive multiples of 3. Statement (2) gives us all the negative multiples of 3, plus 0. The correct answer is choice (A). Joe might have picked (D).

19. **(E)** To solve this "yes or no" question, you have to plug in. Let's begin with statement (1). s must be less than 4 and prime; let's make $s = 3$. The information in the question says that t is a multiple of s. Let's make $t = 9$. Now, let's ask the question: Is t a multiple of s^2? In this case, the answer is "yes." 9 is a multiple of 9. If the answer to this question is *always* "yes" then statement (1) is sufficient, but if we can find even one case where the answer is "no," then statement (1) is no good. Let's try again by keeping $s = 3$, but this time let's plug in 12 for t. Again, let's ask the question: Is t a multiple of s^2? In this case, the answer is "no." 12 is not a multiple of 9. Since the answer is sometimes yes and sometimes no, statement (1) is not sufficient and we're down to (B), (C), or (E).

Statement (2) says that $t = 18$, but gives us no information about s. Let's plug in 3 for s again. 18 is a multiple of 3. Now, let's ask the question: is 18 a multiple of s^2? Yes. 18 is a multiple of 9. If the answer is always yes, then statement (2) is sufficient, but to make sure, let's try plugging in another number. We still have $t = 18$, but make $s = 2$. 18 is a multiple of 2, so now let's ask the question: is 18 a multiple of s^2? In this case, the answer is "no." 18 is not a multiple of 4. Thus statement (2) is not sufficient either, and we are down to (C) or (E).

Combining both statements in this case is not going to help either. The numbers we plugged in above will satisfy both statements, and still sometimes yield a "yes," and other times yield a "no." The correct answer to this question is choice (E). Joe Bloggs is probably pretty tempted by (C), because it appears to give information about both s and t.

20. **(A)** Joe thinks you need both u and t to get s, so he picks choice (C). However, all you need is u. Here's why: We know that $u \times t \times 8 = s \times t \times 4$ so $8u = 4s$. If $u = 6$, here's what the equation would look like:

$$6 \times 8 \times t = s \times 4 \times t$$

Since t is a common term in both, it will cancel out if we divide both sides by t. We're left with $48 = s \times 4$. The correct answer is choice (A).

SECTION 7: SENTENCE CORRECTION

1. **(B)** Go through your checklist of potential errors. Is there a misplaced modifier here? No. Is there a pronoun problem? No. Is there a parallel construction problem? Bingo! The "new rules" have two aims: first, to identify fans and second, to seat them. The correct answer is choice (B).

2. **(C)** The pronoun "it" in this stem sentence is ambiguous. To what noun does it refer? If you said "the status of women" you were right, that was the sentence's *intention*, but the anal ETS test writers want the antecedent of a pronoun to be crystal-clear. Choices (A), (B), (D), and (E) all contain the ambiguous "it." Choice (C), by avoiding the pronoun completely, is the clearest version of the sentence.

3. **(D)** This is a tense question. "In the last twenty years" implies a continued action over time—which needs the perfect tense. This eliminates choices (A) and (B). Choice (C) creates a sentence fragment. Choice (E) isn't bad, but the word "since" is a bit redundant because the sentence began with "in the last twenty years." Choice (D) is best.

4. **(B)** This is an idiom question. Do you debate (A) over if, (B) over whether, (C) about, (D) about if, or (E) concerning? The correct answer is choice (B).

5. **(E)** The clue that let you know this was an apples-and-oranges question was the word "than." In choice (A) the sentence is comparing actions. To make the sentence correct, choice (A) would have had to read, " . . . was more rapid than it *was* in any other American City." Choices (B), (C), (D), and (E) all attempt to get around this by comparing nouns instead (which means, of course, that they will need some version of the replacement noun, "that of." Choice (B) is wrong because, among other things, it suggests that "the nineteenth century" was rapid. To be

correct, it would need to say "those of" other cities. Choices (C) and (D) forget to put in any replacement noun at all. The correct answer is choice (E).

6. (A) This question is about quantity words. Do you use "fewer" or "less" when you are talking about money? It depends. If you had six one-dollar bills, we would say that you had *fewer* than seven, because dollar bills can be counted with assurance. If you had six thousand dollars, we would say that you had *less* than seven thousand, because we have no idea how many actual bills you had. Thus, the correct answer is choice (A).

7. (E) This is a parallel construction question, containing a list of two parts; each must be expressed the same way. There's no point trying to fix the part of the sentence that isn't underlined, so we know that the first part must be correct as is: ". . . for, first of all, failing to . . ."

The second part must mimic the first. The correct answer is choice (E).

8. (D) ETS has an aversion to the word "being," which usually creates a passive voice. This eliminates choice (A). In choice (B), the prepositional phrase "of two weeks" is too far away from "notice" (the noun that it is supposed to modify), giving the mistaken impression that the phrase instead modifies "employers." "Two weeks' notice" is a correct idiomatic expression, but we eliminate choices (C) and (E) due to awkwardness. The correct answer is choice (D).

9. (E) This is a misplaced modifier question. Who was "upset by the recent downturn?" It was the board of directors. This eliminates choices (A), (B), and (C). Choice (E) correctly positions the prepositional phrase "at its quarterly meeting" and avoids the passive "being added."

10. (C) This is a pronoun question. The pronoun in question is the plural "their" which is referring to the singular "S corporation." We can thus eliminate (A), (B), and (D). Choice (E) requires the infinitive "to send." The correct answer is choice (C).

11. (A) The idiom, "Just as . . . so too" is correct as written. Each of the other choices uses variations on unidiomatic expression instead. The correct answer is choice (A).

12. (C) One of ETS's favorite idiomatic expressions is "not only . . . but also." Only choice (C) uses the idiom correctly.

13. (A) This is also an idiom question. Do you attempt *to* do something, do you attempt *at* something, or do you attempt *for* something? The correct answer is choice (A).

14. (A) This question involves parallel construction. The evidence warrants one of two choices, and both must be expressed in the same way. The correct answer is choice (A) which expresses both choices as verbs. Choice (E) might have been correct, but the correct idiomatic expression (as far as ETS is concerned) is to decide *whether*, not to decide *if*.

15. (C) This is also a parallel construction problem. The introductory clause expresses two desirable characteristics of a submarine, but the two characteristics are expressed in different ways. There is no need for a repetition of the verb or a pronoun, and this eliminates all the answers but choice (C).

16. (E) This sentence contains a list of several nouns: "sudden downturns," "hedging, other strategies," etc. The correct answer must contain all nouns. Choices (A), (B), and (C) all contain a verb-like thing. Since "loosening" is an action, you must put the article "a" in front of it to make it a noun. "Fearing" is also an action, but the noun form of "fearing" is simply "fear." This eliminates choices (A), (B), and (C). Choice (D) suggests that it is the "company" that is feared. Choice (E) is best.

17. **(D)** This is a misplaced modifier. What follows "Like the government that came before it" must be an actual government. This eliminates choices (A), (B), and (C). Choice (E) doesn't make much sense, because "laissez-faire" should modify "capitalism," not "cornerstone." So the correct answer is choice (D).

18. **(B)** The stem sentence here has a parallel construction problem: "that soliciting . . . was more efficient than . . . to go . . ." *Going* would have been correct, but this part of the sentence was not underlined. We needed to fix the first part of the sentence to agree with the infinitive construction of the second part of the sentence. The correct answer is choice (B).

19. **(D)** The subject of this sentence is "areas" which is plural, but the verb is singular. This eliminates choices (A) and (E). Choices (B) and (C) are not parallel. As we saw in question 16, some nouns require an "–ing" ending. "Cutting" is one. But, the noun form of "destroy" is not "the destroying," it's "the destruction." The correct answer is choice (D).

20. **(B)** The pronoun "which" is supposed to refer to a particular noun, but in this sentence, that noun does not really exist. (The noun would be "sightings.") This gets rid of (A) and (E). (C) throws in another pronoun, which doesn't help, and (D) gives the impression that it was the UFOs that had reported the sightings. The correct answer is choice (B).

21. **(D)** The sentence as written needs a "but also" to complement its "not only." Choice (A) is gone. In choice (B) the "also" is redundant, since it is next to the word "and." In choice (C), it is implied that "procedures" can "prove themselves." Be careful of this construction. Don't attribute active abilities to things that, in and of themselves, can't act. In choice (E), the pronoun "they" is ambiguous. Choice (D) is best.

22. **(C)** This is an apples and oranges question. The key word here is "than." What is being compared are two actions, which means we need "it was" after the "than." We are down to choices (C) and (E). Choice (E) confuses the participial phrase "making . . ." by the inclusion of the word "in." The correct answer is choice (C).

Afterword

ABOUT THE PRINCETON REVIEW COURSE

The Princeton Review GMAT Course is a six-week course to prepare students for the GMAT.

Students are assigned to small classes (no more than fifteen students) grouped by ability. Everyone in your math class is scoring at your math level; everyone in your verbal class is scoring at your verbal level. This enables your teacher to focus each lesson on your problems because everybody else in your class has precisely the same problems.

Each week you will cover one math area and one verbal area. If you don't understand a particular topic thoroughly, some courses expect you to listen to audiocassettes.

Not so with The Princeton Review.

If you want more work on a topic, you can come to an extra-help session later in the week. If after coming to an extra-help class you want still more practice, you can request free private tutoring with your instructor.

Four times during the course you will take a diagnostic test that is evaluated by computer. Each diagnostic test is constructed according to the statistical design of actual GMATs. The computer evaluation of your diagnostic tests is used to assign you to your class, as well as to measure your progress. The computer evaluation tells you what specific areas you need to concentrate on. We know how busy you are. We don't ask you to spend time on topics you already understand.

Princeton Review instructors undergo a strict selection process and a rigorous training period. All of them have done exceedingly well on standardized tests like the GMAT, and most of them have gone to highly competitive colleges. All Princeton Review instructors are chosen because we believe they can make the course enjoyable as well as instructive.

Our materials are updated each year to reflect changes in the test design and improved techniques.

ARE YOUR BOOKS JUST LIKE YOUR COURSES?

Since our SAT book first came out in 1986, many students and teachers have asked us, "Are your books just like your courses?"

No.

We like to think that this book is fun, informative, and well written, but no book can capture the rigor and advantages of our course structure, or the magic of our instructors. It isn't easy to raise GMAT scores. Our course is spread over six weeks and requires class participation, diagnostic exams, and some homework.

Moreover, this book cannot contain all of the techniques we teach in our course for a number of reasons. Some of our techniques are too difficult to explain, without a trained Princeton Review teacher to describe and demonstrate them. Also, this book is written for the average student. Classes in our course are grouped by ability so that we can gear our techniques to each student's level. A 500-level Princeton Review student learns different techniques from those learned by a 400- or 600-level Princeton Review student.

IF YOU'D LIKE MORE INFORMATION

The Princeton Review offers courses in hundreds of cities around the country and around the world. For the office nearest you, call 1-800-995-5585.

About Computerized Testing

ETS, CBT, CAT, GRE—What Does It All Mean?

In 1990, Howard Wainer, an official of the Educational Testing Service, published a book called *Computer Adaptive Testing: A Primer*, in which he wrote, "There are . . . several aspects of computerized and adaptive testing that raise new issues in the consideration of validity," and went on to admit, "There is, as yet, very little information available about the validity of computerized adaptive tests." The book was co-written by four other ETS functionaries and includes a foreword by ETS Vice President C. Victor Bunderson.

In 1991, despite these reservations, ETS began offering the computer-based GRE. Baffling, isn't it?

Anyway, the world is now graced with two forms of the GRE: the pencil-and-paper (standard) test and the CBT (computer-based test). The CBT has the same format as the standard GRE, except it's on a computer. However, along with its regular (linear) sections, the CBT includes a computer-*adaptive* test

(CAT) which, depending on the individual tester's performance, can be used at the program's discretion as either the scored or the experimental section. "Computer adaptive" means that the computer program molds itself to the individual test taker's performance level. For example, if you answer an easy question correctly, the test will give you a harder one. If you miss a medium question, you'll get an easy one next. Supposedly, this process enables the computer to pinpoint your scoring level more quickly and accurately than a paper-and-pencil test could.

ETS has stated that they plan to eliminate the computer-based tests (CBTs) once they are confident of the validity of their computer-adaptive tests. As of November 17, 1993, in fact, all sections of the GRE—math, verbal, and analytic—will be offered in CAT format. However, ETS is not confident enough in its CAT analytic section to let it stand alone; therefore, immediately following the CAT section, there will be two computer-*based* analytic sections. Just in case. Whichever analytic section you score best on will be the one that counts.

While ETS has not yet made any formal announcement about offering other tests in CBT or CAT format, they do have a tendency to keep their tests uniform. Considering this history of homogeneity, it is highly likely that ETS will, at some time in the near future, come up with a CAT option for its other admissions tests.

ENTER REVIEWARE™

ETS has announced that, as of October 1997, the GMAT will switch to a computer adaptive format. And we at The Princeton Review are ready. We have developed the RevieWare™ Computer Diagnostic, our version of ETS's CBT/CAT. We have attempted to duplicate precisely the format, style, appearance, and workings of the ETS CBT and CAT tests. Aesthetically, ETS's program is rather unattractive, and it's a bit hard to move around in. So is ours. In mirroring the GRE test's look and feel, we made the decision that an accurate test would be more helpful as an instructive and evaluative tool than a fun, attractive test that bore little resemblance to the barren moonscape that is the GRE. They're bland, so we're bland.

If you've purchased the version of *Cracking the GMAT* that comes with a computer disk or CD-ROM enclosed, then you already have our RevieWare package. You can use this as additional practice for the paper-and-pencil version of the test, or as a way to see which version of the test you prefer. If you score higher on our CAT diagnostic than you do on our paper-and-pencil diagnostic, you might consider waiting until after October 1997 and taking the computer adaptive version of the GMAT.

A discussion of the philosophy behind RevieWare isn't really meaningful without an understanding of exactly what computerized testing means to ETS, and what it means to you as a test taker.

WHAT'S IN IT FOR THEM: CASH AND CONVENIENCE

The big question is, if ETS itself questions the validity of these tests, why do they offer the CBT, let alone a fully adaptive CAT?

For one thing, convenience. The standard paper-and-pencil exams are administered five times per year. For each administration, ETS must rent thousands of rooms worldwide, hire proctors, transport materials, and register and collect fees from walk-in testers. In the case of the CBT/CAT, all ETS needs is a room in one of their or Sylvan Learning Centers' (Sylvan's) offices equipped with a couple of computers, and an employee to deal with testers. This room can be open for testing at ETS/Sylvan's discretion, thus eliminating almost all of the hassle associated with administering the paper-and-pencil exam.

Another plus, for ETS and Sylvan, is dollars. The fee for the CBT/CAT is $45 *more* than the fee for the paper-and-pencil exam. At this rate, the expenditure for computer hardware and software will be paid back in very little time. After that, it's straight profit. Or should we say "nonprofit"? That ETS might have financial concerns is often overlooked. Most people assume that ETS is some kind of government organ. Actually, ETS is a nonprofit association of academic organizations, which means that they're not supposed to make a profit. But if they do, well, oops! It's called an "overage," and can be spent on anything from incredibly high salaries and perks to one of the tennis courts or swimming pools in ETS's Princeton, NJ, compound. Sylvan, on the other hand, is a good old-fashioned corporation. They are in business for the bucks, plain and simple.

WHAT'S IN IT FOR YOU: BIAS, EYESTRAIN, TEARS, AND SWEAT

What seem to be the advantages to the test taker? For one, he or she can take the exam virtually any day of the work week. Also, a computerized test can often take far less time than its paper-and-pencil counterpart. That's what ETS would like you to believe, anyway. Now, let's look at these "advantages" and see how they really play out.

First, fourteen states do not have a single test center that offers the CBT/CAT, and ten others have only one. Also, a sampling of test centers showed that none offers testing on the weekends, so anyone interested would have to be in a position to take a day off if he or she wanted to take the CBT/CAT. This means that if you don't live near a test center or if you go to school or work during the week—situations that apply to a large portion of the country—the first "advantage" does not apply.

Second, who in his or her right mind would not use every minute allotted? If you are told, as you are for the GRE CBT, that you have thirty-two minutes per section, then you are going to use thirty-two minutes. In addition, according to our friend from ETS, Mr. Wainer, "...a CAT makes much more stringent demands on its component items than does its paper-and-pencil counterpart. Because the CAT tends to be much shorter . . . each item is more critical. If an item is flawed, its impact on the . . . examinee's proficiency is doubled. Additionally, because not everyone gets the same set of items, a flawed item can affect some examinees and not others. Hence, test fairness, in addition to test validity, can be compromised." So much for the second "advantage."

The difficulties described above begin to bring to light some of the other serious problems with computerized testing. For example, what about the simple, undeniable fact that this test is *on a computer*? Think about the people you know who own and/or spend lots of time with computers and/or video games. Are most of these people members of one gender? Are most of these people members of a specific socioeconomic class? Probably. As Wainer puts it, "It is conceivable that a CAT may be more vulnerable to problems of [bias] than are conventional paper-and-pencil tests, due to the possibility that differences between ethnic groups or genders in familiarity with computers in general may affect scores on computerized tests." In fact, the question of general bias is perhaps the most profound problem facing ETS in creating and administering the CBT/CAT.

For its part, ETS has steadfastly denied that any of its tests exhibit a bias for or against any gender, ethnicity, or race. But for something that doesn't exist, the subject sure does get a lot of attention. In fact, the standardized test-writing community is so worried about bias that its members don't even use the word "bias," opting instead for more comfortable euphemisms. Recently, the term *differential item functioning (dif)* has replaced *item bias* as a less evaluative label. Item bias refers to a specific question that exhibits a bias against a specific group or groups.

Computerized tests, especially computer-adaptive tests like the one that ETS wants to replace the CBT with, are at far greater risk of showing bias than are paper-and-pencil tests. Wainer explains, "Adaptive tests may be more vulnerable to the effects of *dif* on validity than fixed tests. A fixed test may contain items with counterbalancing *dif* that can 'cancel each other out'; however, in an adaptive testing situation, the presence of such [biased] items in the test pool permits the possibility that an unlucky examinee could be administered several items biased against him or her. The resulting test score would not provide a good indication of proficiency." Basically, a paper-and-pencil test is an equal-opportunity bigot, while a CAT can tailor itself to discriminate against you specifically. (See the diagram below for a description of the adaptive flow.)

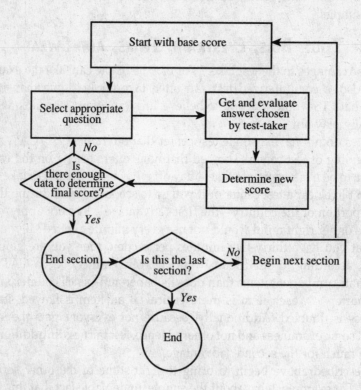

GET IT BEFORE IT GETS YOU

You've been taking multiple-choice, paper-and-pencil, fill-in-the-bubble tests your whole life. So while the prospect of taking another one may not be pleasant, at least it's familiar. But imagine walking into something as completely unfamiliar as a computer-adaptive test. You've never seen anything like it before. You've never practiced on it. You feel like Captain Kirk in that *Star Trek* episode where he has to dress up in a really short toga and act like some live pawn in a game these super-intelligent aliens are playing, but he doesn't know any of the rules.

Well, you don't have to feel that way. RevieWare Computer Diagnostics are here to help. Because adaptive testing is the future, if you don't get familiar with it, you'll regret it. Maybe not today, maybe not tomorrow, but soon, and for the rest of your life. Okay, okay, probably not for the rest of your life. But since you have the option, why not use RevieWare Computer Diagnostics to beat ETS at its own game? Happy testing and good luck!

RevieWare™ Computer Diagnostic Software

ABOUT SYSTEM REQUIREMENTS

WINDOWS™ VERSION

IBM PC or compatible (386 or higher)
MS Windows 3.1 or later *and* MS DOS 3.3 or later
Mouse

Additionally:

For diskette version:
    4 MB RAM
    Local hard disk with 6 MB free

For CD-ROM version:
    Double speed or better CD-ROM drive
    4 MB RAM
    Local hard disk with 6 MB free

MACINTOSH® VERSION

A Macintosh Computer with System 7 or later
High density drive

Additionally:

For diskette version:
    4 MB RAM
    Local hard disk with 6 MB free

For CD-ROM version:
    4 MB RAM
    Local hard disk with 6 MB free

INSTALLING YOUR REVIEWARE COMPUTER DIAGNOSTIC SOFTWARE

CD-ROM

Windows 95

1. Place CD in your CD-ROM drive.

2. A splash screen will automatically appear.

3. Click **Install.** Windows will automatically run an Install Wizard to assist you through the installation process. A series of screens will come up giving you detailed instructions for installation.

4. Click **Next** to proceed through the installation process.

5. Once the setup has completed installation, click **Finish.**

Windows 3.1

1. Place CD in your CD-ROM drive.

2. From the Windows program manager, go into the **File** menu and select **Run.** Then, at the Command line, type **D:SETUP** (where D: is your CD-ROM drive). Press **Enter.**

3. A splash screen will appear. Windows will run an Install Wizard to assist you through the installation process. A series of screens will come up giving you detailed instructions for installation.

4. Click **Next** to proceed through the installation process.

5. Once the setup has completed installation, click **Finish.**

Macintosh

1. Double click on the installer icon.

2. The dialog box will allow you to select an installation folder on your hard drive.

DISKETTE

Windows

1. Place the disk in your floppy drive.

2. From the Program manager, select **Run**.

3. Type **a:\setup** at the Command Line.

4. Click OK.

Macintosh

1. Place diskette in your floppy drive.

2. Double click on "GMAT-Install" to load the program onto your hard drive.

If you have any questions about installing RevieWare™ Computer Diagnostics, please call (800) 546-2102.

USING REVIEWARE COMPUTER DIAGNOSTICS

GETTING STARTED

Open the Program Manager group ("RevieWare"), then double click on the RevieWare icon (the little picture).

THE MENU BAR

The menu bar contains three items: File, Score, and Help.
The **File** menu has four options: **Start New Exam**, **Resume Suspended Exam**, **Preferences**, and **Exit**.

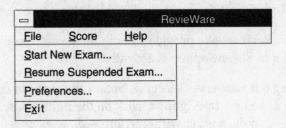

■ **Start New Exam...** Choose this to bring up a window listing all available exams. Select the exam you want and press OK.

▷ Once you've chosen an exam, you will be offered the option of a tutorial, which discusses some of the information we thought you would find useful. If you don't want to read a tutorial, click "Blow Off the Tutorial."

■ **Resume Suspended Exam...** RevieWare Computer Diagnostics give you the option of suspending an exam in progress. Since you can't do this on a real GMAT, *it's a bad thing to do unless absolutely necessary!* But since this is practice, we make it available for emergencies.

▷ To return to a suspended exam, select Resume Suspended Exam from the File menu. Select the exam, click OK or Enter, and the test will restart where you left off.

■ **Preferences...** The Computer Diagnostic allows you to take a test using one of two user interfaces: "Plain Vanilla" or "Flavored." Plain Vanilla is representative of the format in which testing companies will present computer tests. We find it excruciatingly dull, but we provided it so you could see it. "Flavored" is our default, and it spices things up at least a little.

▷ Flavored mode allows you to select from a list of preferences that can be added to the test session. The options are:

- **3D Dialogue in Exam**—Selecting this makes all dialogue boxes 3D, which is the standard interface design.

- **Double-click in Review**—The double-click option gives you direct access to the Review Section screen by double-clicking on a question.

- **Color in Review**—We provide color in the Review Section screen when the Color in Review option is activated.

- **Crossing out answers**—Select this option and you can cross out answer choices as you go. In Windows, click on the right mouse button; on the Mac, click on the answer with SHIFT pressed.

- **LCD clock**—The LCD clock stands out on the screen, making it clear how much time you have left in a section.

- **Timed sounds**—This option gives you scripted sounds that alert you at timed increments and tell you when you have completed a section. *If you find the sounds annoying during an exam, they are easy to turn off: Just type* CONTROL-SHIFT-S.

- **Random sounds**—These sounds are completely random, and are designed to give you a sampling of the sounds you might encounter during an actual test administration.

■ **Exit...** Choose Exit to end your testing session.

The Score Menu has four options: **Load Score**, **Print Score**, **Review Score**, and **Close Score Window**.

- **Load Score...** Select Load Score to review the score report for any completed exam. A window listing all completed exams will open. Select the appropriate exam and click on OK.

▷ You must use Load Score to retrieve a completed exam *before* using the Print Score or Review Score functions.

- **Print Score...** This gives you a printout of your score, including a breakdown by category and question type, for any previously loaded exam. The program will print on your default printer.

- **Review Score...** When you are reviewing an exam, the Computer Diagnostic tells you whether the answer you picked is right or wrong.

- **Close Score Window** Choose this to exit the Score window.

THE TOOLBAR

The Computer Diagnostic toolbar, located just below the menu bar, is another way to navigate through the program. When pressed, the buttons on the toolbar execute the items accessible from the File and Score menus. Included in the exam mode are, from left to right:

 Preferences

 Start New Exam

 Resume Suspended Exam

 Load Score for Review

The Review mode toolbar includes the above icons as well as the following:

 Close Score Window

 Review Score

 Print Score

TAKING A TEST

As soon as you begin a session with the Computer Diagnostic, push your keyboard far to the side. Leave yourself plenty of room for scratch paper, your mouse, mouse pad, and elbows.

Once you begin your test, you will see various buttons on the screen. These buttons are **NEXT, MARK, PREV, TIME, SECTION EXIT, REVIEW, TEST QUIT, CONFIRM,** and **HELP.** Pointing and clicking with your mouse activates them and enables you to navigate through the test. Here is a brief description of each:

 NEXT moves you to the next question. It's the tool you'll use most often. Click it when you've answered (or decided to skip) one question and are ready for the next.

 MARK flags a question to remind you that the question requires further attention. Marking a question is not the same as answering it and has no effect on your score. Unmark a question by clicking the **MARK** tool a second time. Unmarking a question does not erase your answer. This feature is available only on linear exams.

 PREV moves you back to the previous question. Use it if you change your mind, or if one question helps you answer another. This feature is available only on linear exams.

 TIME displays or hides a small digital timer in the upper-left-hand corner of the screen. The timer shows you how much time is left for the current section. When five minutes are left, the timer will flash, display seconds, and remain visible until time is up.

 SECTION EXIT gives you the option of exiting the current section to proceed to the next one, or suspending the exam for later resumption (using Resume Suspended Exam in the File menu).

 REVIEW lets you return to any question in the current section of a linear exam. Clicking on **REVIEW** produces a screen in which questions from the current section are listed in order and described by question type. The status of each question— Answered, Not Answered, or Not Seen—is noted beside it. Any question that you marked earlier using the **MARK** tool will have a small check beside its status designation. To return to one of these questions, select it with the mouse and click the Go to Question button to the right. To return to the place in the test where you were when you clicked **REVIEW**, click on the Return to Where I Was button to the right.

 TEST QUIT works similarly to **EXIT**, but **QUIT** will throw you out of the test entirely if you do not choose the Suspend Exam function.

 HELP reviews directions, lists the tools, and explains their functions.

INTERPRETING SCORE REPORTS

Summary

		Raw Score		Scaled Score	
Verbal	①	39.25	②	470	③
Math		36.56		490	

Scoring Breakdown ⑤

	Correct	Incorrect	Questions
Verbal			
Analogies ④	15	4	19
Reading Comp	15	25	40
Sentence Comp	17	2	19
Section Total	47	31	78
Math			
Arithmetic	24	11	35
Quant Comp	13	2	15
Grid-In	3	7	10
Section Total	40	20	60

Sample exam score report
Question types and scoring ranges will vary among test types.

The score report illustrates your performance on the exam and provides a precise picture of individual test-taking strengths and weaknesses. Descriptions of the score report features are as follows:

1. Depending on the exam type (ACT, SAT, GRE, LSAT, GMAT), scores will be listed by section (just like the real exam).

2. Your **Raw Score** indicates the number of questions answered correctly, minus any penalty (SAT and GMAT only) for wrong answers.

3. Your **Scaled Score** reflects your score after conversion to that exam's specific score curve.

4. Sections from the **Scoring Breakdown** box are divided into specific categories and question types.

5. A breakdown of correctly and incorrectly answered questions enables you to determine specific areas in which you need additional help.

ABOUT THE AUTHORS

Geoff Martz attended Dartmouth College and Columbia University before joining The Princeton Review in 1985 as a teacher and writer. Martz headed the development team that designed the Review's GMAT course. He is the author or coauthor of *Cracking the ACT*, *Paying for College*, *Cracking the GED*, and *How to Survive Without Your Parents' Money*.

Adam Robinson graduated from Wharton before earning a law degree at Oxford University in England. Robinson, a rated chess master, devised and perfected the now-famous "Joe Bloggs" approach to beating standardized tests in 1980, as well as numerous other core Princeton Review techniques. A freelance author of many books, Robinson has collaborated with The Princeton Review to develop a number of its courses.

John Katzman graduated from Princeton University in 1980. After working briefly on Wall Street, he founded The Princeton Review in 1981. Having begun with nineteen high school students in his parents' apartment, Katzman now oversees courses that prepare tens of thousands of high school and college students annually for tests, including the SAT, GRE, GMAT, and LSAT.

All three authors live in New York City.

THE PRINCETON REVIEW WORLDWIDE

Each year, thousands of students from countries throughout the world prepare for the TOEFL and for U.S. college and graduate school admissions exams. Whether you plan to prepare for your exams in your home country or the United States, The Princeton Review is committed to your success.

INTERNATIONAL LOCATIONS: If you are using our books outside of the United States and have questions or comments, or want to know if our courses are being offered in your area, be sure to contact The Princeton Review office nearest you:

- ◆ HONG KONG   852-517-3016
- ◆ JAPAN (Tokyo)   8133-463-1343
- ◆ KOREA (Seoul)   822-508-0081
- ◆ MEXICO CITY   525-564-9468
- ◆ MONTREAL   514-499-0870
- ◆ PAKISTAN (Lahore)   92-42-571-2315
- ◆ SAUDI ARABIA   413-584-6849 (a U.S. based number)
- ◆ SPAIN (Madrid)   341-323-4212
- ◆ TAIWAN (Taipei)   886-27511293

U.S. STUDY ABROAD: *Review USA* offers international students many advantages and opportunities. In addition to helping you gain acceptance to the U.S. college or university of your choice, *Review USA* will help you acquire the knowledge and orientation you need to succeed once you get there.

Review USA is unique. It includes supplements to your test-preparation courses and a special series of *AmeriCulture* workshops to prepare you for the academic rigors and student life in the United States. Our workshops are designed to familiarize you with the different U.S. expressions, real-life vocabulary, and cultural challenges you will encounter as a study-abroad student. While studying with us, you'll make new friends and have the opportunity to personally visit college and university campuses to determine which school is right for you.

Whether you are planning to take the TOEFL, SAT, GRE, GMAT, LSAT, MCAT, or USMLE exam, The Princeton Review's test preparation courses, expert instructors, and dedicated International Student Advisors can help you achieve your goals.

For additional information about *Review USA*, admissions requirements, class schedules, F-1 visas, I-20 documentation, and course locations, write to:

The Princeton Review • Review USA
2315 Broadway, New York NY 10024
Fax: 212/874-0775

The Princeton Review
Diagnostic Test Form ○ Side 1

1.

YOUR NAME:_____
(Print)   Last   First   M.I.

SIGNATURE:_____   DATE: ___/___/___

HOME ADDRESS:_____
(Print)   Number and Street

_____
City   State   Zip Code

PHONE NO.:_____
(Print)

IMPORTANT: Please fill in these boxes exactly as shown on the back cover of your test book.

2. TEST FORM

_____

3. TEST CODE

4. REGISTRATION NUMBER

5. YOUR NAME

First 4 letters of last name				FIRST INIT	MID INIT

(A) (A) (A) (A) (A) (A)
(B) (B) (B) (B) (B) (B)
(C) (C) (C) (C) (C) (C)
(D) (D) (D) (D) (D) (D)
(E) (E) (E) (E) (E) (E)
(F) (F) (F) (F) (F) (F)
(G) (G) (G) (G) (G) (G)
(H) (H) (H) (H) (H) (H)
(I) (I) (I) (I) (I) (I)
(J) (J) (J) (J) (J) (J)
(K) (K) (K) (K) (K) (K)
(L) (L) (L) (L) (L) (L)
(M) (M) (M) (M) (M) (M)
(N) (N) (N) (N) (N) (N)
(O) (O) (O) (O) (O) (O)
(P) (P) (P) (P) (P) (P)
(Q) (Q) (Q) (Q) (Q) (Q)
(R) (R) (R) (R) (R) (R)
(S) (S) (S) (S) (S) (S)
(T) (T) (T) (T) (T) (T)
(U) (U) (U) (U) (U) (U)
(V) (V) (V) (V) (V) (V)
(W) (W) (W) (W) (W) (W)
(X) (X) (X) (X) (X) (X)
(Y) (Y) (Y) (Y) (Y) (Y)
(Z) (Z) (Z) (Z) (Z) (Z)

6. DATE OF BIRTH

MONTH	DAY		YEAR	
○ JAN				
○ FEB				
○ MAR	(0) (0)	(0) (0)		
○ APR	(1) (1)	(1) (1)		
○ MAY	(2) (2)	(2) (2)		
○ JUN	(3) (3)	(3) (3)		
○ JUL	(4)	(4) (4)		
○ AUG	(5)	(5) (5)		
○ SEP	(6)	(6) (6)		
○ OCT	(7)	(7) (7)		
○ NOV	(8)	(8) (8)		
○ DEC	(9)	(9) (9)		

Test Code bubbles:
(0) (A)(J) (0) (0) (0) (0) (0) (0) (0) (0) (0)
(1) (B)(K) (1) (1) (1) (1) (1) (1) (1) (1) (1)
(2) (C)(L) (2) (2) (2) (2) (2) (2) (2) (2) (2)
(3) (D)(M) (3) (3) (3) (3) (3) (3) (3) (3) (3)
(4) (E)(N) (4) (4) (4) (4) (4) (4) (4) (4) (4)
(5) (F)(O) (5) (5) (5) (5) (5) (5) (5) (5) (5)
(6) (G)(P) (6) (6) (6) (6) (6) (6) (6) (6) (6)
(7) (H)(Q) (7) (7) (7) (7) (7) (7) (7) (7) (7)
(8) (I)(R) (8) (8) (8) (8) (8) (8) (8) (8) (8)
(9) (9) (9) (9) (9) (9) (9) (9) (9) (9)

7. SEX
○ MALE
○ FEMALE

⚡ **SCANTRON** FORM NO. F-591-KIN
© SCANTRON CORPORATION 1989 3289-C553-5 4 3 2 1
ALL RIGHTS RESERVED.

Begin with number 1 for each new section of the test. Leave blank any extra answer spaces.

SECTION 1

1 (A) (B) (C) (D) (E)					26 (A) (B) (C) (D) (E)				
2 (A) (B) (C) (D) (E)					27 (A) (B) (C) (D) (E)				
3 (A) (B) (C) (D) (E)					28 (A) (B) (C) (D) (E)				
4 (A) (B) (C) (D) (E)					29 (A) (B) (C) (D) (E)				
5 (A) (B) (C) (D) (E)					30 (A) (B) (C) (D) (E)				
6 (A) (B) (C) (D) (E)					31 (A) (B) (C) (D) (E)				
7 (A) (B) (C) (D) (E)					32 (A) (B) (C) (D) (E)				
8 (A) (B) (C) (D) (E)					33 (A) (B) (C) (D) (E)				
9 (A) (B) (C) (D) (E)					34 (A) (B) (C) (D) (E)				
10 (A) (B) (C) (D) (E)					35 (A) (B) (C) (D) (E)				
11 (A) (B) (C) (D) (E)					36 (A) (B) (C) (D) (E)				
12 (A) (B) (C) (D) (E)					37 (A) (B) (C) (D) (E)				
13 (A) (B) (C) (D) (E)					38 (A) (B) (C) (D) (E)				
14 (A) (B) (C) (D) (E)					39 (A) (B) (C) (D) (E)				
15 (A) (B) (C) (D) (E)					40 (A) (B) (C) (D) (E)				
16 (A) (B) (C) (D) (E)					41 (A) (B) (C) (D) (E)				
17 (A) (B) (C) (D) (E)					42 (A) (B) (C) (D) (E)				
18 (A) (B) (C) (D) (E)					43 (A) (B) (C) (D) (E)				
19 (A) (B) (C) (D) (E)					44 (A) (B) (C) (D) (E)				
20 (A) (B) (C) (D) (E)					45 (A) (B) (C) (D) (E)				
21 (A) (B) (C) (D) (E)					46 (A) (B) (C) (D) (E)				
22 (A) (B) (C) (D) (E)					47 (A) (B) (C) (D) (E)				
23 (A) (B) (C) (D) (E)					48 (A) (B) (C) (D) (E)				
24 (A) (B) (C) (D) (E)					49 (A) (B) (C) (D) (E)				
25 (A) (B) (C) (D) (E)					50 (A) (B) (C) (D) (E)				

SECTION 2

1 (A) (B) (C) (D) (E)					26 (A) (B) (C) (D) (E)				
2 (A) (B) (C) (D) (E)					27 (A) (B) (C) (D) (E)				
3 (A) (B) (C) (D) (E)					28 (A) (B) (C) (D) (E)				
4 (A) (B) (C) (D) (E)					29 (A) (B) (C) (D) (E)				
5 (A) (B) (C) (D) (E)					30 (A) (B) (C) (D) (E)				
6 (A) (B) (C) (D) (E)					31 (A) (B) (C) (D) (E)				
7 (A) (B) (C) (D) (E)					32 (A) (B) (C) (D) (E)				
8 (A) (B) (C) (D) (E)					33 (A) (B) (C) (D) (E)				
9 (A) (B) (C) (D) (E)					34 (A) (B) (C) (D) (E)				
10 (A) (B) (C) (D) (E)					35 (A) (B) (C) (D) (E)				
11 (A) (B) (C) (D) (E)					36 (A) (B) (C) (D) (E)				
12 (A) (B) (C) (D) (E)					37 (A) (B) (C) (D) (E)				
13 (A) (B) (C) (D) (E)					38 (A) (B) (C) (D) (E)				
14 (A) (B) (C) (D) (E)					39 (A) (B) (C) (D) (E)				
15 (A) (B) (C) (D) (E)					40 (A) (B) (C) (D) (E)				
16 (A) (B) (C) (D) (E)					41 (A) (B) (C) (D) (E)				
17 (A) (B) (C) (D) (E)					42 (A) (B) (C) (D) (E)				
18 (A) (B) (C) (D) (E)					43 (A) (B) (C) (D) (E)				
19 (A) (B) (C) (D) (E)					44 (A) (B) (C) (D) (E)				
20 (A) (B) (C) (D) (E)					45 (A) (B) (C) (D) (E)				
21 (A) (B) (C) (D) (E)					46 (A) (B) (C) (D) (E)				
22 (A) (B) (C) (D) (E)					47 (A) (B) (C) (D) (E)				
23 (A) (B) (C) (D) (E)					48 (A) (B) (C) (D) (E)				
24 (A) (B) (C) (D) (E)					49 (A) (B) (C) (D) (E)				
25 (A) (B) (C) (D) (E)					50 (A) (B) (C) (D) (E)				

The Princeton Review
Diagnostic Test Form ○ Side 2

Begin with number 1 for each new section of the test. Leave blank any extra answer spaces.

SECTION 3	SECTION 4	SECTION 5	SECTION 6

Each section contains numbered rows 1 through 50, each with answer bubbles A B C D E.

FOR TPR USE ONLY

V1	V2	V3	V4	M1	M2	M3	M4	M5	M6	M7	M8

This License Agreement is your proof of license. Please treat it as valuable property.

REVIEWARE® LICENSE AGREEMENT

This is a legal agreement between you (either an individual or an entity), the end user, and Princeton Review Publishing, L.L.C., ("TPRP"). By using the software enclosed, you and any transferees and/or multiple licensees hereunder agree to be bound by the terms of this RevieWare® License Agreement. If you do not agree to its terms, promptly return the disk package and accompanying items (including written materials and binders or other containers) to the place you obtained them for a full refund.

REVIEWARE® SOFTWARE LICENSE

1. GRANT OF LICENSE This RevieWare® License Agreement ("License") permits you to use one copy of the specified version of the RevieWare software product identified above ("SOFTWARE") on any single computer, provided the SOFTWARE is in use on only one computer at any time. If you have multiple Licenses for the SOFTWARE, then at any time you may have as many copies of the SOFTWARE in use as you have Licenses. The SOFTWARE is "in use" on a computer when it is loaded into the temporary memory (i.e., RAM) or installed into the permanent memory (e.g., hard disk, CD-ROM, or other storage device) of that computer, <u>except</u> that a copy installed on a network server for the sole purpose of distribution to other computers is not "in use." If the anticipated number of users of the SOFTWARE will exceed the number of applicable Licenses, then you must have a reasonable mechanism or process in place to ensure that the number of persons using the SOFTWARE concurrently does not exceed the number of Licenses. If the SOFTWARE is permanently installed on the hard disk or other storage device of a computer (other than a network server) and one person uses that computer more than 80% of the time it is in use, then that person may also use the SOFTWARE on a portable or home computer.

2. COPYRIGHT The SOFTWARE is owned by TPRP or its suppliers and is protected by United States copyright laws and international treaty provisions. Therefore, you must treat the SOFTWARE like any other copyrighted material (e.g., a book or musical recording) except that you may either (a) make one copy of the SOFTWARE solely for backup or archival purposes, or (b) transfer the SOFTWARE to a single hard disk provided you keep the original solely for backup or archival purposes. You may not copy the written materials accompanying the SOFT-WARE.

3. OTHER RESTRICTIONS This License is your proof of license to exercise the rights granted herein and must be retained by you. You may not rent or lease the SOFTWARE, but you may transfer your rights under this License on a permanent basis provided you transfer this License, the SOFTWARE, and all accompanying written materials and retain no copies, and the recipient agrees to the terms of this License. You may not reverse engineer, decompile, or disassemble the SOFTWARE. Any transfer of the SOFTWARE must include the most recent update and all prior versions.

LIMITED WARRANTY

LIMITED WARRANTY. TPRP warrants that (a) The SOFTWARE will perform substantially in accordance with the accompanying written materials for a period of ninety (90) days from the date of receipt; and (b) any hardware accompanying the SOFTWARE will be free from defects in materials and workmanship under normal use and service for a period of one (1) year from the date of receipt. Any implied warranties on the SOFTWARE and hardware are limited to ninety (90) days and one (1) year, respectively. Some states or jurisdictions do not allow limitations on duration of an implied warranty, so the above limitation may not apply to you.

CUSTOMER REMEDIES. TPRP's entire liability and your exclusive remedy shall be at TPRP's option, either (a) return of the price paid or (b) repair or replacement of the SOFTWARE or hardware that does not meet TPRP's Limited Warranty and that is returned to TPRP with a copy of your receipt. This Limited Warranty is void if failure of the SOFTWARE or hardware has resulted from accident, abuse, or misapplication. Any replacement SOFTWARE will be warranted for the remainder of the original warranty period or thirty (30) days, whichever is longer. These remedies are <u>not</u> available outside the United States of America.

<u>NO OTHER WARRANTIES.</u> TPRP disclaims all other warranties, either express or implied, including but not limited to implied warranties of merchantability and fitness for a particular purpose with respect to the SOFTWARE, the accompanying written materials, and any accompanying hardware. This limited warranty gives you specific legal rights. You may have others, which vary from state or jurisdiction to state or jurisdiction.

<u>NO LIABILITY FOR CONSEQUENTIAL DAMAGES.</u> In no event shall TPRP or its suppliers be liable for any damages whatsoever (including, without limitation, damages for loss of business profits, business interruption, loss or business information, or other pecuniary loss) arising out of the use or inability to use this TPRP product, even if TPRP has been advised of the possibility of such damages. Because some states or jurisdictions do not allow the exclusion or limitation of liability for consequential or incidental damages, the above limitation may not apply to you.

U.S. GOVERNMENT RESTRICTED RIGHTS

The SOFTWARE and documentation are provided with RESTRICTED RIGHTS. Use, duplication, or disclosure by the Government is subject to restrictions as set forth in subparagraph (c)(1)(ii) of the Rights in Technical Data and Computer Software clause at DFARS 252.227-7013 or subparagraphs (c)(1) and (2) of the Commercial Computer Software—Restricted Rights at 48 CFR 52.227-19, as applicable. Contractor manufacturer is TPRP/2315 Broadway/New York, 10024. This Agreement is governed by the laws of the State of New York. For more information about TPRP's licensing policies, please call RevieWare Customer Service at (800) 546-2102, or write: RevieWare Customer Sales and Service/2315 Broadway/New York, NY 10024.